1

Helen Stephenson

Paul Dummett

John Hughes

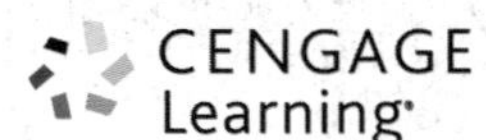

Life Level 1 Student Book

Helen Stephenson

Paul Dummett

John Hughes

Publisher: Sherrise Roehr

Executive Editor: Sarah T. Kenney

Associate Development Editor: Nathan A. Gamache

Director of Global Marketing: Ian Martin

Senior Product Marketing Manager: Caitlin Thomas

Director of Content and Media Production: Michael Burggren

Senior Content Project Manager: Daisy Sosa

Senior Print Buyer: Mary Beth Hennebury

Cover Designers: Scott Baker and Alex Dull

Cover Image: Sarah Palmer/Getty Images

Compositor: MPS Limited

Cover image

Sea nettle jellyfish swim off the coast of San Francisco.
Photo by Sarah Palmer.

Student Book
ISBN-13: 978-1-305-25572-2

Student Book + CD-ROM
ISBN-13: 978-1-305-25576-0

Student Book + PAC
ISBN-13: 978-1-305-26072-6

National Geographic Learning/Cengage Learning
20 Channel Center Street
Boston, MA 02210
USA

Cengage Learning is a leading provider of customised learning solutions with office locations around the globe, including Singapore, the United Kingdom, Australia, Mexico, Brazil and Japan. Locate our local office at **international.cengage.com/region**

Cengage Learning products are represented in Canada by Nelson Education Ltd.

Visit National Geographic Learning online at **NGL.cengage.com**
Visit our corporate website at **www.cengage.com**

Printed in the United States of America
4 5 6 7 8 19 18 17 16

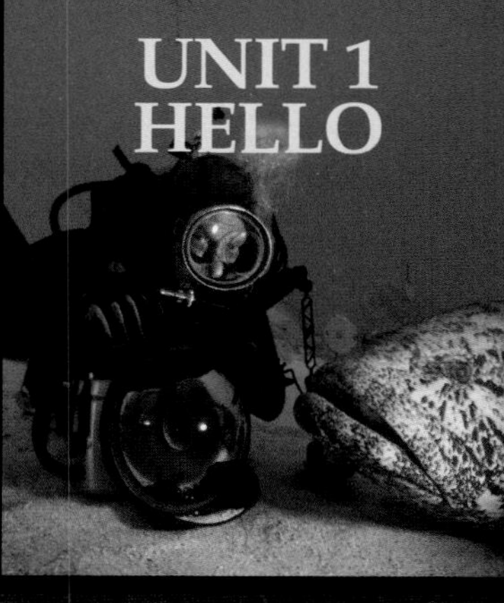
UNIT 1
HELLO

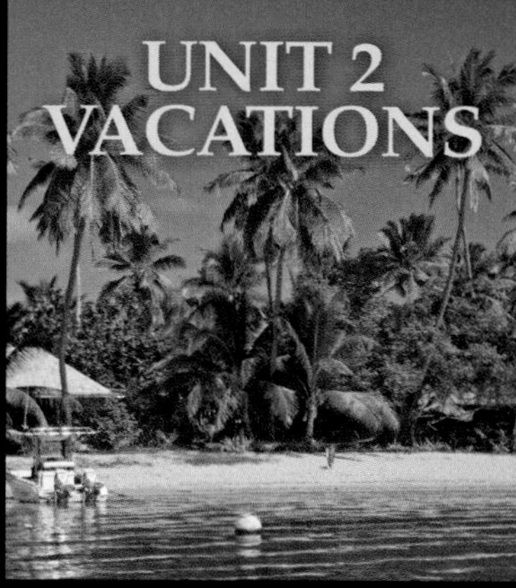
UNIT 2
VACATIONS

UNIT 3
FAMILIES

UNIT 4
CITIES

UNIT 5
INVENTIONS

UNIT 6
PASSIONS

UNIT 7
DIFFERENT
LIVES

UNIT 8
ROUTINES

UNIT 9
TRAVEL

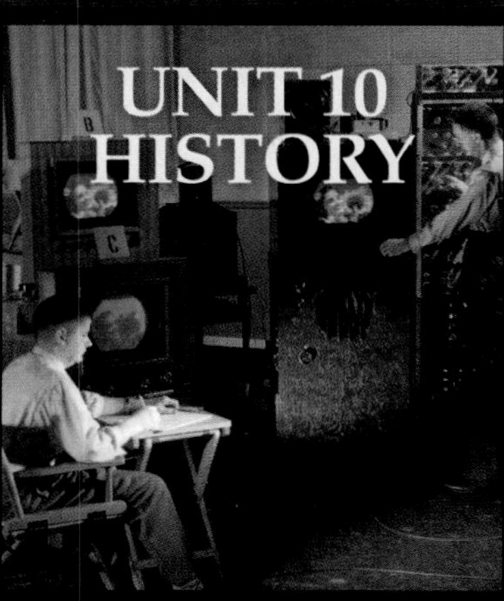
UNIT 10
HISTORY

UNIT 11
DISCOVERY

UNIT 12
THE WEEKEND

Contents

PRONUNCIATION	LISTENING	READING	SPEAKING	WRITING
word stress questions	introductions	a description of two people in the Himalayas an article about phone calls from New York	personal information a quiz phone numbers	text type: an identity badge writing skill: capital letters (1)
we're, they're *isn't, aren't* *be* questions and short answers plural nouns syllables	a description of a place a conversation on vacation	a blog about a vacation a quiz about vacation places	vacation photos on vacation general knowledge	text type: a form writing skill: capital letters (2)
possessive *'s* linking with *at* exclamations	information about a family from India a description of the Cousteau family	a description of a wedding in Thailand an article about population pyramids in different countries	your family tree a wedding your family pyramid	text type: a greeting card writing skill: contractions
th /ð/ linking with *can*	a description of Shanghai at a tourist information center	information about a town center a description of two famous towers an article about times around the world	locations famous places times and timetables	text type: a postcard writing skill: *and*
can/can't numbers	information about Yves Rossy an interview with a robot expert	an article about a robot a blog about technology an article about cooking with the sun	your abilities your favorite object buying online	text type: an email writing skill: *but*
do you … ? *likes, doesn't like* intonation	information about soccer and the World Cup an interview with a man about his likes and dislikes	an article about giant vegetables a profile of a TV presenter an article about racing with animals	a food survey things in common a sports event	text type: a review writing skill: pronouns

PRONUNCIATION	LISTENING	READING	SPEAKING	WRITING
don't intonation in questions sentence stress	information about the Holi festival an interview with a teacher an interview with a student	an article about traditional life an article about the seasons of the year	you and your partner a survey activities in different seasons	text type: a profile writing skill: paragraphs
-s and *-es* verbs /s/ and /z/	an interview with a man about his job a conversation about a National Geographic explorer	an article about a typical day an article about a job in tiger conservation	routines your friends and family a quiz	text type: an email writing skill: spelling: double letters
there is/are *I'd like*	four people talking about travel a conversation in which two people plan a trip	an article about things in your suitcase an article about a Trans-Siberia trip	things in your suitcase hotel rooms travel tips	text type: travel advice writing skill: *because*
was/were weak forms strong forms sentence stress	information about an important moment in TV history a radio show about heroes	a quiz about "firsts" in exploration an article about the first people on the American continents	dates and events people in the past famous Americans	text type: a blog writing skill: *when*
-ed verbs *did you … ?* *didn't*	information about discoveries in Papua New Guinea a story about the investigation of a discovery an interview about discovering your local area	an article about an unusual discovery an interview with an adventurer an article about an accident in Madagascar	your family's past what did you do last year? telling a story	text type: an email writing skill: expressions in emails
going and *doing* *would you … ?*	information about the weekend in different countries a description of a family in Indonesia a conversation between two friends about this weekend	an article about helping people on the weekend	your photos next weekend a special weekend	text type: an invitation writing skill: spelling: verb endings

Life around the world

Unit 4 Where's that?

A video quiz about four cities.

Unit 6 At the market

Meet people at a market in an English city.

Unit 7 The people of the reindeer

Life with the Sami people in Scandinavia.

Unit 12 Saturday morning in São Tomé

Meet some local artists in this small African country.

Unit 3 A Mongolian family

Meet a family in Mongolia.

Unit 1 My top ten photos

A photographer talks about his favorite photos.

Unit 10 The space race

What was the "space race"? Find out in this video.

Unit 9 Along the Inca Road

Discover South America with writer Karin Muller.

Unit 5 The Owl and the Pussycat

A video about an unusual pair of friends

Unit 11 Perfumes from Madagascar

Why do scientists love Madagascar?

Unit 2 Antarctica

Vacations in Antarctica.

Unit 8 The elephants of Samburu

Meet a man who photographs elephants.

Unit 1 Hello

Pacific Ocean, Australia
Photo by David Doubilet

FEATURES

1 **1** Look at the photo. Listen and mark (✓).

a Hi! My name's Mike.
b Hello! I'm Mike.
c Hi! I'm Mike.

2 **1** Listen again and repeat.

3 Write your name.

Hi! I'm ....

4 Work in pairs.

Hello! I'm Meera.

Hi! My name's Jared.

1a National Geographic people

Vocabulary jobs

1 2 Look at the photos. Listen to the people.

Hi. I'm Mattias. I'm a filmmaker.

2 3 Listen and repeat the jobs.

explorer	filmmaker	
photographer	scientist	writer

3 Look at the photos. Write the jobs.

1 Hi. I'm Carolyn. I'm a Wriler
2 Hello. I'm Alex. I'm a Photographer
3 Hi. I'm Mireya. I'm a acientist
4 Hi. I'm Mattias. I'm a filmmaker
5 Hello. I'm Robert. I'm an explore.

4 Complete the sentence with your job.

I'm studen .

5 Talk to four people in your class.

Hi. I'm Katya. I'm a student.

NATIONAL GEOGRAPHIC PEOPLE

Mattias Klum in Malaysia

Mattias Klum
filmmaker

Carolyn Anderson
writer

Robert Ballard
explorer

Mireya Mayor
scientist

Alex Treadwa
photographer

Grammar *a/an*

6 Look at the grammar box and the example. Then look at the jobs in Exercise 2. Underline the first letter.

Example: <u>e</u>xplorer

A	*AN*
a + noun with *b, c, d, f, ...* *a filmmaker*	*an* + noun with *a, e, i, o, u* *an explorer*

For more information and practice, see page 161.

7 Complete the sentences with ***a*** or ***an***.

1 

2 

3 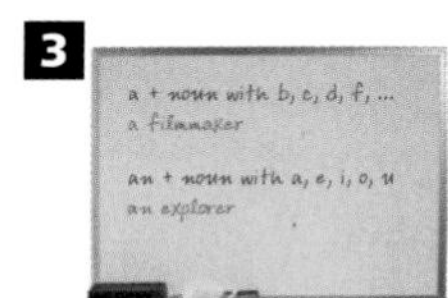

4 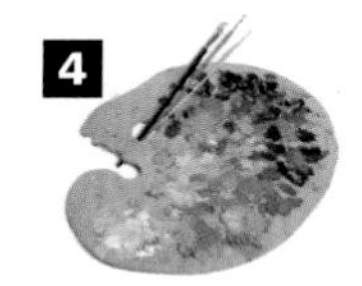

5 

6 

1 I'm ___a___ photographer.
2 I'm ___a___ doctor.
3 I'm ___a___ teacher.
4 I'm ___a___ artist.
5 I'm ___a___ engineer.
6 I'm ___an___ driver.

Listening

8 4 Listen and put the conversation in order.

a Yes.
b Oh, you're a photographer!
c Hello. 1
d I'm Alex Treadway.
e Hi.

9 5 Listen and complete the conversation.

you're	I'm	Hi	Hello

YOU: [1] ________.
MATTIAS: [2] ___Hi___. [3] ________ Mattias Klum.
YOU: Oh, [4] ___He___ a filmmaker!
MATTIAS: Yes, for National Geographic.

Grammar *I + am, you + are*

▶ *I + AM, YOU + ARE*	
I'm	Katya.
You're	a student.
(I'm = I am, You're = You are)	

For more information and practice, see page 161.

10 Work in pairs. Look at the photos on page 10. Practice the conversations in Exercises 8 and 9.

11 Work in groups. Play a game. Take turns.

Student A: Act a job.

Students B, C, D: Say the job.

Take turns.

Vocabulary the alphabet

12 6 Listen and repeat the alphabet.

Aa	Bb	Cc	Dd	Ee	Ff	Gg
Hh	Ii	Jj	Kk	Ll	Mm	
Nn	Oo	Pp	Qq	Rr	Ss	Tt
Uu	Vv	Ww	Xx	Yy	Zz	

13 7 Listen and choose the correct name.

1 Paula / Paola
2 Bryan / Brian
3 Shaun / Sean
4 Anna / Ana

14 Work in pairs. Spell your name.

15 Work in pairs. Spell words.

Student A: Turn to page 153.

Student B: Turn to page 157.

Speaking

16 Work in groups. Play a memory game. Introduce yourself. Then give information about other people.

I'm Katya.
I'm a student.

You're Katya. You're a student.
I'm Paola. I'm a doctor.

You're Katya. You're a student.
You're Paola. You're a doctor.
I'm Jason. I'm a scientist.

1b People and places

Reading

1 Read the article. Complete the table.

	Photo 1	Photo 2
Name	Manu	Dechen
Country	Nepal	Ladakh
Nationality	Nepalese	Indian

1

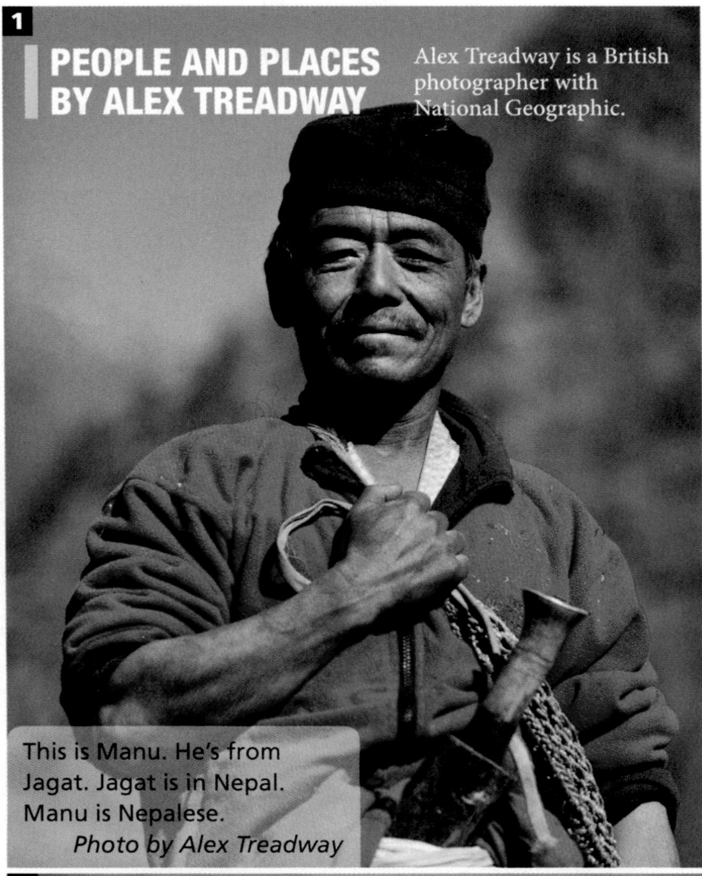

PEOPLE AND PLACES BY ALEX TREADWAY
Alex Treadway is a British photographer with National Geographic.

This is Manu. He's from Jagat. Jagat is in Nepal. Manu is Nepalese.
Photo by Alex Treadway

2

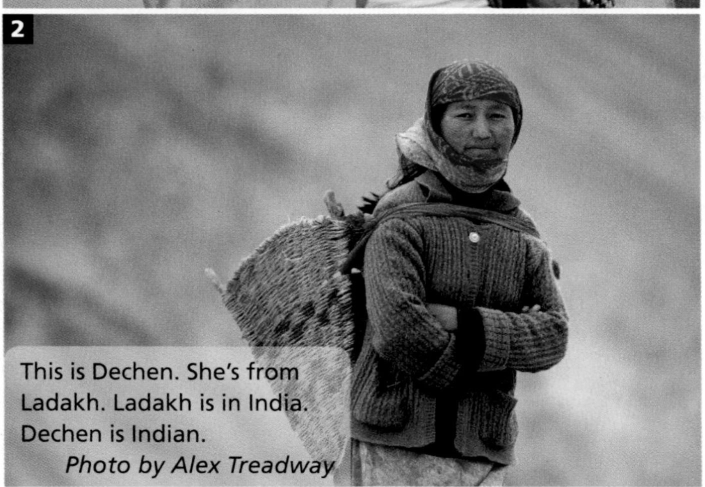

This is Dechen. She's from Ladakh. Ladakh is in India. Dechen is Indian.
Photo by Alex Treadway

Vocabulary countries and nationalities

2 Complete the table.

British China Spanish the United States

Country	Nationality
Brazil	Brazilian
Canada	Canadian
....	Chinese
Egypt	Egyptian
France	French
Germany	German
Great Britain	....
Italy	Italian
Japan	Japanese
Mexico	Mexican ✓
Oman	Omani
Spain	....
....	American

3 **Pronunciation word stress**

8 Listen and repeat the countries from Exercise 2. Notice the stress.

Grammar *he/she/it + is*

▶ *HE / SHE / IT + IS*

He	is	from India.
She	is	Indian.
It	he	in India.

(He's, She's = He is, She is)

For more information and practice, see page 161.

4 Complete the table for you. Then work in pairs. Complete the table for your partner.

	You	Your partner
Name	Lucina	Martha
Country	Mexico	Columbia
Nationality	Mexican	Columbian

5 Work in groups of four. Tell the other pair about your partner.

This is Kira. She's from France. She's French.

6 Look at the photos (a–d). Then read the sentences. Write true (T) or false (F).

1 Miu is from Japan.
2 John is French.
3 Jai is Indian.
4 Marita is from China.

7 Write sentences (true or false) like Exercise 6. Read your sentences to your partner.

Miu is a writer.

False. She's a filmmaker.

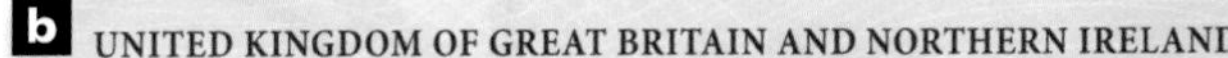

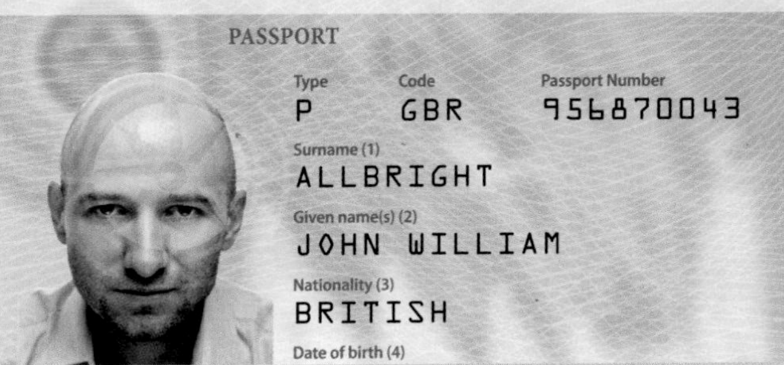

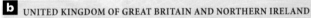

Speaking and writing

8 Work in pairs. Do the quiz.

Toshiba is French.

False. It's Japanese.

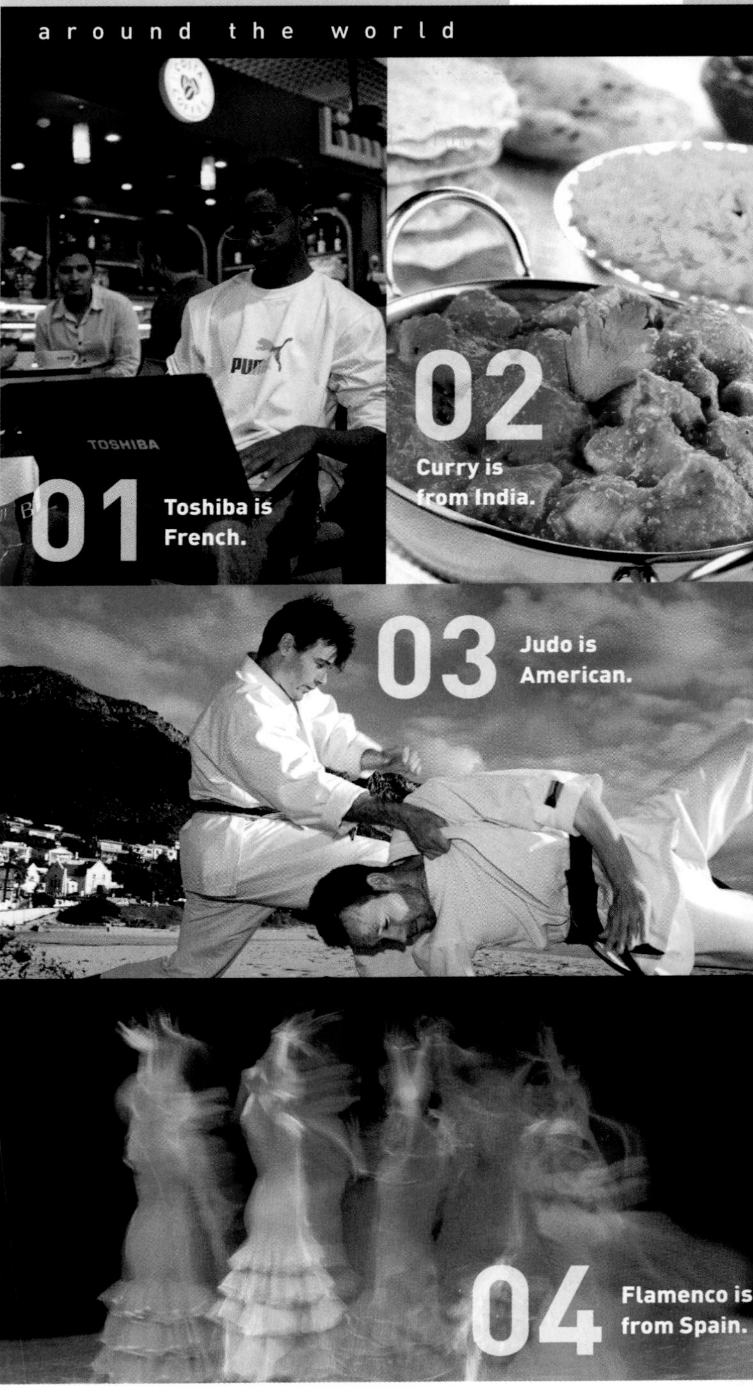

QUICK QUIZ: TRUE OR FALSE
around the world
01 Toshiba is French.
02 Curry is from India.
03 Judo is American.
04 Flamenco is from Spain.

9 Work in pairs. Write an "Around the world" quiz. Write four sentences. Test the class.

1c International phone calls

Vocabulary continents

1 Look at the map on page 15. Complete the names of the continents.

1 Af..........
2 As..........
3 Au..........
4 E..........
5 N.......... A..........
6 S.......... A..........

2 Look at the map again. Complete the sentences.

1 India is in ....
2 Italy is in ....
3 Germany is in ....
4 Canada is in ....
5 Brazil is in ....

3 Work in pairs. Write five sentences (true or false). Test your partner.

Brazil is in Africa.

Reading

4 Read the article on page 15. Underline the names of four countries.

5 Read the article again. Complete the sentences with the correct name.

1 .... is a student.
2 .... is Mexican.
3 .... is an artist.
4 .... is from Brazil.
5 .... is from Canada.
6 .... is a doctor.

6 Word focus ***from***

Underline *from* in the sentences. Then match the sentences (1–3) with the pictures (a–c).

1 I'm from Spain.
2 Pizza is from Italy.
3 This phone call is from John.

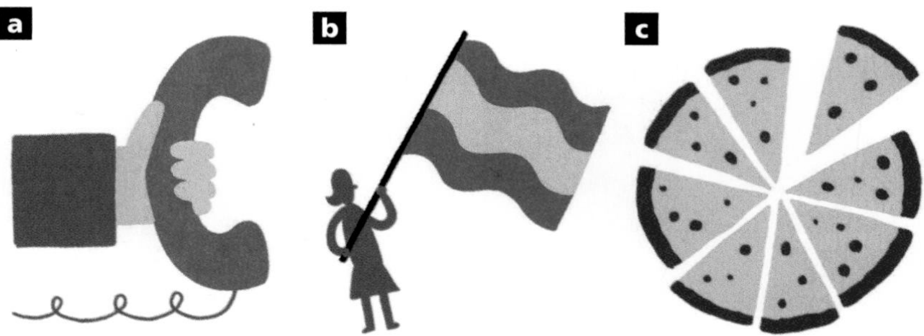

Vocabulary numbers 1–10

7 9 Write the numbers (1–10). Then listen and repeat the numbers.

0	zero	....	four	....	eight
....	one	....	five	....	nine
....	two	....	six	....	ten
....	three	....	seven		

8 Work in pairs. Look at the map and say a number. Your partner says the country. Switch roles.

Grammar *my, your*

9 10 Listen to the conversation. Choose the correct cell phone number (a–c).

a 619 507 7132. b 619 408 7132. c 619 401 6235.

10 10 Listen again. Write the work phone number.

> ▶ ***MY, YOUR***
>
> What's **your** phone number?
> **My** cell phone number is 619 408 7132.
> Note: we often say *oh* for 0 (zero) in phone numbers.
>
> For more information and practice, see page 161.

Speaking

11 Work in pairs. Ask and answer questions.

cell phone number

work number

home number

GEOGRAPHY

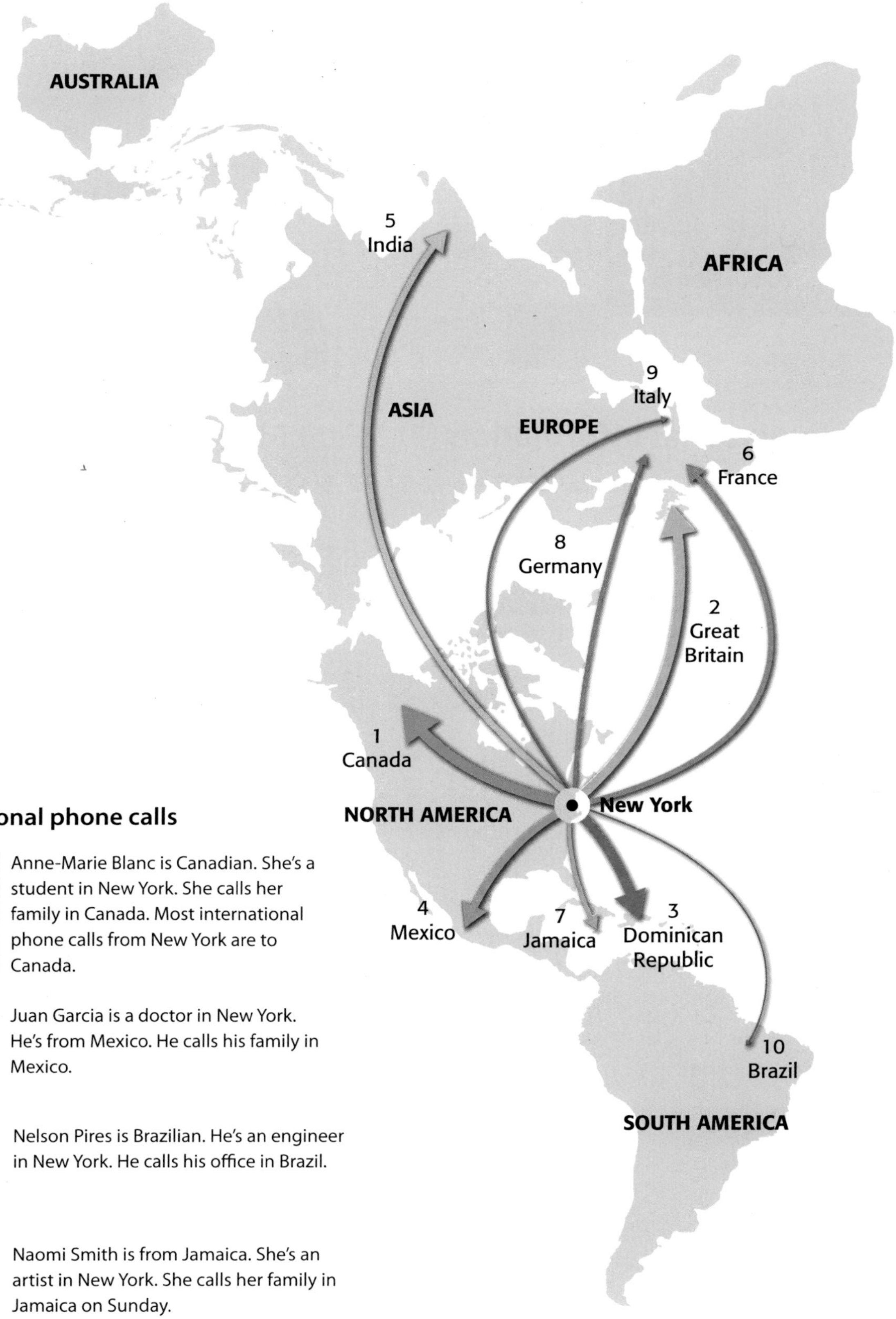

AUSTRALIA
AFRICA
ASIA
EUROPE
NORTH AMERICA
SOUTH AMERICA
New York
1 Canada
2 Great Britain
3 Dominican Republic
4 Mexico
5 India
6 France
7 Jamaica
8 Germany
9 Italy
10 Brazil

International phone calls

Anne-Marie Blanc is Canadian. She's a student in New York. She calls her family in Canada. Most international phone calls from New York are to Canada.

Juan Garcia is a doctor in New York. He's from Mexico. He calls his family in Mexico.

Nelson Pires is Brazilian. He's an engineer in New York. He calls his office in Brazil.

Naomi Smith is from Jamaica. She's an artist in New York. She calls her family in Jamaica on Sunday.

1d Nice to meet you

Vocabulary greetings

1 Write *Bye* and *Hello* in the correct places.

Hi.
[1] ....

Real life personal information (1)

2 11 Listen to the conversation. Mark (✓) the greetings in Exercise 1.

3 11 Listen again. Complete the visitor book.

Date	Name	Company	Signature
5/17/2015	Elias Brich	EB Consulting	E Brich
5/18/2015	Suzi Lee	New Start	Suzi Lee
5/18/2015	James Watt	New Start	James Watt
5/18/2015			

4 Pronunciation questions

a 12 Listen and repeat three questions from the conversation.

b Work in pairs. Look at the audioscript on page 169. Practice the conversation.

5 Look at the expressions for asking for PERSONAL INFORMATION. Complete the questions with these words.

first name phone

PERSONAL INFORMATION

What's your ....?
What's your .... name?
What's your last name?
What's your .... number?
What's your job?
I'm Liam. / My name's Liam.

Real life meeting people

6 13 Listen to the conversation. Put the conversation in order.

a Hi, Katya. How are you? *1*
b Nice to meet you too.
c Fine, thanks. And you?
d I'm OK. This is Silvia. She's from Madrid.
e Nice to meet you, Silvia.

7 Work in groups of three. Practice the conversation from Exercise 6. Use your own names.

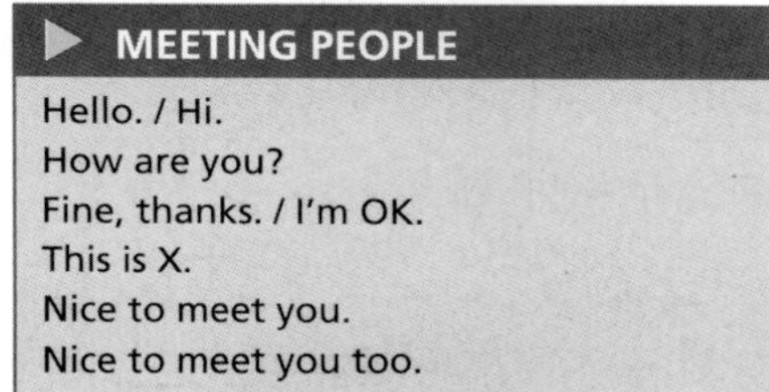

MEETING PEOPLE

Hello. / Hi.
How are you?
Fine, thanks. / I'm OK.
This is X.
Nice to meet you.
Nice to meet you too.

8 You are at a meeting. Invent an identity: name, job, company, phone number. Talk to people. Write the names and phone numbers of people with the same job.

Good afternoon. I'm Vicente.

Nice to meet you.

1e My ID

Writing an ID badge

1 Look at the ID (identity) badge and find:

1 the name of the company
2 the name of the visitor

2 Writing skill capital letters (1)

a Underline the capital letters on the ID badge.

b Write these words in the table.

Brazil	Nelson Pires
Brazilian	Rio de Janeiro
Portuguese	South America

a city	Washington ....
a continent	North America ....
a country	the United States of America ....
a language	English ....
a name	Carolyn Anderson ....
a nationality	American ....

c Rewrite the sentences with the correct capital letters.

1 riyadh is in saudi arabia.
2 I'm chinese.
3 He's from tokyo.
4 She's from canada.
5 I speak french.

3 Complete the IDs with the information. Use capital letters.

1 houston sean booth

2

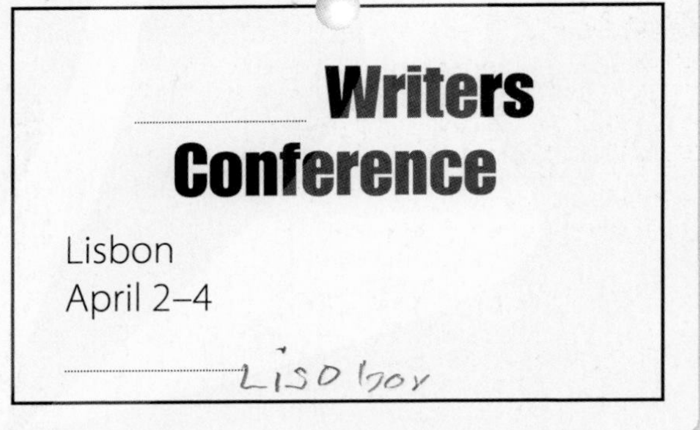

3 honolulu bangkok sydney jan sastre

4 Write an ID badge for yourself.

5 Check your badge. Check the capital letters.

1f My top ten photos

Video

Before you watch

1 Work in pairs. Look at this photo. Complete the information about Tom Brooks.

Hi. My name [1] .... Tom Brooks. I'm [2] .... photographer. This [3] .... my top ten—my favorite National Geographic photos of people and places.

While you watch

2 Watch the video. Mark (✓) the correct column for each photo.

	a man	a woman	people	an animal / animals
Photo 1		✓		
Photo 2				
Photo 3				
Photo 4				
Photo 5				
Photo 6				
Photo 7				
Photo 8				
Photo 9				
Photo 10				

3 Work in pairs. Compare your answers from Exercise 2.

Photo 2 is a man. *Yes, I agree.*

4 Watch the video again. Choose the correct country.

Photo 1 Nepal / India
Photo 2 China / Mongolia
Photo 3 Mongolia / Nepal
Photo 4 the United States / Canada
Photo 5 Brazil / Bangladesh
Photo 6 Canada / New Zealand
Photo 7 Australia / the United States
Photo 8 South Africa / Namibia
Photo 9 Namibia / Kenya
Photo 10 Kenya / South Africa

5 Work in pairs. Read the sentences. Write true (T) or false (F). Then watch the video again and check.

Photo 1 The photographer is Alex Treadway.
Photo 2 This man is a hunter.
Photo 3 This woman is happy.
Photo 4 This fisherwoman is from Alaska.
Photo 5 This is a photo of water buffalo.
Photo 6 This whale is in the ocean.
Photo 7 This climber is Jimmy Chin.
Photo 8 The photographer is South African.
Photo 9 This photo is in Africa.
Photo 10 Tom says, "This photo is my favorite."

6 Watch the video again. Choose your favorite photo. Tell your partner.

After you watch

7 Complete the information about three of the photos.

Photo 5 is by Jim Blair. He's [1] .... American photographer. The photo is in Dhaka in Bangladesh. It's [2] .... photo of water buffalo in [3] .... river and [4] .... man.

Photo 7 [5] .... by Jimmy Chin. This [6] .... Kate Rutherford. She's [7] .... the United States. She's [8] .... climber.

Photo 8 is by David Cartier. [9] .... Australian. He's [10] .... student. This [11] .... a photo of a student too. She's a student [12] .... South Africa.

8 Write about your favorite photo.

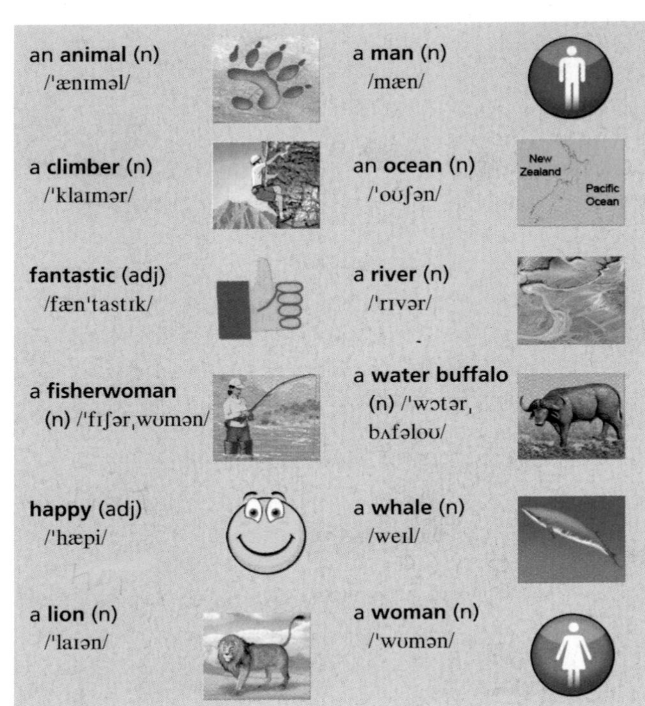

UNIT 1 REVIEW

Grammar

1 Complete the sentences with these words.

I'm	you're	he's	he's	she's	she's	it's	it's

1 Hi. My name's Rosa. ________ from Brazil.
2 This is Carolyn. ________ an engineer.
3 I'm from Ottawa. ________ in Canada.
4 "My name's Claude Lefevre."
"Oh! ________ a writer!"
5 Mattias is a doctor. ________ from Germany.
6 Marina is from Italy. ________ Italian.
7 This is Nelson. ________ a student.
8 John is from Sydney. ________ in Australia.

2 Circle the correct option.

1 *a* / *an* country
2 *a* / *an* explorer
3 *a* / *an* family
4 *a* / *an* identity badge
5 *a* / *an* office
6 *a* / *an* passport

I CAN	
introduce people (*be*)	☐
use *a* and *an* correctly	☐
use *my* and *your* correctly	☐

Vocabulary

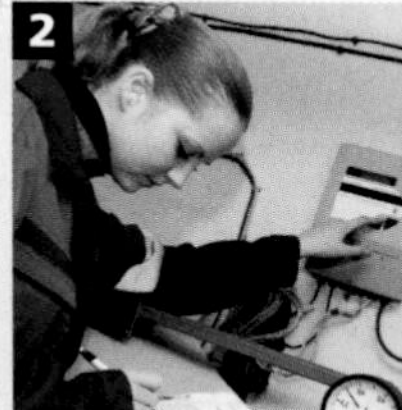

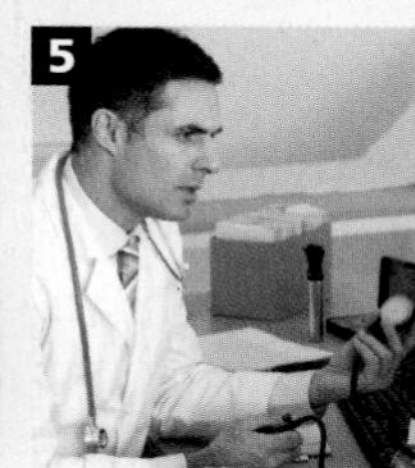

3 Look at the pictures. Complete the sentences.

1 I'm a *teacher*. I'm from Italy. I'm ________.
2 Lisa's an ________. She's French. She's from ________.
3 Joe's British. He's from ________. He's an ________.
4 I'm a ________. I'm from China. I'm ________.
5 Enrique is a ________. He's from Mexico. He's ________.
6 Sam's American. He's from ________. He's a ________.

4 Work in pairs. Take turns.

Student A: Write five numbers. Then say the numbers to your partner.

Student B: Write the numbers. Then check your answers.

5 Work in pairs. Complete the names of the continents. Spell the names to your partner.

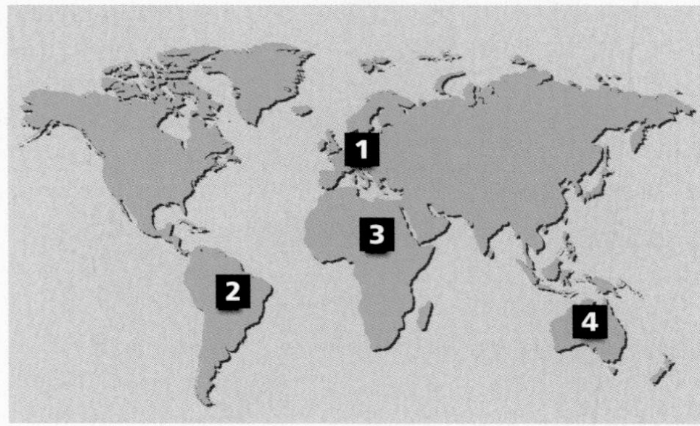

1 _ _ r _ p _
2 S _ _ th _ m _ r _ c _
3 _ fr _ c _
4 _ _ str _ l _ _

I CAN	
talk about jobs, countries, and nationalities	☐
count to ten	☐
say the alphabet, and spell names and words	☐

Real life

6 Complete the conversations with the right option.

Can you spell your last name?
How are you?
Nice to meet you too.
What's your name, please?

A: Hello. I'm from *World Film* magazine.
B: Ah yes! Good morning. [1] ________
A: My name's Amy Lewis.
B: [2] ________
A: Yes. Lewis. L–E–W–I–S.
B: Thanks. Nice to meet you, Amy.
A: [3] ________
B: This is Chanda. She's a photographer.
A: Hi, Chanda.[4] ________
C: Fine, thanks.

I CAN	
ask for and give personal information	☐
meet and greet people	☐

Speaking

7 Work in groups of three. Practice the conversation in Exercise 6.

Unit 2 Vacations

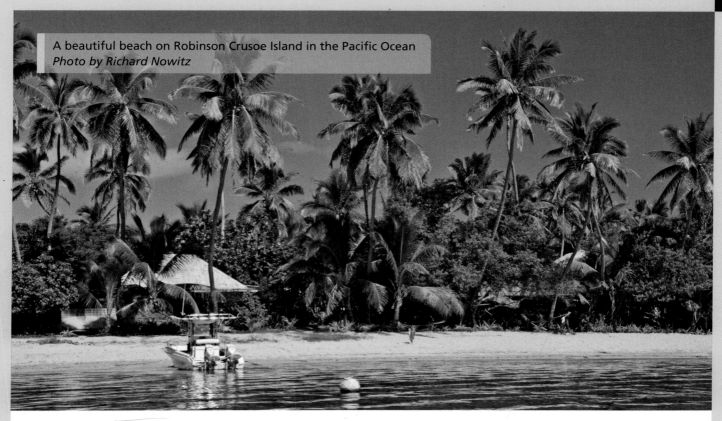

A beautiful beach on Robinson Crusoe Island in the Pacific Ocean
Photo by Richard Nowitz

FEATURES

1 Look at the photo. Choose the correct option (a–c).

a This is in Canada. It's a beach. It's evening.
b This is in France. It's a city. It's night.
c This is in Fiji. It's an island. It's morning.

2 14 Look at these two pictures. Listen and repeat the words.

3 Complete the sentences with words from Exercise 2.

1 Rio de Janeiro is a .... in Brazil.
2 Titicaca is a .... in Bolivia and Peru.
3 Tahiti is an .... in the Pacific Ocean.
4 Everest is a .... in Nepal.

4 Write four sentences about places and read them to your partner.

Loch Ness is a lake in Scotland.

2a My vacation

MY VACATION BLOG by Laura
03 JAN
This is in Tunisia. It's beautiful! It's evening. I'm with Brad, Andy, and Jessica. We're on a beach. We're happy. Andy and Jessica are Canadian. They're doctors. They're on vacation too.

Reading

1 Work in pairs. Look at the photos. Choose the place (a–c).

a North America b Europe c Africa

2 Read about the photo above. Find:

1 the name of the country
2 the names of the people

Grammar *we/they + are*

3 Look at the grammar box. Then look at the blog. Underline the contractions *we're* and *they're*.

▶ *WE/THEY + ARE*		
We **They**	**are**	in Tunisia. Canadian.
(We're, They're = We are, They are)		
For more information and practice, see page 161.		

4 Complete the sentences.

1 This is Jane. This is Paul. They .... Australian.
2 I'm Meera. This is Suri. We .... from India.
3 In this photo, I'm with my friend Jack. ....'re in Egypt.
4 Laura is with Brad, Andy, and Jessica. .... on vacation.
5 Jeanne and Claude are from France. .... French.

5 Pronunciation ***we're, they're***

a 15 Listen and repeat six sentences.

b Work in pairs. Write three true sentences with *We're*. Read your sentences to a new pair.

We're in Moscow.

6 Read these sentences about the photo on page 22. Write true (T) or false (F). Correct the false sentences.

1 It isn't Tunisia.
2 They are on a beach.
3 Andy and Jessica aren't from Canada.
4 Laura isn't in the photo.
5 They aren't happy.

Grammar *be* negative forms

7 Look at the grammar box and the sentences in Exercise 6. Note the negative forms of *is* and *are*.

▶ *BE* NEGATIVE FORMS		
I You	**am not (I'm not)** **are not (aren't)**	happy. on a beach.
He/She/It	**is not (isn't)**	
We/You/They	**are not (aren't)**	

For more information and practice, see page 162.

8 Complete the blog. Use these words.

not aren't isn't isn't

9 **Pronunciation *isn't, aren't***

a 16 Listen and repeat the sentences.

b Write true sentences. Read them to your partner.

We aren't on a beach.

I'm (not) You're You aren't We're We aren't	a student. a doctor. in a city. in a classroom. in Asia. happy. on a lake. on a beach. on vacation. from Morocco.

Speaking

10 Work in groups. Show a photo on your cell phone to the group. Tell the group about your photo.

This is a photo of my friends, Carlos and Enrique. We're in Egypt.

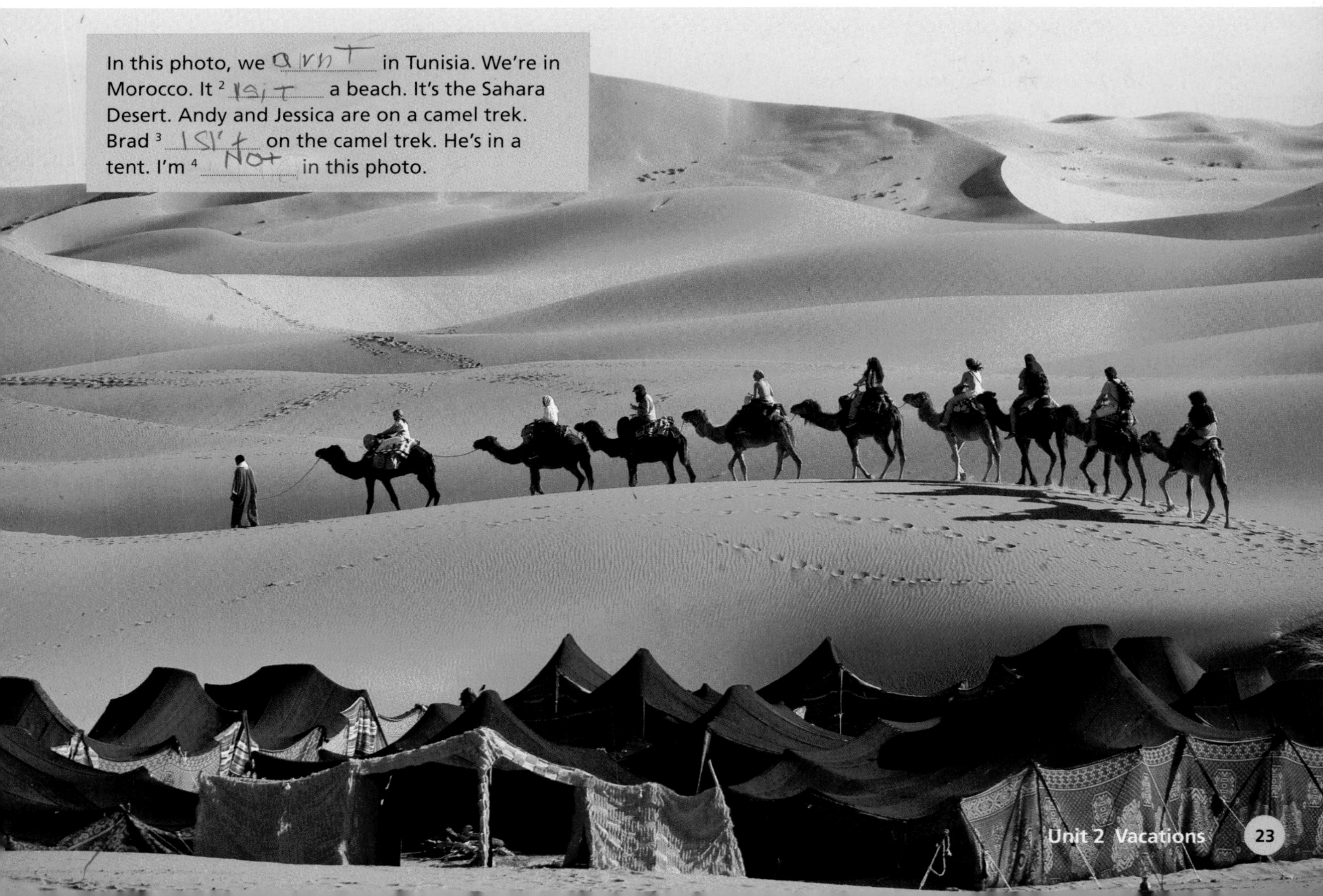

In this photo, we [1] ______ in Tunisia. We're in Morocco. It [2] ______ a beach. It's the Sahara Desert. Andy and Jessica are on a camel trek. Brad [3] ______ on the camel trek. He's in a tent. I'm [4] ______ in this photo.

2b Where are you?

Vocabulary numbers 11–100

1 Write the numbers. Repeat them after your instructor.

11	eleven
______	twelve
______	thirteen
______	fourteen
______	fifteen
______	sixteen
______	seventeen
______	eighteen
19	nineteen

2 Write the numbers in order. Check your answers with your instructor.

eighty	fifty	forty	ninety
seventy	sixty	thirty	twenty

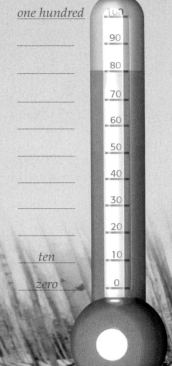

one hundred
______
______
______
______
______
______
______
______
ten
zero

3 17 Look at the temperatures. Then listen. Are the numbers the same or different?

It's twelve degrees.
the same

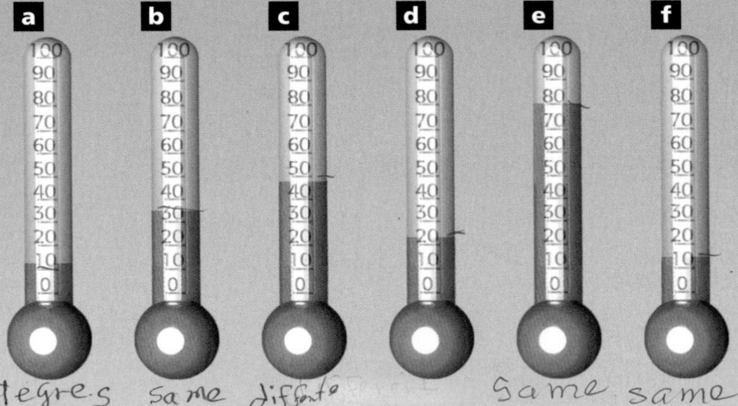

4 17 Listen again. Write the correct numbers.

5 Work in pairs. Say the correct temperatures to your partner.

6 Complete the sentences with ***hot*** or ***cold***.

1 It's eleven degrees in London today. It's ________ .
2 It's eighty degrees in Sydney today. It's ________ .

7 Work in pairs. Make sentences with *hot* and *cold*.

Iceland is cold.

Cairo is hot.

Reading and listening

8 Lorna is Australian. She's on vacation in Europe. Read the conversation. Answer the questions.

1 Where's Lorna?
2 Where's Greg?
3 Where are Kara and Ona?

9 18 Listen and choose the correct option.

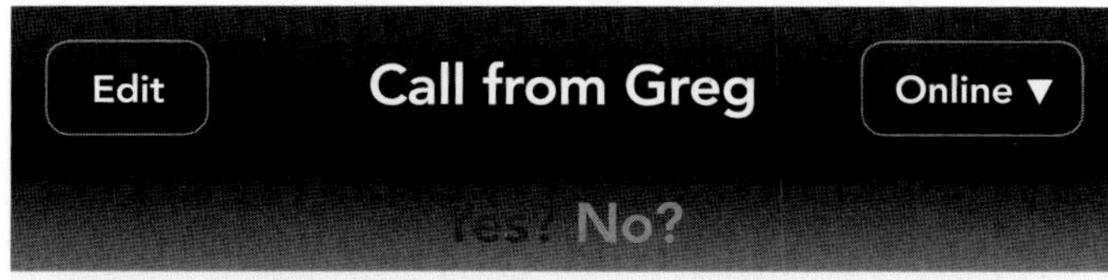

Greg:	Hi! Where are you now? Are you in [1] *France / Italy*?
Lorna:	Yes, I am. I'm in the Alps. It's beautiful!
Greg:	Are you OK?
Lorna:	No, I'm not. It's [2] *two / seventy-two* degrees!
Greg:	Wow! Is it [3] *cold / hot* in your hotel?
Lorna:	No, it isn't. The hotel is nice.
Greg:	It's [4] *eighty-six / sixteen* degrees in Sydney today.
Lorna:	Oh! That's [5] *hot / cold*!
Greg:	Are Kara and Ona in France?
Lorna:	No, they aren't. They're on a [6] *beach / lake* in Morocco!

Grammar *be* questions and short answers

10 Look at the grammar box. Then underline the questions in Exercise 9.

▶ *BE* QUESTIONS and SHORT ANSWERS		
Am I	in France? cold?	Yes, I **am**. No, **I'm not**.
Are you/we/they		Yes, you/we/they **are**. No, you/we/they **aren't**.
Is she/he/it		Yes, she/he/it **is**. No, she/he/it **isn't**.

For more information and practice, see page 162.

11 Put the words in order to make questions. Then match the questions (1–6) with the answers (a–f).

1 you / OK / are / ?
2 is / in France / Kara / ?
3 in Sydney / you and Paul / are / ?
4 in London / is / Greg / ?
5 Kara and Ona / in Morocco / are / ?
6 nice / your hotel / is / ?

a Yes, they are.
b No, he isn't.
c Yes, I am.
d Yes, it is.
e No, she isn't.
f Yes, we are.

12 Pronunciation ***be* questions and short answers**

a 19 Listen and repeat these questions and answers.

b Work in pairs. Practice the questions and answers.

Speaking

13 Work in pairs. You are on vacation. Have a telephone conversation with your friend.

Student A: Turn to page 153.

Student B: Turn to page 157.

2c A vacation quiz

La Defense, Paris, France

Vocabulary colors

1 Match the colors with the numbers.

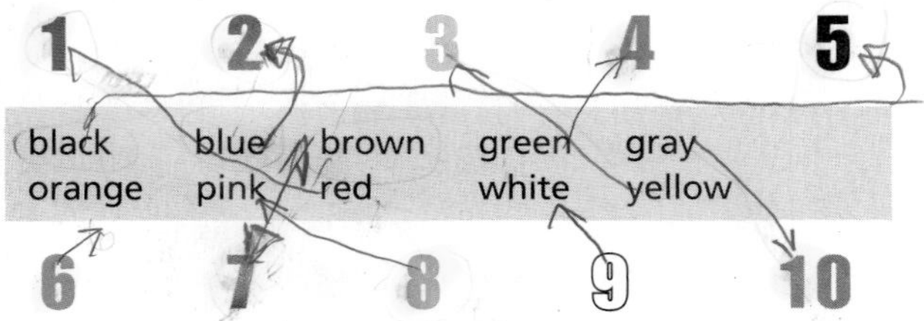

2 Find the colors in the photo.

Reading

3 Read the quiz on page 27. Match the photos with four sentences.

4 Complete the sentences in the quiz in pairs.

Grammar plural nouns

5 Look at the grammar box. Find these plural nouns in the quiz. Then find TWO more plural nouns in the quiz.

▶ NOUNS

Singular	Plural
a lake	lakes
a car	cars
a country	**cities**
a beach	**beaches**

For more information and practice, see page 162.

6 Pronunciation plural nouns

a 20 Listen and repeat these nouns.

/s/	/z/	/ɪz/
lakes airports	cars countries	beaches buses

b 21 Write the plural of these nouns. Then listen and repeat.

a city	a doctor	a friend
a hotel	a mountain	an office
a phone	a student	a tent

7 Word focus *in*

Write the expressions in the correct place.

in Australia	in French	in a hotel
in Japanese	in Moscow	in a tent

1 in English ....
2 in Europe ....
3 in a classroom ....

Speaking

8 Work in pairs. Test your partner. Take turns.

cities countries continents lakes

Name three cities.

London, Lima, Bangkok.

A Vacation Quiz

airports	black	China
Cuba	lakes	London

1. In ________, cars are old.
2. In ________, buses are red.
3. In Hawaii, beaches are ________.
4. In Iceland, the ________ are hot.
5. Hong Kong, Shanghai, and Beijing are cities in ________.
6. John Lennon, Charles de Gaulle, and John F. Kennedy are ________.

d

A 1951 Chevy on Playa Ancon, Cuba

2d Here are your keys

Vocabulary car rental

1 Match 1–5 with a–e.

1 a license plate number
2 an email address
3 an address
4 a zip code
5 keys

2 Work in pairs. Take turns.

Student A: Read an email address.

Student B: Identify the email address.

1 smith23@hotmail.com
2 ryan.law@google.com
3 barry@yahoo.com
4 smnrss@msn.com

3 Work in pairs. Ask your partner his or her address, zip code, email address, and license plate number.

Real life personal information (2)

4 **22** Listen to the conversation. Answer the questions.

1 Is the man from Tokyo?
2 Is he on vacation or on business?

5 **22** Listen again. Choose the correct option.

1 Name: *Mr. Sato / Mrs. Ono*
2 Zip code: *08597 / 170-3293*
3 Email address: *epsato@hotmail.com / ep@hotmail.com*
4 License plate number: *BD5 ACR / BD6 ATR*

6 Work in pairs. Practice the conversation on page 169.

PERSONAL INFORMATION

This is my ID.
Where are you from?
Is this your (email) address?
What's the zip code?
What's your telephone number in the US?
Sign here, please.
Here's your key.
The license plate number is BD6 ATR.
Note: in email addresses we say *at* for @ and *dot* for "."

7 **Pronunciation syllables**

23 Listen and repeat these words. Count the syllables.

vacation va – ca – tion = 3

address car email key number telephone

8 Work in pairs. Practice the conversation again with new information.

Good evening.

Hello, I'm Mrs. Ono.

2e Contact details

Writing a form

1 Match 1 and 2 with the options (a and b).

a a hotel online reservation form
b an Internet profile

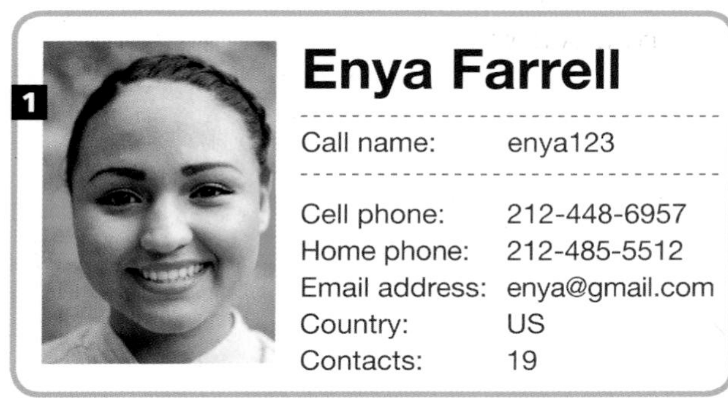

1

Enya Farrell

Call name:	enya123
Cell phone:	212-448-6957
Home phone:	212-485-5512
Email address:	enya@gmail.com
Country:	US
Contacts:	19

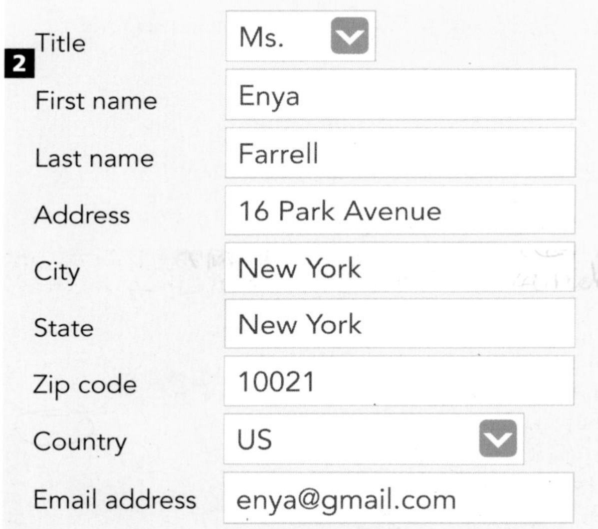

2

Title	Ms.
First name	Enya
Last name	Farrell
Address	16 Park Avenue
City	New York
State	New York
Zip code	10021
Country	US
Email address	enya@gmail.com

2 What's your title? Is it Mr., Mrs., or Ms.?

3 Writing skill **capital letters (2)**

a Look at the information in form 2. Underline the capital letters.

b Rewrite this information with the correct capital letters.

1 11 hill view
2 california
3 san francisco
4 esposito
5 mr.
6 ryan

4 Complete the college registration form with the information from Exercise 3b.

REGISTRATION FORM

Title ________
First name ________
Last name ________
Address ________
City ________ State ________
Zip code *94122*
Contact number *415 - 489 - 1453*
Email address *ryan@aol.com*

5 Complete the online reservation form with your own information. Check the capital letters.

Title	Choose...
First name	
Last name	
Address	
City	
State	
Zip code	
Contact number	
Email address	

2f Antarctica

Video

People and penguins in Antarctica

Before you watch

1 Look at the photo and the caption on page 30. What are the animals?

2 Look at the map. Write the number (1–4) next to the place.

Africa	Australia	New Zealand	South America

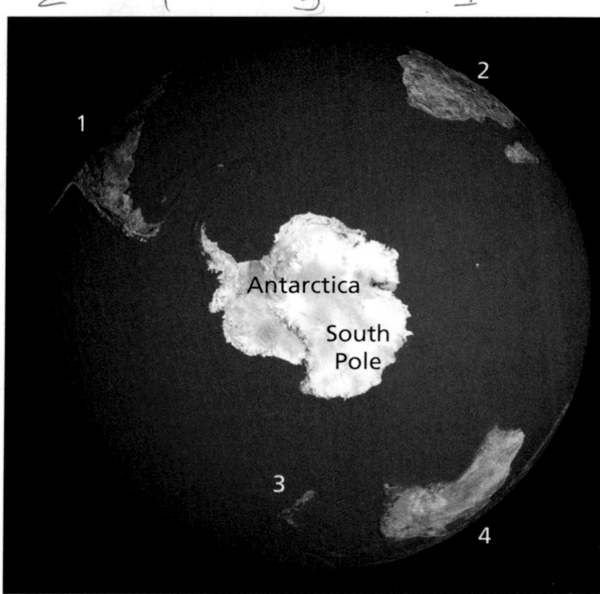

While you watch

3 Watch the video without sound. Write at least five words.

4 Work in pairs. Read your words to your partner. Watch the video again. Check your partner's words.

5 Watch and listen to the video. Listen to information about these things. Put the words in the order you hear them.

a animals
b beaches
c boats
d temperatures
e the ocean

6 Read the sentences. Watch the video again. Write true (T) or false (F).

1 The typical temperatures in Antarctica are 90 degrees below zero.
2 The people on the boat are scientists.
3 The animals in the ocean are whales and penguins.
4 The temperature of the ocean in Antarctica is from two degrees below zero to ten degrees.

7 Read the sentences. Underline the correct option. Watch the video again. Check your answers.

1 Antarctica *is / isn't* a continent.
2 Antarctica *is / isn't* a good place for scientists and explorers.
3 The beaches *are / aren't* yellow.
4 Cold temperatures *are / aren't* good for the animals.

After you watch

8 Work in pairs. Test your memory. Ask and answer the questions.

1 Where are the boats from?
2 What color are penguins?
3 What color are whales?
4 What color is ice?

9 Work in pairs. Write questions about Antarctica with these words.

1 mountains / beautiful
2 beaches / nice
3 animals / amazing
4 Antarctica / a good place for a vacation

10 Work as a class. Ask three people your questions. Write their names and answers.

Are the mountains beautiful?

Yes, they are. *No, they aren't.*

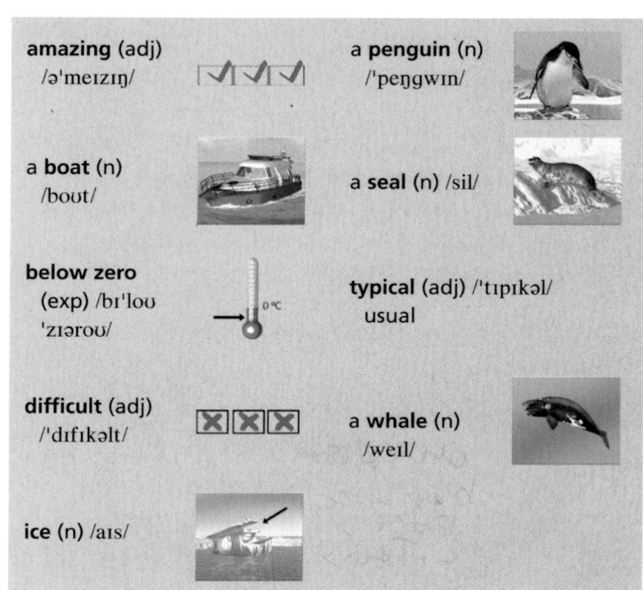

amazing (adj) /ə'meɪzɪŋ/
a boat (n) /bout/
below zero (exp) /bɪ'lou 'zɪərou/
0°C
difficult (adj) /'dɪfɪkəlt/
ice (n) /aɪs/
a penguin (n) /'peŋgwɪn/
a seal (n) /sil/
typical (adj) /'tɪpɪkəl/ usual
a whale (n) /weɪl/

UNIT 2 REVIEW

Grammar

1 Complete the texts with the words. Then match the photo with Greg or Kara.

'm isn't not we're

GREG
I'm in the mountains. I [1] ________ with my friends. We're in Canada. [2] ________ on vacation. I'm [3] ________ happy—the hotel [4] ________ nice.

are aren't isn't they're we

KARA
I'm in Brazil with my friends Jorge and Ana. [5] ________ Brazilian. I'm on vacation. Jorge and Ana [6] ________ on vacation. [7] ________ 're in Rio de Janeiro. The beaches [8] ________ beautiful. The ocean [9] ________ cold—it's warm!

2 Write questions.

1 your teacher / American?
2 we / in an office?
3 you / from Europe?
4 your friends / teachers?
5 this classroom / cold?
6 you / OK?

3 Work in pairs. Ask and answer the questions in Exercise 2.

4 Write the plurals.

1 airport ________ 5 country ________
2 beach ________ 6 friend ________
3 bus ________ 7 office ________
4 city ________ 8 photo ________

I CAN
- talk about more than one person (*we, you, they*)
- ask and answer questions (*be*)
- use regular plural nouns

Vocabulary

5 Write the numbers.

a eleven + twelve = ________
b twenty-three + sixty = ________
c forty-five + fifteen = ________
d thirty-eight + fifty-one = ________

6 Choose the correct color.

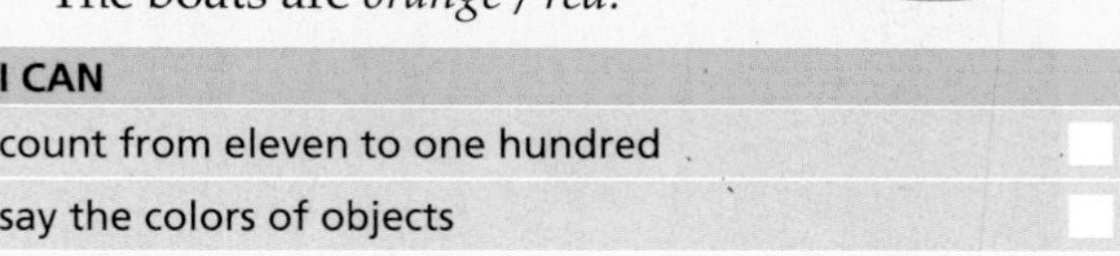

1 My car is *red / yellow.*
2 My phone is *gray / black.*
3 The buses are *yellow / green.*
4 The lake is *brown / blue.*
5 The boats are *orange / red.*

I CAN
- count from eleven to one hundred
- say the colors of objects

Real life

7 Complete 1–4 with four of these words. Then match 1–4 with a–d.

a are is my your zip code

1 Where ________ you from?
2 ________ this your address in the US?
3 What's the ________?
4 Here are ________ keys.

a 10007.
b Thank you.
c I'm from Poland.
d Yes, it is.

I CAN
- ask for and give personal information
- rent a car

Speaking

8 Work in pairs.

Student A: You are a car rental agent.

Student B: You are a customer.

Ask and answer questions to complete the car rental form. Take turns.

SuperCar

title	
first name	
last name	
address	
city	
state	
zip code	
contact number	
email address	

Unit 3 Families

A father in India takes his two sons to school.

FEATURES

1 24 Look at the photo and read the information about the family. Complete the information for Ravi and Mohan. Then listen and check.

Danvir and Mohan are brothers. Ravi and Danvir are father and son. Ravi and Mohan are ______ and ______ .

2 Write the words in the correct place.

daughter parents sister

♂		♀		
brother		______		
son		______		
father	&	mother	=	______

3 Complete the sentences with a family word.

1 I'm a ______ . 2 I'm not a ______ .

4 Work in pairs. Read your sentences to your partner.

I'm a father. I'm not a brother.

I'm a sister. I'm not a mother.

3a Unusual families

Vocabulary **family**

1 Look at the words. Add *grand-* to six of the words to make words for more family members.

brother	child	cousin
daughter	father	mother
parent	sister	son

2 Look at the Cousteau family tree. Find the names of:

1 the grandparents
2 two grandsons
3 two granddaughters
4 two brothers
5 four cousins

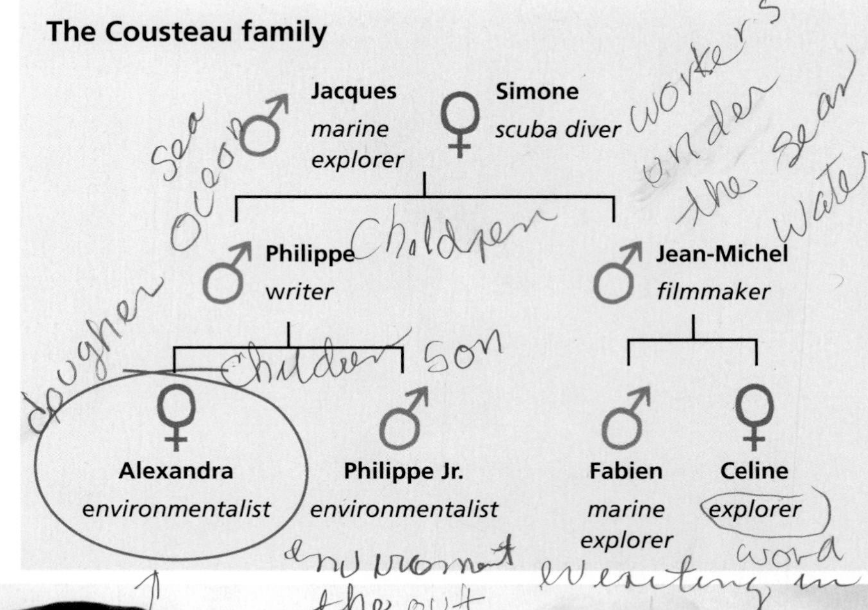

Reading and listening

3 🔊 **25** The woman in the photo is Alexandra Cousteau. Look at the family tree. Mark (✓) the correct options (a–d) about Alexandra. Then listen and check.

Who's Alexandra?

a She's Jacques Cousteau's daughter.
b She's Philippe's daughter.
c She's Philippe Jr.'s sister.
d She's Simone's mother.

4 🔊 **25** Listen again. Match A and B to make sentences.

A	B
Alexandra Cousteau is	Philippe's children.
Jean-Michel Cousteau is	Jean-Michel's children.
Fabien and Celine are	Jacques Cousteau's granddaughter.
Alexandra and Philippe Jr. are	Alexandra's brother.
Philippe Jr. is	Jacques Cousteau's son.

Grammar **possessive *'s***

5 Look at the grammar box. Then look at the sentences in Exercise 4. Find *'s* five times.

> **▶ POSSESSIVE 'S**
>
> Alexandra Cousteau is Jacques Cousteau**'s** granddaughter.
>
> For more information and practice, see page 162.

6 Explain the use of *'s* in these sentences.

1 Who's Celine?
2 She's Fabien's sister.

7 Work in pairs. Test your memory.

Who's Jacques?

He's Alexandra's grandfather.

8 Look at the photo. Then look at the example. Write sentences about this family.

Example: Bolormaa – Bat
Bolormaa is Bat's mother.

1 Bat – Sukh
2 Bat – Bolormaa
3 Bold – Bat
4 Bolormaa – Sukh

9 Pronunciation **possessive *'s***

26 Listen and repeat the sentences.

Speaking and writing

10 Work in pairs. Draw your family tree. Tell your partner about people in your family.

Who's David?

He's my sister's son.

11 Write about your family tree.

Three generations of a family in Mongolia

3b Celebrations

Vocabulary months and ages

1 Look at the calendar. Write the months in the correct place.

August December February June November

FAMILY EVENTS

January	....
....	Jim's birthday (49)
March	Rory's birthday (34)
April	Sue and Colin's wedding anniversary
May	Jack and Rosie's wedding anniversary
....	Matt's birthday (19)
July	....
....	Eve's birthday (21!)
September	....
October	....
....	Kate and Paul's wedding anniversary
....	Our wedding anniversary

2 Work in pairs. Look at the calendar. Ask and answer questions.

When's Sue and Colin's wedding anniversary?

In April.

3 Write a list of five family members. Then work in pairs. Exchange lists. Take turns to ask and answer questions about people's ages.

mother
grandmother
sister – Pilar
sister – Erika
brother

How old is your sister Erika?

She's twenty-three.

Reading

4 Look at the photo of a wedding. Find:

the bride the groom a boy a girl

5 Read about the wedding. Complete the sentences with five of these words.

bride cousin groom
husband wedding wife

1 This is Jao and Sunisa's ....
2 The ....'s name is Sunisa.
3 The ....'s name is Jao.
4 Deng is Jao's ....
5 Deng's .... is at the wedding.

Celebrations around the world

This is a wedding in Thailand in October 2010. The bride is 23 years old. Her name's Sunisa. The groom is 30 years old. His name's Jao. Their family and friends are at the wedding. Jao's cousin Deng is there with his wife and their children. "Today we are all happy," says Deng.

Grammar *his, her, our, their*

6 Look at the sentences in the grammar box. When do we use *his* and *her*? When do we use *our* and *their*?

> **▶ *HIS, HER, OUR, THEIR***
>
> He is the groom. **His** name's Jao.
> She is the bride. **Her** name's Sunisa.
> They are from Thailand. This is a photo of **their** wedding.
> We are married. **Our** wedding anniversary is in June.
>
> For more information and practice, see page 162.

7 Complete the sentences with *his, her, our,* and *their.*

1 Deng's daughter is three. ______ name's Areva.
2 Sunisa's father is fifty. ______ name's Thaksin.
3 This is a photo of my father. ______ name's Andrew.
4 Kate and Paul are parents. ______ baby's name is Louisa.
5 My sister and I are twins. ______ birthday is the same day.

8 Look at the answers. Complete the questions about the people in the photo with these words.

her	his	their	they

1 "Where are ______ ?"
"In Thailand."
2 "What's ______ name?"
"Jao."
3 "What are ______ names?"
"Sunisa and Areva."
4 "What's ______ husband's name?"
"Jao."

Speaking

9 Work in pairs. Ask and answer questions about two weddings.

Student A: Turn to page 153.

Student B: Turn to page 157.

3c Young and old

Vocabulary adjectives

1 Match these adjectives with the pictures (1–6). Then check your answers with your instructor.

big old poor rich small young

2 Find three pairs of opposite adjectives in Exercise 1.

3 Write three sentences with words from Exercise 1. Then read your sentences to your partner.

My grandfather isn't young.

Reading

4 Read the article on page 39. Choose the correct option (a or b) for what the diagrams show.

a The ages of people in two different countries.
b The family size in two different countries.

5 Read the article again. Answer the questions.

1 Where are families big?
2 Where are people old?

6 Work in groups. Answer the questions.

1 Are families in your country big or small?
2 Are people old or young?

I'm from Italy. In my country, families are small.

Grammar irregular plural nouns

7 Look at the grammar box. Underline examples of two of these nouns in the article on page 39.

▶ IRREGULAR PLURAL NOUNS

a child → two **children**
a man → three **men**
a woman → four **women**
a person → five **people**

For more information and practice, see page 163.

8 Choose the correct option.

1 Daughters and mothers are *men / women.*
2 Grandsons are *men / women.*
3 Boys and girls are *children / men.*

9 Word focus *at*

Look at the expressions with ***at***. Complete the exchanges with two of the expressions. Check your answers with your instructor.

at a meeting	at home
at a wedding	at work

1 A: Where are Paul and Jen today?
B: They're .... The bride is Jen's sister.

2 A: Where are you?
B: We're .... ! My parents are here.

10 Pronunciation linking with *at*

27 Listen and repeat these sentences.

1 They're at‿a wedding.
2 He's at‿a meeting.

Speaking

11 Work in pairs. Draw a population pyramid for your family. Tell your partner about it.

The people in my family are all young.

FAMILIES AROUND THE WORLD ARE DIFFERENT

This is Mulogo and his friends. They are from Uganda. Their families are big—with seven or eight children. Mulogo's brothers and sisters are under sixteen years old. In Uganda, people are young. Half the people are under fifteen. Uganda is a poor country.

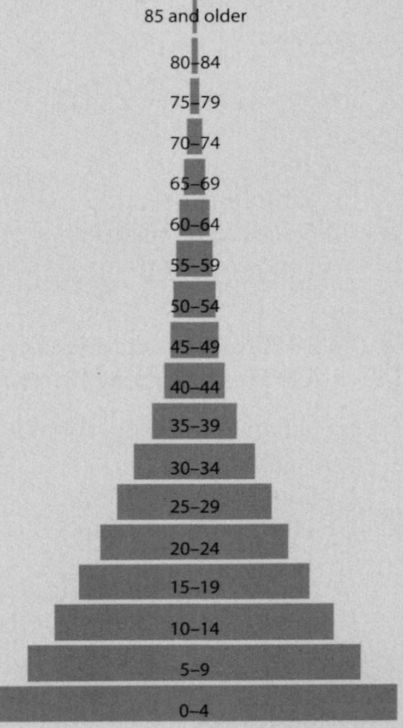

UGANDA

JAPAN

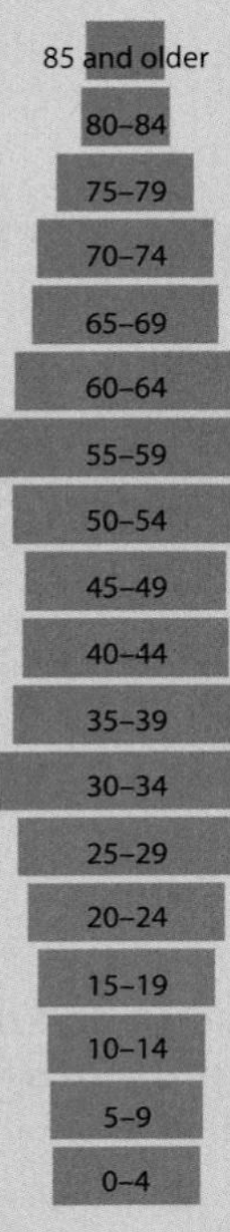

This is Amaya. She's Japanese. Her family is small—one daughter, one son, and one grandson. Japan is a rich country. In Japan, people are old. Twenty percent of the people are over sixty-five. In rich countries, people are old.

3d Congratulations!

Vocabulary special occasions

1 28 Look at these words. Then look at the photo and listen to a conversation. What's the special occasion?

a new baby
a birthday
a party
a wedding
a wedding anniversary
an engagement

2 28 Put the conversation in order. Then listen again and check.

a Ah, she's lovely. What's her name?
b Congratulations!
c Hello, Juba.
d It's Juba.
e Thank you. We're very happy.

Real life special occasions

3 29 Listen to three more conversations. Number (1–3) the occasions in Exercise 1.

4 29 Look at the expressions for SPECIAL OCCASIONS. Listen again. Write the number of the conversation.

▶ SPECIAL OCCASIONS

Congratulations!
Happy birthday!
Happy anniversary!
I'm very happy for you.
How old are you?
When's the wedding?

5 Pronunciation exclamations

a 30 Listen and repeat three expressions for SPECIAL OCCASIONS.

b Work in pairs. Practice the conversations on page 170.

Real life giving and accepting presents

6 Work in pairs. Answer the questions.

1 Is it traditional to give presents in your country?
2 What are some special occasions for giving presents?
3 What's a good present for these special occasions?

a new baby
new parents
your best friend's birthday
your cousin's wedding
your parents' wedding anniversary

7 Look at the occasions in Exercise 1. Which expression would you use for each one?

▶ GIVING AND ACCEPTING PRESENTS

This is for you / the baby.
That's nice / very kind.
You're welcome. / My pleasure.
Thanks. / Thank you very much.

8 Work in pairs. Choose a special occasion. Create a conversation. Take turns.

Hi. This is for ...

3e Best wishes

Writing a greeting card

1 Writing skill contractions

a Underline the contractions in these sentences. What's the missing letter?

1 I'm Mexican.
2 She's French.
3 It isn't my birthday.
4 What's your name?
5 They're engaged.
6 Who's this?
7 You aren't married.
8 Where's your husband?

b Find and underline eight contractions in these messages.

1 It's Javi's birthday tomorrow. He's with his grandparents in Chicago. What's their address?

2 Diana and Albert are engaged. They're really happy! The engagement party's at Albert's house.

3 Ingrid and Karl's wedding's in June. Sonia's the bridesmaid. I'm the best man!

c Rewrite these messages. Use contractions.

1 It is Karin's birthday tomorrow. She is twenty-one. Where is her present?

2 I am engaged to Miguel. Our wedding is in May.

3 Hi. What is Katya's husband's name? Is it Bruno or Silvio? Thanks.

2 Read the greeting. Answer the questions.

1 What's the occasion?
2 Who's the card from?
3 Who's the card to?

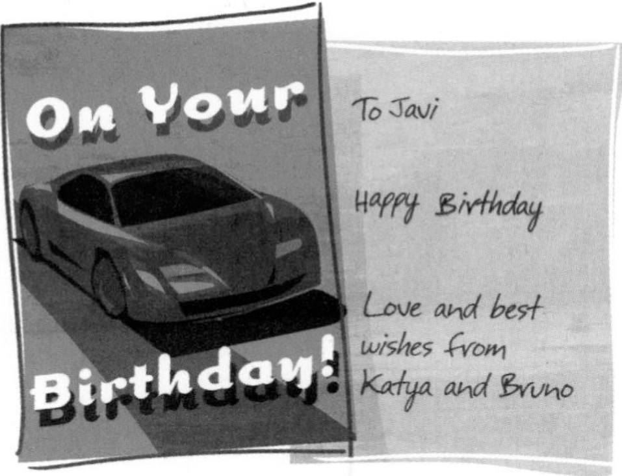

On Your
Birthday!
To Javi
Happy Birthday
Love and best wishes from Katya and Bruno

3 Write a card for Diana and Albert, and for Karin. Use these words. You can use some words more than once.

best wishes	birthday	congratulations	
engagement	from	love	
happy	on	to	your

4 In pairs, read your cards. Check the capital letters.

5 Work in pairs. Compare your cards with your partner's cards.

3f A Mongolian family

Video

Mongolian children in Ulaanbaatar

Before you watch

1 Read about Mongolia. Complete the article with three of these words.

country family hot people

Mongolia

Mongolia is a [1] ______ in Asia. It's big. It's cold in January and it's [2] ______ in July. Sixty percent of the [3] ______ are under thirty. Forty percent of the people are in Ulaanbaatar, the capital.

2 Look at the word box in the next column.

3 Look at the photo on page 42. Find:

a ger children houses

While you watch

4 Watch the video. Mark (✓) the things you see.

a ger	a city
children	a wedding
animals	mountains

5 The young man's name is Ochkhuu Genen. Watch the video again. Match the names with the people.

1 Anuka	his wife's mother
2 Norvoo	his daughter
3 Jaya	his wife's father
4 Chantsal	his wife

6 Watch the video again. Choose the correct option.

1 Where is Ochkhuu's ger?
a in Ulaanbaatar c in the mountains
b in the country

2 How old is Ochkhuu's daughter?
a two years old c ten years old
b six years old

3 How old are Norvoo's parents?
a fifty-five years old c sixty-five years old
b sixty years old

4 What is Norvoo's father's job?
a a taxi driver c a teacher
b a farmer

5 What is Ochkhuu's job?
a a taxi driver c a teacher
b a farmer

After you watch

7 Work in pairs. Answer the questions.

1 Is Ochkhuu's family big or small?
2 Are Norvoo's parents young or old?

8 Work in pairs.

Student A: Look at photo A. You are in Mongolia. These people are your neighbors. What are their names and ages? What are the relationships?

Tell your partner about the people in the photo.

Student B: Look at photo B. You are in the United States. These people are your neighbors. What are their names and ages? What are the relationships?

Tell your partner about the people in the photo.

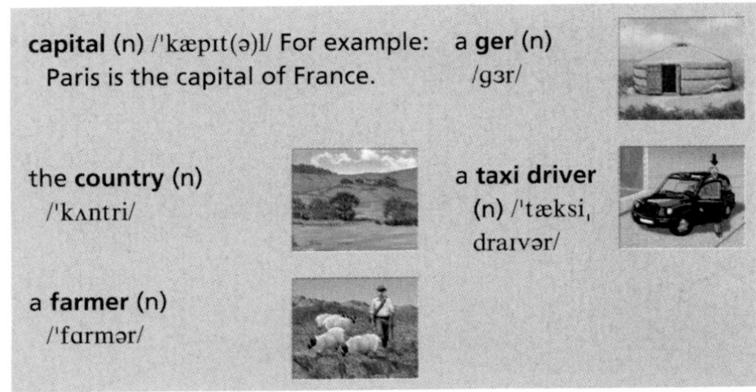

capital (n) /ˈkæpɪt(ə)l/ For example: Paris is the capital of France.

a **ger** (n) /gɜr/

the **country** (n) /ˈkʌntri/

a **taxi driver** (n) /ˈtæksi, draɪvər/

a **farmer** (n) /ˈfɑrmər/

UNIT 3 REVIEW

Grammar

1 Complete the sentences.

1 Look at the photo. This is Jin's family.
(Jin / family)

2 This is ______ .
(Sandra / car)

3 They're ______ .
(Toni / keys)

4 Is this ______ ?
(Diana / phone)

5 This is ______ .
(Michael / passport)

6 Is this ______ ?
(Enya / email address)

enya@bt.com

2 Complete the sentences with these words.

he's his our their they're

1 This card is for Ellie and Greg. What's ______ address?
2 Suzi and Ryan are engaged. ______ very happy!
3 It's David's birthday. The party's at ______ house.
4 Dirk and I are married. It's ______ anniversary in March.
5 It's my grandfather's birthday today. ______ eighty-nine.

I CAN	
talk about families and possessions (possessive *'s* and possessive adjectives)	☐
use irregular plural nouns	☐

Vocabulary

3 Match the words for women and men.

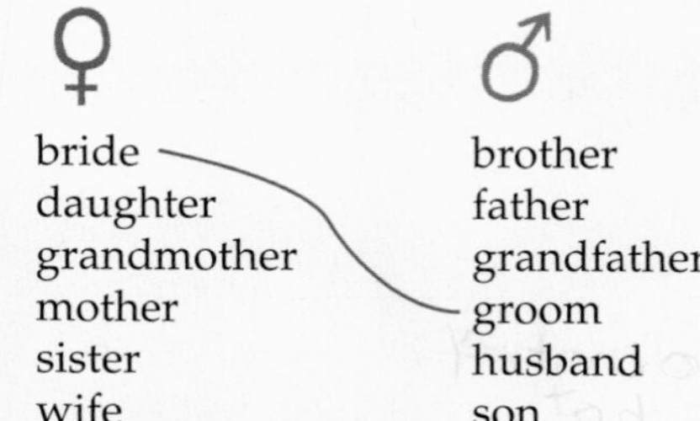

♀	♂
bride	brother
daughter	father
grandmother	grandfather
mother	groom
sister	husband
wife	son

4 Work in pairs. Take turns.

Student A: Say a month.

Student B: Say the next month.

5 Choose the correct option.

1 Our class is *big / small*—3 students!
2 "Are your grandparents *old / young*?"
"Yes, they are. They're 89 and 92."
3 We aren't rich. We're *big / poor*.
4 This wedding is *rich / small*—the bride and groom and their families.

I CAN	
talk about my family	☐
talk about months and ages	☐
describe people	☐

Real life

6 Put the words in order. Then match 1–4 with a–d.

1 the / is / wedding / when / ?
2 are / how old / you / ?
3 for / this / is / you / .
4 you / much / thank / very / .

a are / welcome / you / .
b am / eighteen / I / .
c in / is / July / it / .
d very / kind / is / that / .

7 Work in pairs. Practice the exchanges in Exercise 6. Use contractions.

I CAN	
talk about special occasions	☐
give and accept presents	☐

Speaking

8 Write the names of people from three generations in your family. Then work in pairs. Ask and answer questions using *who* and *how old*.

Unit 4 Cities

The Pearl TV tower and the Huang Pu River in Shanghai, China
Photo by Justin Guariglia

FEATURES

1 Look at the photo. Find these things:

buildings a river a tower

2 Read the photo caption. Find the name of the city and the country.

3 **31** Listen. Are these items true (T) or false (F)?

1 Shanghai is the capital of China.
2 Shanghai isn't rich.
3 The buildings in Shanghai are old.
4 The Pearl TV tower is famous.

4 Work in pairs. Tell your partner about famous things in your city or town.

I'm from Tokyo. Mt. Fuji is famous.

4a In the city

Vocabulary places in a town

1 Match the words and the pictures. Check your answers with your instructor.

a bank	a bus station
a café	a parking lot
a movie theater	a market
a museum	a park
an information center	a train station

1 

2 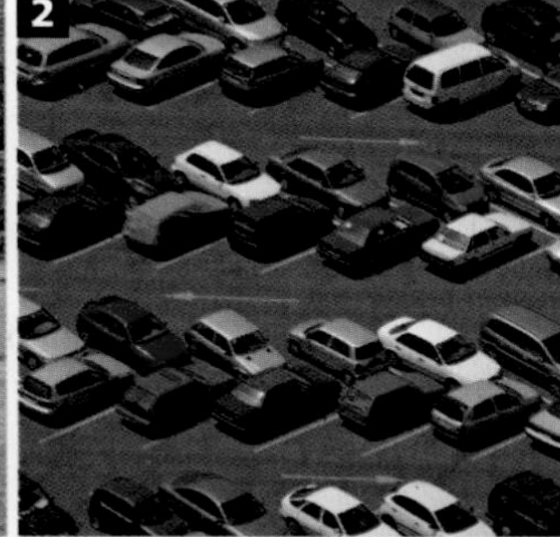

3 

4 

5 

6 

7 

8 

9 

10 

2 Are the places in Exercise 1 in your town? What are their names?

Reading

3 Read the information about downtown Northville. Complete the sentences with the places in the comments.

1 The ________ is great.
2 The ________ is new.
3 The ________ is old.
4 The ________ is on Milk Street.

a bank
b Transportation Museum
c bus station
d café
e parking lot
f City Information Center
g Roxy movie theater
h Central Market
i train station
j Green Park

The museum isn't very good. It's old. It's near the train station. *Berta*

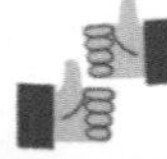

This café is great! It's next to a movie theater. *Artem*

Grammar **prepositions of place**

4 Look at the grammar box. Then look at the comments about Northville. Underline the prepositions.

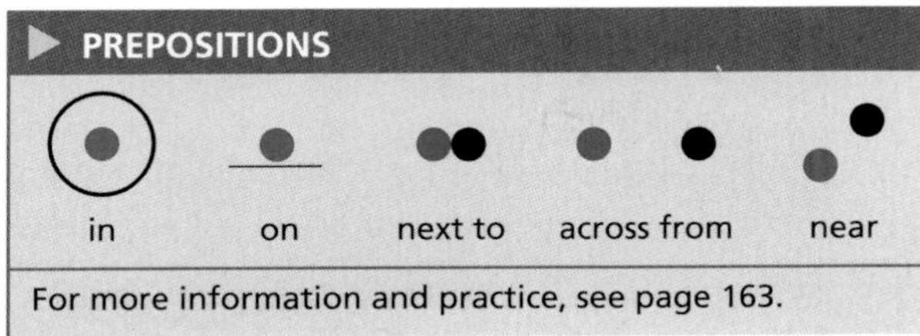

5 Look at the map. Are the sentences true (T) or false (F)?

1 The café is next to the movie theater.
2 The museum is in the park.
3 The park is near the information center.
4 The market is across from the movie theater.
5 The train station is on Exeter Street.
6 The transportation museum is across from the parking lot.

6 Look at the map. Choose the correct option.

1 The bank is *next to / across from* the market.
2 The movie theater is *on / near* South Street.
3 The information center is *next to / across from* the bus station.
4 The bus station is *in / next to* the park.
5 The train station is *across from / near* the museum.

7 32 Listen to four conversations about these places. Write the number of the conversation (1–4) next to the places.

a bank
b parking lot
c information center
d train station

Speaking

8 Work in pairs. Ask and answer questions about places on the map.

Excuse me?

Yes?

Where's the market?

9 Work in pairs. Ask and answer questions about four places in your town.

Where's the Coffee Pot café?

I'm not sure!

DOWNTOWN NORTHVILLE

Exeter Street

Milk Street

South Street

i b e a d g j h f c

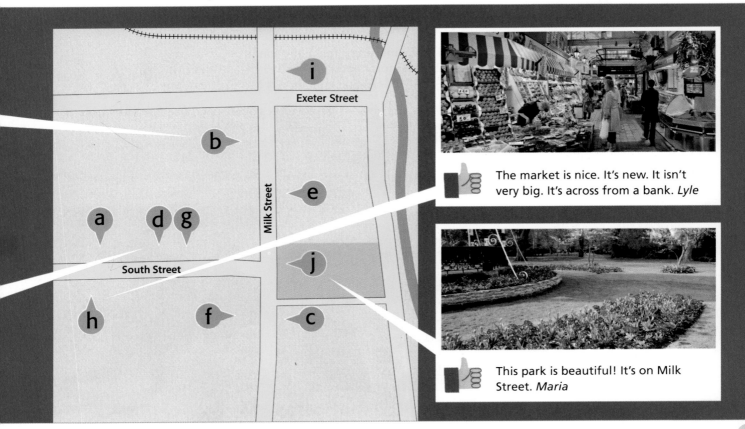

The market is nice. It's new. It isn't very big. It's across from a bank. *Lyle*

This park is beautiful! It's on Milk Street. *Maria*

4b Tourist information

Listening

1 33 Listen to the conversation and put it in order.

a Good morning.
b Is **this** a map of the city?
c Hi. *1*
d No, it isn't. **That's** a map of the city.
e OK. And where's Tokyo Tower?
f Yes, it is.
g Oh yes. Is it open on Sunday?
h It's near the Prince Park … here it is.

Grammar *this, that*

THIS, THAT

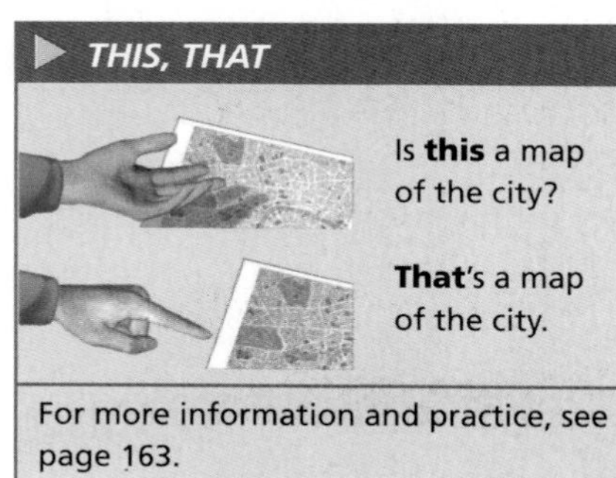

Is **this** a map of the city?

That's a map of the city.

For more information and practice, see page 163.

2 Complete the conversations with *this* and *that*.

Excuse me. Is .... a map of Tokyo?
Yes, it is.

1

Is .... a train schedule?
No, it's a bus schedule.

2

Is .... guidebook in English?
Where?
The book next to you.
No, it isn't. It's in Spanish.

3

3 Pronunciation *th* /ð/

a 34 Listen and repeat the conversations from Exercise 2.

b Practice the *th* sound in these words.

this that there they

Vocabulary days of the week

4 Put the days of the week in order. Check your answers with your instructor.

Friday Monday Saturday Sunday Thursday Tuesday Wednesday

5 35 Read the questions about places in Tokyo. Then listen to the conversation and answer *yes* or *no*.

1 Are museums open on Monday? yes no
2 Are stores open every day? yes no
3 Are banks open on Sunday? yes no

6 Work in pairs. When are places open—and not open—in your country?

Banks aren't open on Saturday or Sunday.

The Tower of Pisa

Tokyo Tower

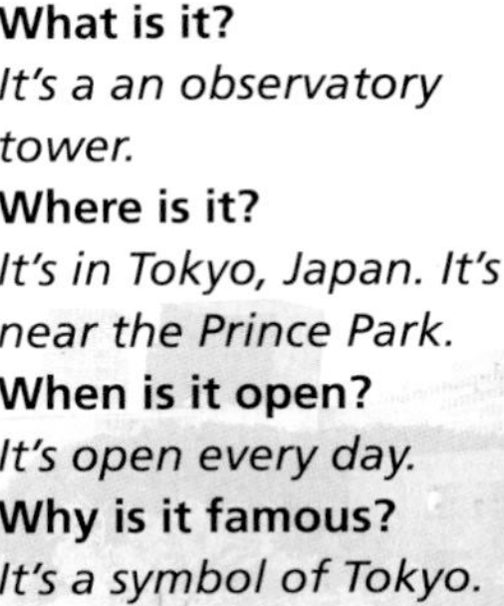

What is it?
It's a bell tower.
Where is it?
It's in Pisa, Italy. It's next to the cathedral.
When is it open?
It's open every day.
Why is it famous?
It isn't vertical.

What is it?
It's a an observatory tower.
Where is it?
It's in Tokyo, Japan. It's near the Prince Park.
When is it open?
It's open every day.
Why is it famous?
It's a symbol of Tokyo.

bell (n) /bel/

observatory

vertical (n) /ˈvɜrtɪkəl/

Reading

7 Read about two famous towers. Choose the correct option.

1 *Tokyo Tower / The Tower of Pisa / both* is an observatory.
2 *Tokyo Tower / The Tower of Pisa / both* is open to tourists.
3 *Tokyo Tower / The Tower of Pisa / both* is near a park.

Grammar **question words**

8 Look at the grammar box and the words in **bold** in the questions. Then look at the article about towers. Find the words in **bold** in the article.

▶ QUESTION WORDS

What is it?	**When** is it open?
Where is it?	**Why** is it famous?

For more information and practice, see page 163.

9 Complete the questions with the correct question word.

1 Q: .... are you?
A: I'm in the park.
2 Q: .... is the museum open?
A: Every day.
3 Q: .... is the name of this street?
A: Main Street.
4 Q: .... is this place famous?
A: It's very old.
5 Q: .... is this?
A: It's in Italy.
6 Q: .... is your birthday?
A: In June.

10 Work in pairs. Ask and answer questions about two more towers.

Student A: Turn to page 154.

Student B: Turn to page 158.

Speaking

11 Work in pairs. Ask and answer questions about famous places you know.

4c Time zones

Vocabulary the time

1 Match the times with the clocks.

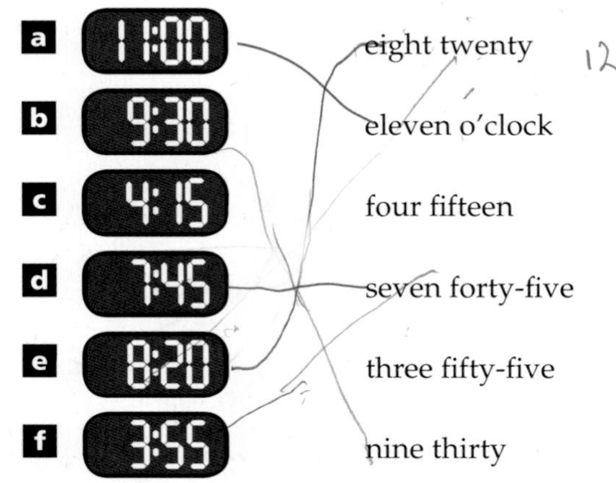

2 36 Listen and write the times.

1 .... 4 ....
2 .... 5 ....
3 .... 6 ....

3 Match the word with the time.

1 noon 12:00 pm (☼)
2 midnight 12:00 am (☾)

4 Work in pairs. Ask and answer questions.

What time is	your the	English class? office open? bus in the morning? train to work?

Grand Central Station, New York

Reading

5 Read the article and look at the map on page 51. Where is the International Date Line?

6 Read the article again. Look at the time in London. Then write the names of the two cities.

London: 12:00 pm

1 ....: 8:00 pm 2 ....: 4:00 am

7 Work in pairs. It's noon in London. What time is it in these places?

Cairo Sydney Rio de Janeiro Japan
Argentina South Africa

In Cairo, it's two o'clock in the afternoon.

8 Word focus *of*

a Underline *of* in the sentences. Then match the sentences (1–4) with the pictures (a–d).

1 What's the name of this street?
2 Rome is the capital of Italy.
3 It's a symbol of Tokyo.
4 This is a map of the city.

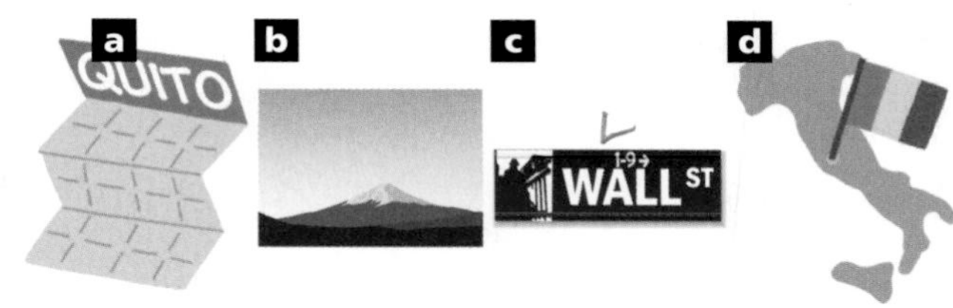

b Complete the sentences. Then tell your partner.

1 The name of my street is ....
2 The capital of my country is ....
3 .... is a symbol of my ....

Speaking

9 Work in pairs. Talk about your city at different times of the day. Take turns.

Student A: Say a time.

Student B: Make sentences.

Five o'clock in the afternoon.

Stores are open. Children aren't at school.

TIME ZONES

In London, it's twelve o'clock noon. Stores and offices are open. People are at work. Children are at school. In Hong Kong, it's eight o'clock in the evening. Schools are closed and children are at home. People are in cafés and restaurants. In Los Angeles, it's four o'clock in the morning. People aren't at work. They're at home.

The time is different in the 24 time zones around the world. The International Date Line is from north to south "in" the Pacific Ocean. The Date Line is the end of one day and the beginning of the next day. It's 80 kilometers from Russia to Alaska, but Sunday in Russia is Saturday in Alaska.

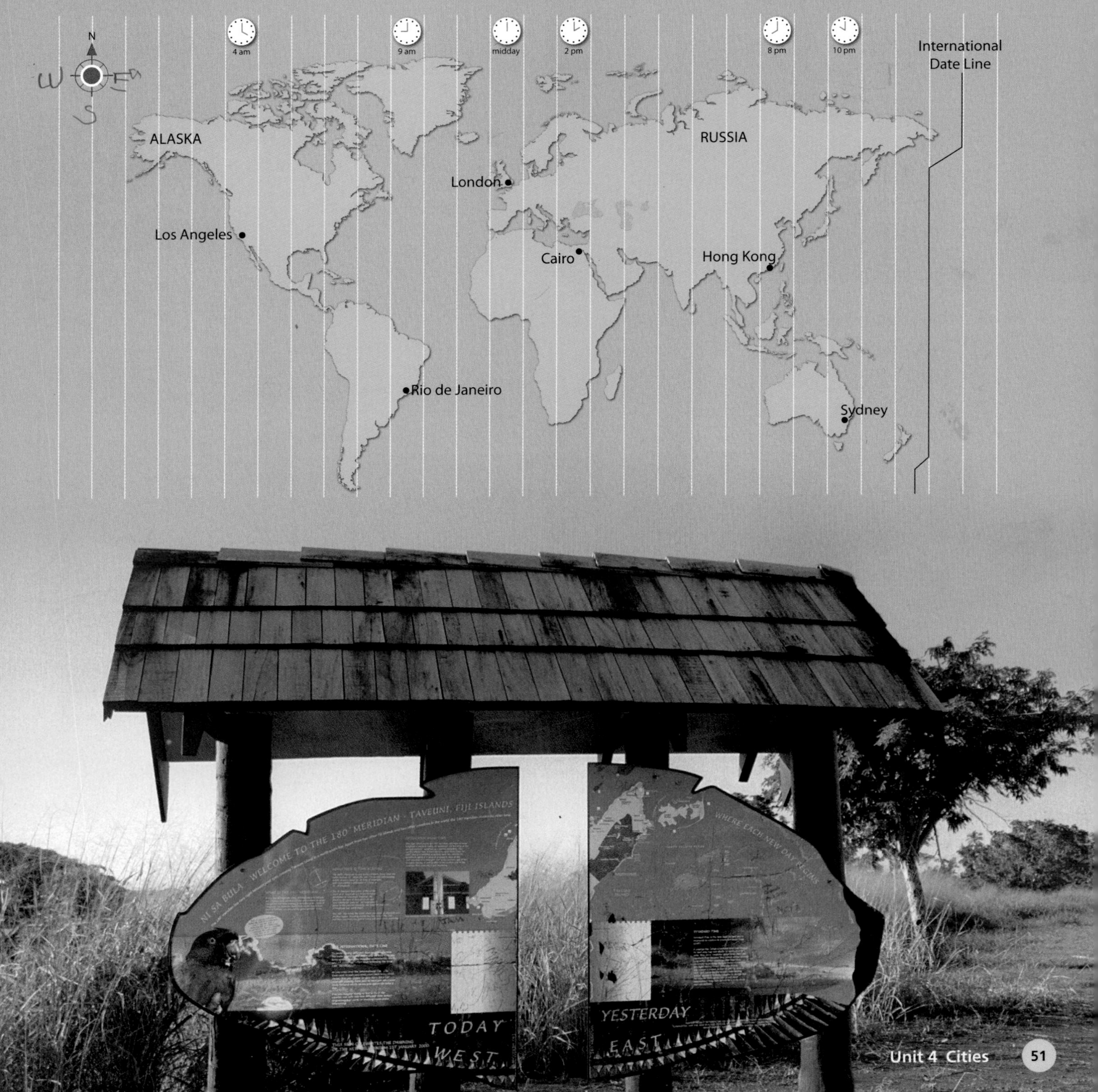

4d Two teas, please

Vocabulary snacks

1 Look at the photo. Choose the correct caption (a–c).

a Fruit juice, India
b Mint tea, Morocco
c Black coffee, Turkey

2 Write the words with the pictures (1–7).

pastry coffee fruit juice water
salad sandwich tea

Real life buying snacks

3 37 Listen to three conversations. Number the snacks (1–3) in Exercise 2.

4 37 Complete the conversations with expressions for BUYING SNACKS. Then listen again and check.

1 A: Hi. Can I help you?
B: 1 ....
A: 2 ....
B: Small.
A: Anything else?
B: 3 ....

2 A: Hi. Can I help you?
B: 4 ....
A: Anything else?
B: Yes. A salad.
A: OK. 5 ....

3 A: 6 ....
B: A tea and a fruit juice, please.
A: 7 ....
B: Yes. Two pastries, please.
A: OK. Here you are. Seven dollars, please.
B: 8 ....

5 **Pronunciation linking with *can***

38 Listen and repeat these sentences.

1 Can‿I help you?
2 Can‿I have a water, please?

BUYING SNACKS

Can I help you?
Two coffees, please.
Can I have a water, please?
Large or small?
Anything else?
No, thanks.
Four dollars, please./
Here you go.

6 Work in pairs. Take turns buying a snack from your partner.

Hi. Can I help you?

Two teas, please.

4e See you soon

Writing a postcard

1 Read the postcard. Answer the questions.

1 Who is the postcard to?
2 Who is it from?
3 Where are they?

2 Read the postcard again. Underline:

1 two adjectives to describe the hotel
2 one adjective to describe the markets
3 two adjectives to describe the people
4 one adjective to describe the food

Hi Sandra
We're in Thailand. We're in Bangkok. It's great! Our hotel is big and new. It's near the market on this postcard. The markets are famous here. Thai people are nice and friendly. Oh, and the food is great too.
See you soon.
Jen and Chris

3 Writing skill *and*

a Read the postcard again. Circle *and* in three sentences.

b Look at the example. Then rewrite the sentences with *and*.

Example: The hotel is small. The hotel is new.
The hotel is small ***and*** *new.*

1 The museums are big. The museums are old.
2 The town is old. The town is beautiful.
3 It's famous in America. It's famous in Europe.
4 It's a drink with sugar. It's a drink with mint.

4 Choose a place you know. Write a postcard to your partner. Write about these three things. Use ***and***.

- the town/city
- places in the town/city
- the food
- the hotel
- the people

5 Work in pairs. Exchange postcards. Where is your partner?

4f Where's that?

Video

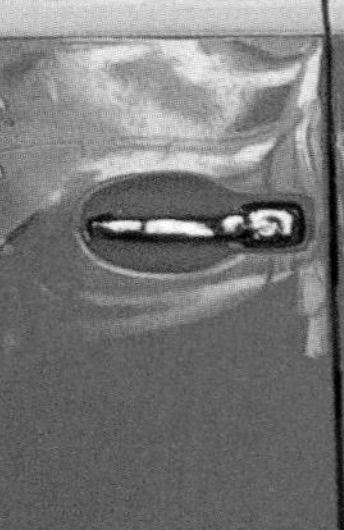

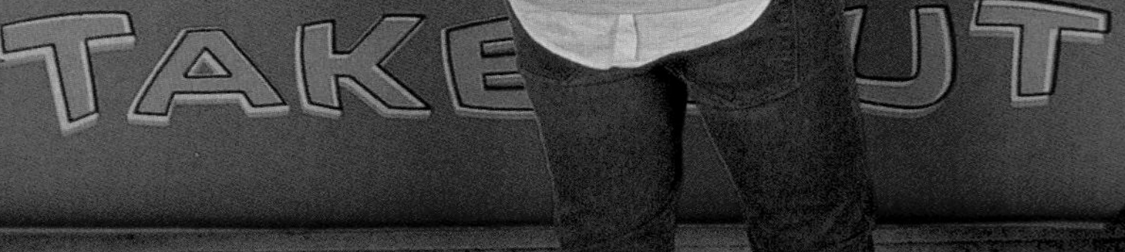

Coffee and a sandwich, please.

Before you watch

1 Look at the photo and the caption on page 54. Find the name for this place in the word box in the next column.

2 Work in pairs. Are these places in your town? Where?

a bridge	a shopping area
a garden	a snack bar

3 Work in pairs. Mark (✓) what's in your city or town.

a bank
a bus station
a café
a parking lot
a movie theater
a market
a museum
a park
an information center
a train station

4 This video is a quiz about cities. What do you think the title will be?

- ▢ **Where's that?**
- ▢ **Four cities around the world.**
- ▢ **What are their names?**

While you watch

5 Watch the video. Are the things in your list from Exercise 3 in the video?

6 Watch the video again. Where are the cities? Write the number of the city (1–4) with the continent. Two cities are in one continent.

America Asia Europe

7 Work in pairs. What are the names of the four cities? Choose the correct option (a–c). Do you agree?

1 a Beijing b Hong Kong c Tokyo
2 a Madrid b Paris c Rome
3 a New York b San Francisco c Washington
4 a Lisbon b London c St. Petersburg

8 Watch the video again and check.

After you watch

9 Look at the questions and answers from the video. Complete the questions.

A: That's beautiful. [1] ....'s that?
B: It's in the city. It's a park with a lake.

A: [2] ....'s that? Is that you next to the lake?
B: No, it isn't.

A: [3] ....'s that? A park?
B: It's a garden—and a nice café next to the garden.

A: Look at the two people. [4] .... are they there?
B: I don't know.

A: [5] .... are the people?
B: They're tourists, I think.

10 Match two places with each city from the video. Then write sentences about one of the cities.

Atocha Station
Fisherman's Wharf
Greenwich Naval College
Shinjuku district
the Golden Gate Bridge
the Imperial Palace
the London Eye and the Houses of Parliament
the Prado museum

11 Write a postcard from one of the cities in the video.

12 Send your postcard to a classmate.

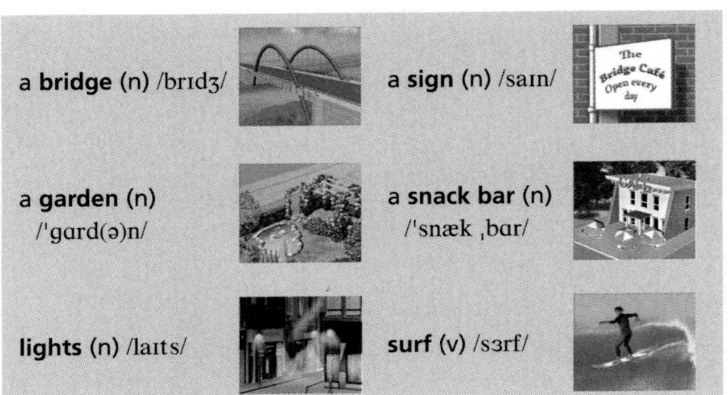

UNIT 4 REVIEW

Grammar

1 Read about the café. Then complete the questions.

New!
The Art Café
We are in the Modern Art Museum.
We are next to the Museum Store.
We are open Monday – Saturday, 10:00 – 6:00. On Sunday we are open 10:00 – 2:30.
Hot and cold snacks.

1 .... is the café's name?
2 .... is the café?
3 .... is the café open?
4 .... old is the café?

2 Work in pairs. Ask and answer the questions from Exercise 1. Take turns.

3 Look at the pictures. Choose the correct option.

Is this / that *the bus to downtown?*

Is this / that *fruit juice?*

I CAN	
describe the location of places (prepositions of place)	☐
use *this* and *that* correctly	☐
ask and answer questions (question words)	☐

Vocabulary

4 Complete the words for places in a town.

1 tr _ _ n st _ t _ _ n
2 p _ rking l _ t
3 m _ s _ _ m
4 m _ vi _ th _ _ t _ r

5 Work in pairs. Where are the places in Exercise 4 in your town?

6 Work in pairs. Say the days in order. Take turns. Start with Monday.

7 Work in pairs. Take turns.

Student A: Choose a clock and say the time.

Student B: Point to the clock.

8 Complete the menu with these snacks.

salad fruit juice coffee sandwiches

The Art Café

Hot drinks	
tea	$2.00
1	$2.50

Cold drinks	
mineral water	$2.50
2	$3.00
Snacks	
3	$7.50
4	$7.50
pastries	$3.00

I CAN	
talk about places in a town	☐
say the days of the week	☐
say the time	☐
talk about snacks	☐

Real life

9 Complete the conversation in a café with a–d.

a OK. Four dollars, please.
b Large or small?
c Thanks.
d Hello. Can I help you?

A: 1 ....
B: Can I have two teas, please?
A: 2 ....
B: Small, please.
A: 3 ....
B: Here you are.
A: 4 ....

I CAN	
buy snacks	☐

Speaking

10 Work in pairs. Practice the conversation in Exercise 9. Change the snacks.

Unit 5 Inventions

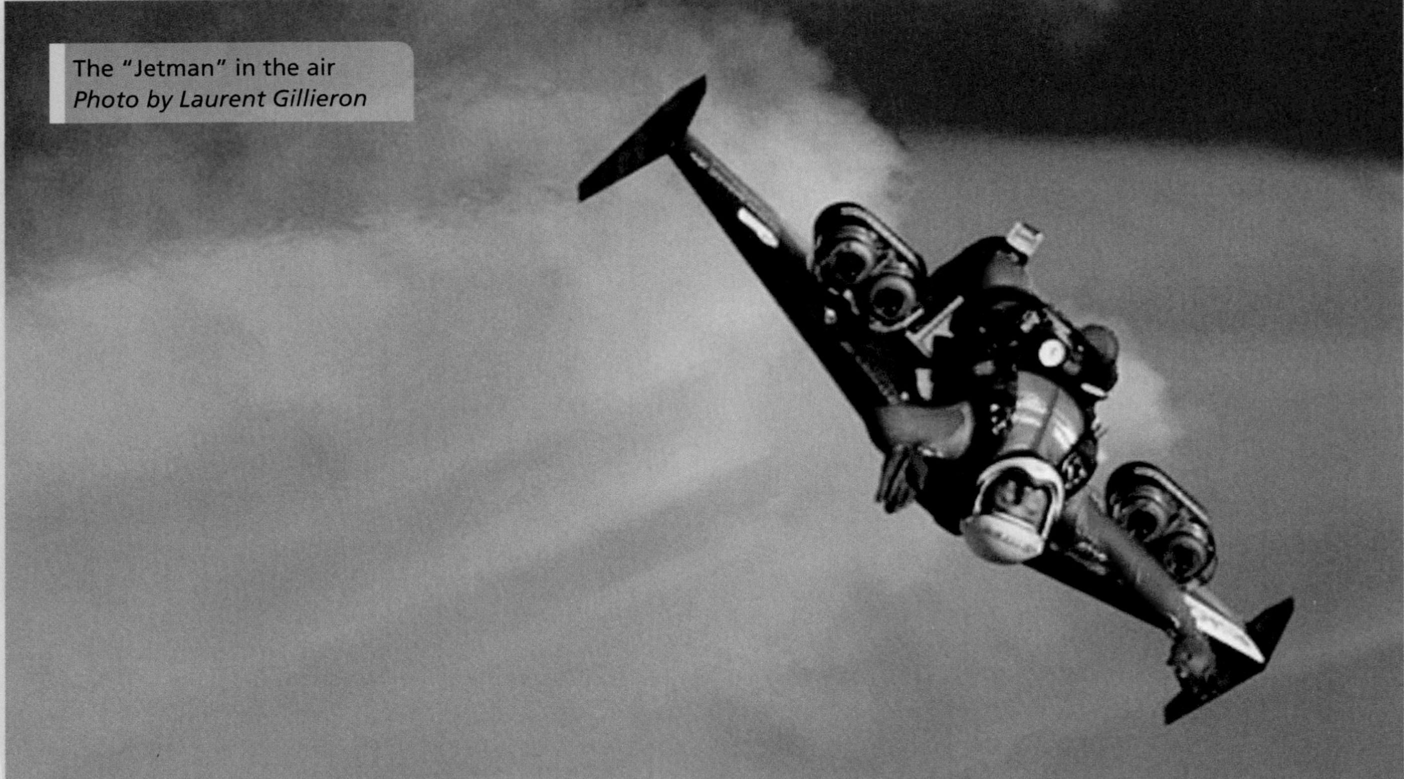
The "Jetman" in the air
Photo by Laurent Gillieron

FEATURES

1 Work in pairs. Look at the photo. What is it?

a a toy
b a person
c a robot

2 **39** Listen to the information about the photo. Check your answer from Exercise 1.

3 **39** Listen again. Choose the correct option.

1 Yves Rossy is from *France / Switzerland.*
2 In the photo, he's above the Swiss *Alps / capital.*
3 He's in the air for *five / nine* minutes.

4 Work in groups. Yves Rossy is an inventor. Name some inventors and their inventions.

Steve Jobs – iPod

5a Robots and people

ROBOTS AND PEOPLE

This is 69-year-old Nabeshima Akiko. She's in a supermarket in Japan. She's with a robot. The robot is from Keihanna Science City near Kyoto. This robot can see and it can speak. It can move, but it can't run. It can carry things—for example, Nabeshima's basket.

Robots are amazing. They can help people in their lives.

Photo by Randy Olson

Reading

1 Look at the photo. Find:

two women   a robot   a child   a basket

2 Read the article. Underline:

1 the woman's name
2 four things this robot can do
3 one thing this robot can't do

Grammar *can/can't*

3 Choose the correct option to make a true sentence.

Robots *can* / *can't* help people.

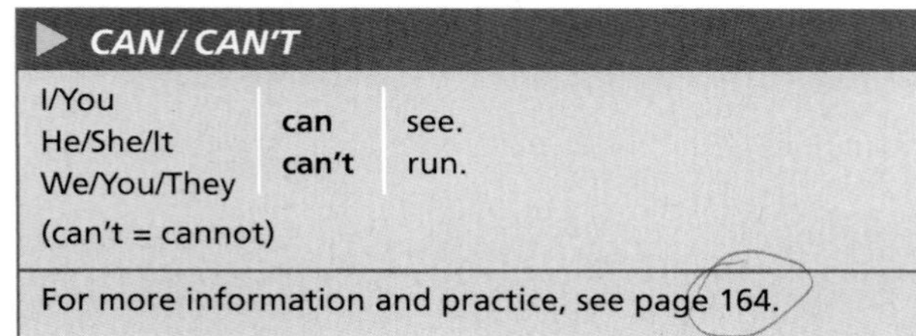

▶ *CAN / CAN'T*

I/You He/She/It We/You/They	**can** **can't**	see. run.

(can't = cannot)

For more information and practice, see page 164.

4 Write sentences with ***can*** and ***can't***.

Example:
robots / move ✓ *Robots can move.*

1 robots / speak ✓
2 robots / carry things ✓
3 people / fly ✗
4 I / speak English ✓
5 my grandfather / run ✗

5 **Pronunciation *can/can't***

40 Listen and check your sentences from Exercise 4. Then listen again and repeat.

Vocabulary abilities

6 Mark (✓) the sentences that are true about you. Make the other sentences negative.

1 I can cook.

2 I can speak English.

3 I can play soccer.

4 I can drive a car.

5 I can ride a bike.

6 I can swim.

7 I can sing.

8 I can play the piano.

7 Work in pairs and take turns.

Student A: Read your sentences to your partner.

Student B: Write the number of the sentence. Then write ✓ (*can*) or ✗ (*can't*).

Listening

8 41 Listen to an interview with Christine Black, a robot expert. Are the sentences true (T) or false (F)?

1. The robot's name is Tomo.
2. Tomo is an American robot.
3. Tomo is from a new generation of robots.
4. "Tomo" is Japanese for "intelligent."

9 41 Listen again and answer the questions with ✓ (*can*) or ✗ (*can't*).

1. Can Tomo speak Japanese?
2. Can she sing?
3. Can she play the piano?
4. Can she swim?

Grammar *can* questions and short answers

10 Look at the grammar box. Write full answers to the questions in Exercise 9.

▶ ***CAN* QUESTIONS and SHORT ANSWERS**

Can	I/you he/she/it we/you/they	speak Japanese? swim?
Yes, **No,**	I/you he/she/it we/you/they	**can.** **can't.**

For more information and practice, see page 164.

Speaking

11 Work in pairs. Ask and answer questions about the abilities in Exercise 6.

Can you cook?

No, I can't.

5b Technology and me

Vocabulary technology

1 Look at the objects. Number the words (1–5). Check your answers with your instructor.

a camera
headphones
an MP3 player
a video camera
a webcam

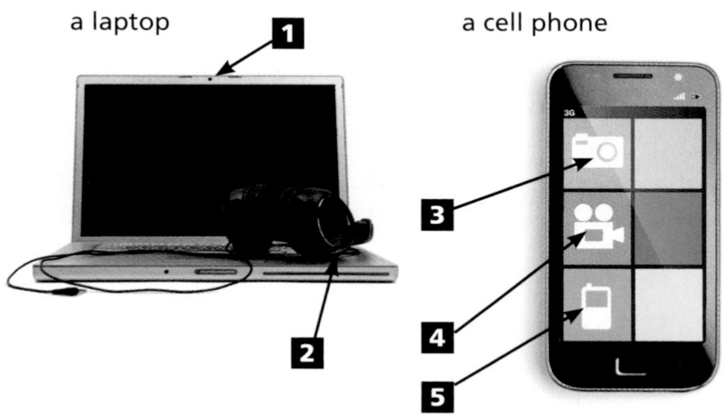

Grammar *have/has*

2 Look at the grammar box. Then look at the sentences. Choose the correct option.

1 This laptop *have / has* a webcam.
2 Cell phones *have / has* MP3 players.

HAVE/HAS		
I/You/We/You/They	**have**	a camera.
He/She/It	**has**	headphones.

For more information and practice, see page 164.

3 Work in pairs. Tell your partner about your laptop, cell phone, or computer.

I have a cell phone. It has a camera.

intelligent travel blog

We ask six travelers about their favorite piece of technology. Here are their comments.

This is my "mobile office." These things are in my backpack.
Posted by **Ian Walker**

I can take hundreds of photos with my new camera. It has a big memory.
Posted by **Sacha Brown**

I have an old webcam, but it's OK. I can see and talk to my family at home.
Posted by **Luis dos Santos**

I can work on the train with my laptop. It has a good battery.
Posted by **Adela Law**

My phone has a fantastic video camera. I can take great videos.
Posted by **Hon Yin**

My MP3 player is small and light. It's in my bag all the time.
Posted by **Adam LeBlanc**

a **backpack (n)** /ˈbækˌpæk/

Reading

4 Work in pairs. Complete the sentences with objects from Exercise 1. Then read the *Intelligent Travel* blog. Which objects are in the blog?

1 You can listen to music with ....
2 You can take photos with a ....
3 You can take videos with a ....

5 Read the blog again. Find these adjectives. What do they describe?

new big fantastic great small light

Grammar **adjective + noun**

6 Look at the words in **bold** in the grammar box. Circle the adjectives and underline the nouns.

▶ ADJECTIVE + NOUN	
My **camera** is **fantastic**.	I have an **old webcam**.
For more information and practice, see page 164.	

7 Look at the example. Then write sentences.

Example:
This is my camera. It's new.
This is my new camera.

1 It's an MP3 player. It's new.
2 My phone has a battery. It's small.
3 They are headphones. They are light.
4 I have a video camera. It's digital.

Writing and speaking

8 What's your favorite piece of technology? Write a comment for the blog.

9 Work in groups. Talk about your favorite pieces of technology.

What's your favorite piece of technology?
My cell phone.
Why?
It's new and it has a great camera.

5c Solar ovens

Reading

1 Work in pairs. Match the words with the photos (1–3). Are these ovens popular in your country?

an electric oven   a gas oven
a microwave oven

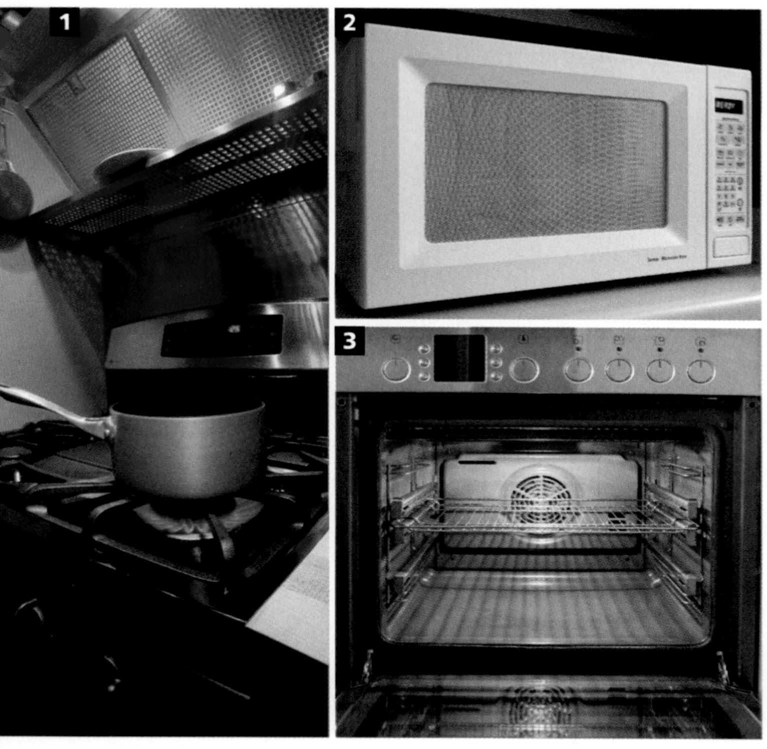

2 Read the article. Write this information for the two ovens.

	Bøhmer	HotPot
Number of parts		
Price		
Maximum temperature		

3 Read the article again. Are the sentences true (T) or false (F)?

1 Solar ovens can heat water.
2 You can buy the Bøhmer oven in stores.
3 The Bøhmer oven has five parts.
4 The HotPot oven has a glass bowl.
5 You can buy the HotPot oven online.

Grammar *very, really*

4 Look at the sentences in the grammar box. Which sentences are from the article?

▶ *VERY, REALLY*

This oven is **very** basic.	This oven is **really** basic.
It's **very** cheap.	It's **really** cheap!

Note: really great ✓ really fantastic ✓
BUT ~~very great~~ ✗ ~~very fantastic~~ ✗

For more information and practice, see page 164.

5 Put the words in order to make sentences.

1 basic / this / is / design / very
2 basic / this / a / oven / is / really
3 is / a / designer / very / he / good
4 phone / this / really / a / has / good / video camera

6 **Word focus *this***

a Match the sentences (1–4) with the pictures (a–d).

1 This is my new camera.
2 What's this in English?
3 This is my sister Anita.
4 Is the Plaza Hotel on this street?

b Work in pairs. Change the underlined words in the sentences in Exercise 6a.

This is my new phone.

It's very nice.

Speaking

7 Work in pairs. Ask and answer questions about two microwave ovens.

Student A: Turn to page 154.

Student B: Turn to page 158.

TECHNOLOGY

Solar ovens

People in some parts of the world can't cook with gas or electric ovens, but they can cook with the sun! Solar ovens are really fantastic. They can cook food and heat water. Here are two solar ovens.

The Bøhmer oven

This oven is very basic. The designer is Jon Bøhmer. He's Norwegian, but he lives in Kenya. You can't buy this oven, but you can make it. It has five parts: a lid, a pot, two boxes, and newspaper. The total price of the parts is about $7. It's really cheap! The maximum temperature is about 90°C (194°F). This oven is very good for people in poor parts of the world.

The HotPot oven

The HotPot oven is a basic design too. It has three parts: a pot, a bowl, and aluminum panels. The pot is in the glass bowl. The maximum temperature is about 150°C (300°F). It's really hot! You can buy this oven online and in stores. The price is about $100.

MAKE IT
The Bøhmer oven

BUY IT
The HotPot oven

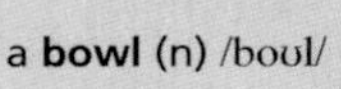
a **bowl** (n) /boʊl/

the **sun** (n) /sʌn/

5d How much is it?

Vocabulary money and prices

1 Match the symbols with the money (currency).

1	$	euros
2	£	pounds
3	€	dollars

2 Work in pairs. What's the currency of these countries?

> Australia Brazil China the United States
> Ireland Canada the United Kingdom
> Egypt Germany Saudi Arabia

3 42 Listen and repeat the prices.

4 Pronunciation numbers

a 43 Listen and mark the correct price.

1	$13.00	$30.00	4	$16.00	$60.00
2	$14.00	$40.00	5	$17.00	$70.00
3	$15.00	$50.00	6	$18.00	$80.00

b Work in pairs. Take turns to dictate three prices to your partner.

Real life shopping

5 44 Listen to three conversations in stores. Write the number of the conversation (1–3) next to the product. There is one extra product.

an alarm clock
flash drives
speakers
a video camera

6 44 Listen again. Mark the correct price.

1	$15	$50	$80
2	$46.50	$65.60	$95.50
3	$5.99	$9.99	$99

7 Look at the expressions for SHOPPING. Write customer (C) or salesperson (S).

> **SHOPPING**
>
> Excuse me.
> Can I help you?
> I'd like this video camera, please.
> How much is this alarm clock?
> How much are these flash drives?
> It's / They're 15 dollars.
> That's $95.50, please.
> Can I pay with pesos / cash / a card?
> Here you go.

8 Work in pairs. Take turns to buy a product from your partner.

Salesperson: Decide the price of the products.

Customer: Decide how much you can pay.

a digital camera

headphones

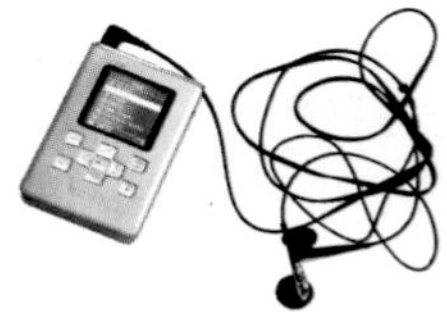
an MP3 player

a webcam

5e Can you help me?

Writing an email

1 Read the emails and answer the questions.

1 Who is Eliza?
2 Who is Mike?
3 What is Eliza's question?
4 What is Mike's answer?

2 Read Mike's reply again. Complete the table.

	Positive +	Negative –
Tables	small, ... screens special pen	.... small screens
Laptops	.... screens keyboard	

Computer Life *Weekly*

can help with your IT questions.

Email mike@computerlifeweekly.com.

Hi Mike

I'm in my first semester at college and I'd like a new computer. My PC is old and slow. I can buy a laptop or a tablet. I can't decide. Can you help me?

Eliza

Hi Eliza

Tablets are small and light, but they are expensive. Tablets have good screens, but they are small. Laptops have big screens. Can you type? Laptops have a keyboard. Tablets have a special pen and you can write on the screen. This is great, but it's slow. Good luck in your studies!

Mike, Computer Life Weekly

3 Writing skill *but*

a Look at the example. Then underline two sentences with *but* in Mike's reply.

Example: Tablets are small and light. They are expensive.
Tablets are small and light, ***but*** *they are expensive.*

b Read the pairs of sentences. Which pair can you not rewrite with *but*?

1 This tablet is great. It's expensive.
2 Tablet screens aren't big. They are good quality.
3 This computer is old. It's slow.
4 With this phone, you can watch videos. You can't edit videos.

c Rewrite the pairs of sentences with *but*.

4 Write a reply to this email. Before you write, make notes on the two things. Use a table.

> Hi Jo,
>
> I'm in my first term at college. The bus to college is slow. I'd like a bike or a motorbike. I can't decide. Can you help me?
>
> Billie

5 Work in pairs. Exchange replies. Is your partner's reply useful?

5f The Owl and the Pussycat

Video

Technology can make some animals famous.

Before you watch

1 Read the list of objects and animals. Write what they can do.

fly	take photos and videos
climb trees	have information about things, people, etc.
make calls	take videos
connect to the Internet	have special pens

Cameras	*They can take photos and videos.*
Owls	
Laptops	
Webcams	
Cats	
Websites	
Cell phones	
Tablets	

2 Look at the word box below. Listen and repeat the words after your instructor.

3 In the video, Jordi Amenos takes videos of his owl and cat. Which items from Exercise 1 do you think are in the video that you will see? What do you think Amenos does with the videos he takes?

While you watch

4 As you watch the video, match these items. One answer is used two times.

1 Gebra	a owl
2 Fum and Gebra	b web developer
3 Fum	c cat
4 Facebook	d website
5 Amenos and Marti	e friends
6 Marti	

5 Watch the video again. Put these items in order from 1–8.

☐ Amenos edits the video.
☐ Visitors to the website post comments.
☐ 300,000+ people see the video.
☐ Jordi Amenos takes videos of Fum and Gebra.
☐ Amenos puts the video on the Internet.
☐ 1,000 people see the video.
☐ Amenos goes to bed.
☐ Ferran Marti helps Amenos make a website about Fum and Gebra.

6 Choose the correct words to complete each sentence.

1 Fum is very ________, but he ________ fly.
  a big; can
  b heavy; likes to
  c agile; can't
2 Jordi Amenos takes ________ and puts them on a ________.
  a videos; memory stick
  b photos; cell phone
  c videos; website
3 Thousands of people ________ Amenos's ________.
  a visit; website
  b visit; owl
  c post videos on; website

After you watch

7 What is your favorite piece of technology for watching videos? Why? Share your answers with a partner. Then describe the piece of technology to your partner.

8 Do you watch interesting or funny videos with animals? Where can you see them online? Get together with another pair and talk about the videos.

I can see funny videos on …

agile (adj) /ˈædʒəl/ able to move quickly and easily

airborne (adj) /ˈeərˌbɔrn/ moving in the air

leap (v) /lip/ to jump

link (n) /lɪŋk/ a web address that you can click on

post (v) /poʊst/ to put something online

profile (n) /ˈproʊfaɪl/ information about someone

web developer (n) /ˈweb dɪˌveləpər/ someone who makes web pages

web traffic (n) /ˈweb ˌtræfɪk/ how many people visit a website

UNIT 5 REVIEW

Grammar

1 Work in pairs. Ask and answer questions about Lynn. Use *can*. Take turns.

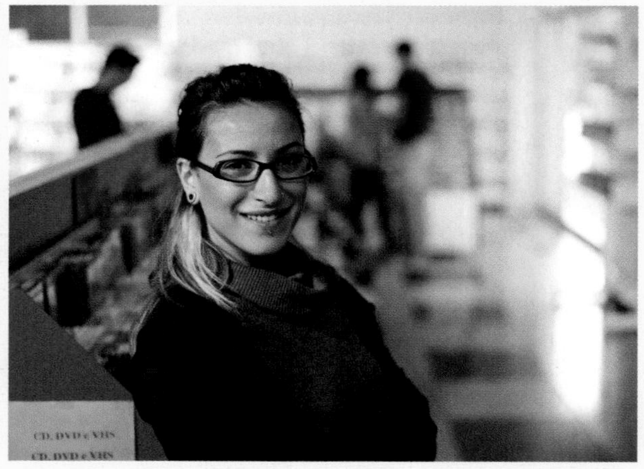

1 drive a car ✓
2 drive a motorbike ✗
3 cook ✓
4 type ✓
5 speak Arabic ✗
6 speak Russian ✓
7 write in Arabic ✗
8 write in Russian ✗

2 Work in pairs. Make sentences about Lynn.

3 Complete the text with these words.

's fantastic has invention really

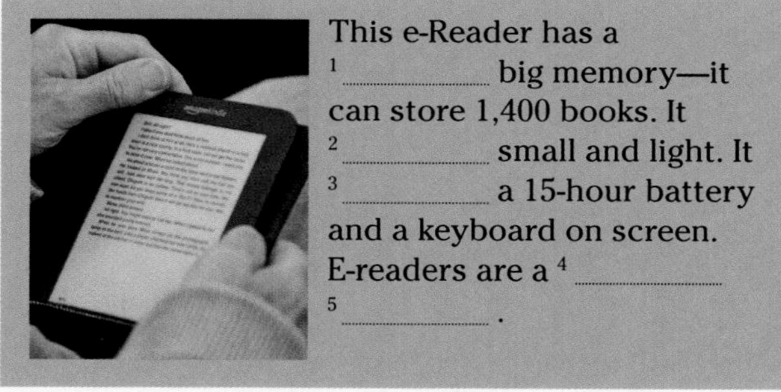

This e-Reader has a [1] ______ big memory—it can store 1,400 books. It [2] ______ small and light. It [3] ______ a 15-hour battery and a keyboard on screen. E-readers are a [4] ______ [5] ______ .

I CAN	
talk about ability (*can*)	☐
talk about possessions and features (*have*)	☐
describe objects (adjective + noun)	☐
use *very* and *really* correctly	☐

Vocabulary

4 Match the verbs from A with words from B.

A	B
drive	a bike
play	a car
play	the piano
ride	three languages
speak	tennis

5 Write ✓ or ✗ next to the objects.

1 You can listen to music with:
a phone   headphones   an MP3 player
2 You can take a photo with:
speakers   a phone   a camera
3 You can speak to people with:
a video camera   a laptop   a memory stick

6 Work in pairs. Tell your partner about the objects in Exercise 5.

I have a phone. It's in my bag.

7 Work in pairs. Take turns.

Student A: Choose a price tag and say the price.

Student B: Point to the price tag.

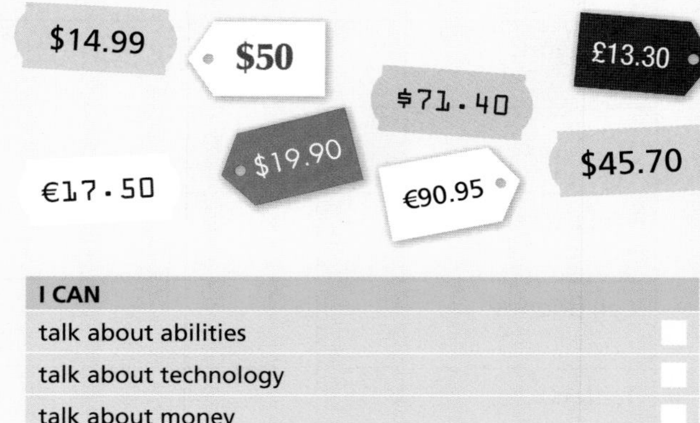

I CAN	
talk about abilities	☐
talk about technology	☐
talk about money	☐

Real life

8 Complete the conversation between a customer (C) and a salesperson (S) with these words.

help here like much pay that's they're

S: Can I [1] ______ you?
C: How [2] ______ are these webcams?
S: [3] ______ 37 dollars.
C: OK. I'd [4] ______ this webcam and a flash drive please.
S: [5] ______ you are. [6] ______ 47.50, please.
C: Can I [7] ______ with a card?
S: Yes, of course.

I CAN	
ask and talk about prices	☐
buy things in a store	☐

Speaking

9 Work in pairs. Practice the conversation in Exercise 8. Change the objects and the prices.

Unit 6 Passions

Passionate sports fans in Soweto, South Africa

FEATURES

1 45 Look at the photo. What's the sport? Listen and check.

basketball	rugby	soccer	tennis

2 45 Look at these numbers. Then listen again and choose the correct option. Practice saying the numbers.

100 = one hundred
1,000 = one thousand
1,000,000 = one million

1 About 270 *thousand / million* people play soccer around the world.
2 Soccer is popular in more than two *hundred / thousand* countries.
3 The World Cup prize is 30 *thousand / million* US dollars.

3 Work in pairs. Take turns to say the numbers. Then dictate three numbers to your partner.

300	9,000	20,000	800	70,000,000

4 Work in groups. Answer the questions.

1 Which sports are popular in your country?
2 What's the national sport in your country?
3 What sports can you play?

6a A passion for vegetables

Reading

1 Look at the photo and the caption. What is Steve Weston's passion?

2 Read about Steve Weston. Answer the questions.

1. Where is Steve Weston in the photo?
2. What's the name of this kind of vegetable?
3. How much does the vegetable weigh?
4. Can you eat this vegetable?

Grammar *like*

3 Look at the grammar box. Underline the sentences in the article with *like* and *don't like*.

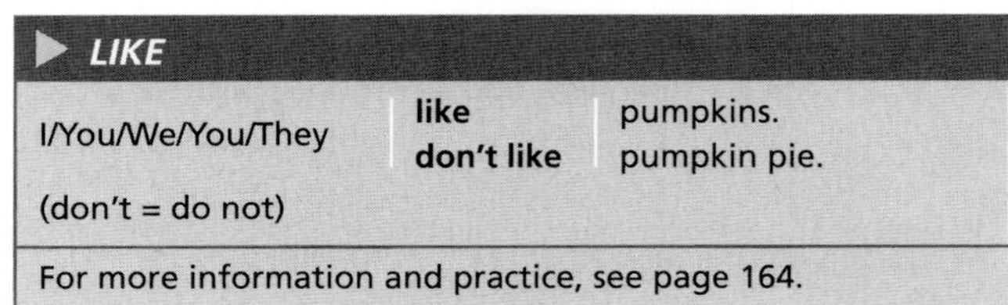

▶ LIKE

I/You/We/You/They	**like** **don't like**	pumpkins. pumpkin pie.
(don't = do not)		

For more information and practice, see page 164.

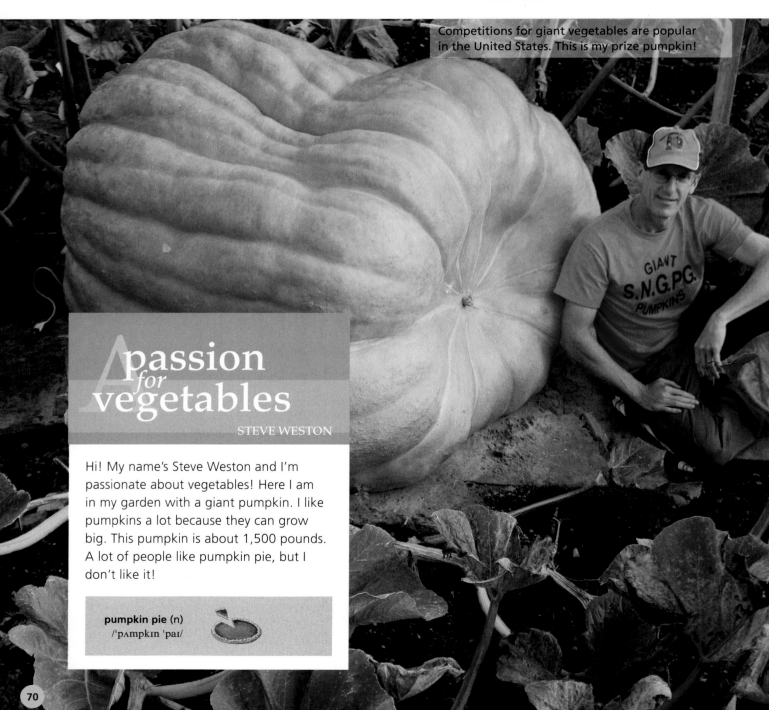

Competitions for giant vegetables are popular in the United States. This is my prize pumpkin!

A passion for vegetables

STEVE WESTON

Hi! My name's Steve Weston and I'm passionate about vegetables! Here I am in my garden with a giant pumpkin. I like pumpkins a lot because they can grow big. This pumpkin is about 1,500 pounds. A lot of people like pumpkin pie, but I don't like it!

pumpkin pie (n) /ˈpʌmpkɪn ˈpaɪ/

4 Look at the example. Then complete the sentences with ***like*** (☺) or ***don't like*** (☹).

Example:
I / vegetables. ☺
I like vegetables.

1 I / my garden. ☺
2 I / competitions. ☹
3 My friends / sports. ☺
4 I / soccer. ☹
5 We / tennis. ☺

5 Change the sentences in Exercise 4 so they are true for you. Read the sentences to your partner.

I don't like vegetables.

Vocabulary **food**

6 Write these words with the photos.

pasta chocolate vegetables salad

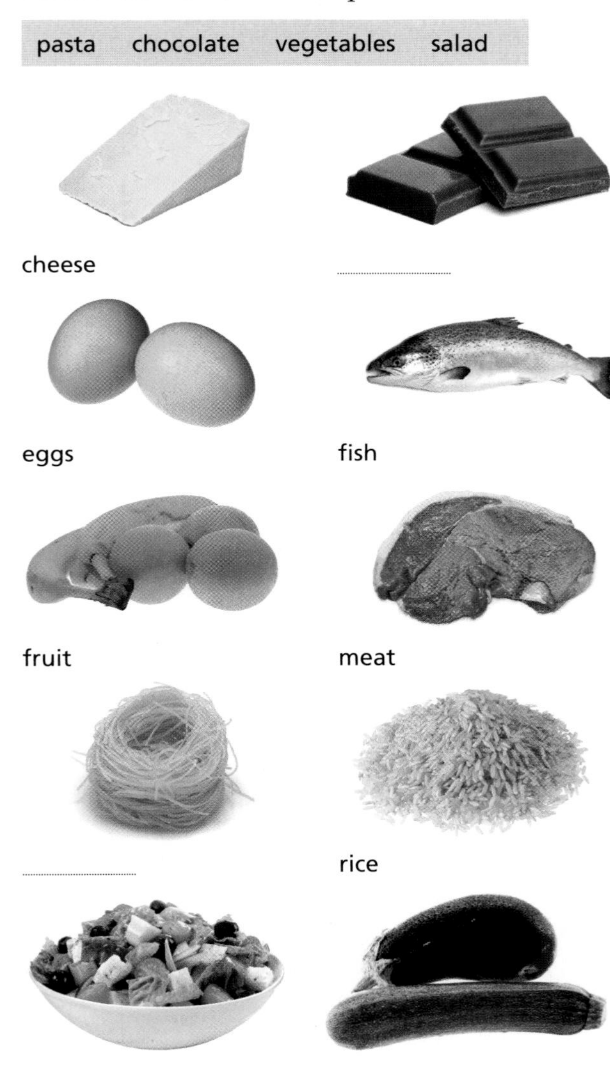

7 Work in pairs. Talk about the food in the photos.

I like cheese.

I don't like cheese very much.

Listening

8 46 Listen and mark the questions you hear.

1 Do you like fruit?
2 Do you like salad?
3 Do you like meat?
4 Do you like pasta?

9 46 Listen again and choose ***like*** (☺) or ***don't like*** (☹).

1 fruit ☺ / ☹
2 salad ☺ / ☹
3 meat ☺ / ☹
4 pasta ☺ / ☹

Grammar ***like*** questions and short answers

10 Look at the grammar box. What's the question form of *like*?

▶ *LIKE* QUESTIONS and SHORT ANSWERS

Do	I/you/we/you/they	like	fruit?
Yes, No,	I/you/we/you/they	do. don't.	

For more information and practice, see page 164.

11 Pronunciation ***do you … ?***

a 47 Listen and repeat four questions from the interview.

b Work in pairs. Ask and answer the questions in Exercise 11a.

Speaking and writing

12 Prepare questions for a food survey. Write six questions with *Do you like … ?*

13 Work in groups. Ask and answer the questions.

Alex, do you like pizza?

Yes, I do.

Krish, do you like pizza?

No, I don't.

14 Which foods are popular? Write sentences about your results. Compare with other groups.

In our group, three people like pizza.

6b My favorite things

Vocabulary interests

1 Match the categories in box A with the examples in box B. Check your answers with your instructor.

Example:
birds, fish – animals

A

animals

books

movies

music

sports

TV

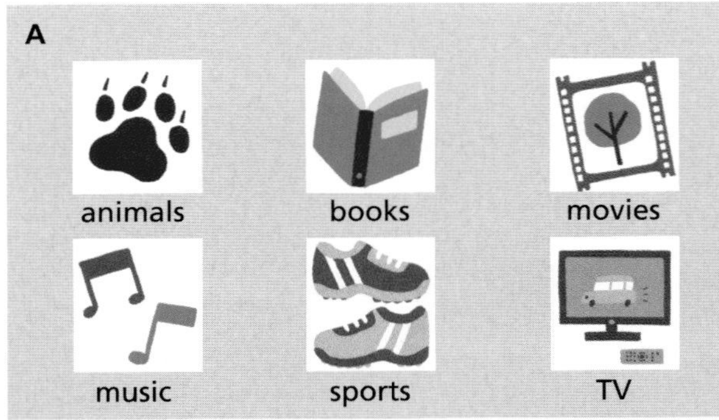

B		
	jazz	pop
	detective stories	novels
	action movies	comedies
	birds	fish
	reality shows	wildlife shows
	scuba diving	swimming

2 Work in pairs. Ask and answer questions about your favorite TV show, book, movie, and sport.

Do you like TV?

Yes, I do.

What's your favorite TV show?

Reading

3 Read the article about Zeb Hogan. Underline four interests from Exercise 1.

4 Read the article again. Are the sentences true (T) or false (F)?

1 Zeb Hogan has two jobs.
2 He's a fisherman.
3 He's from Botswana.
4 His favorite sports are swimming and tennis.

My favorite things | Zeb Hogan

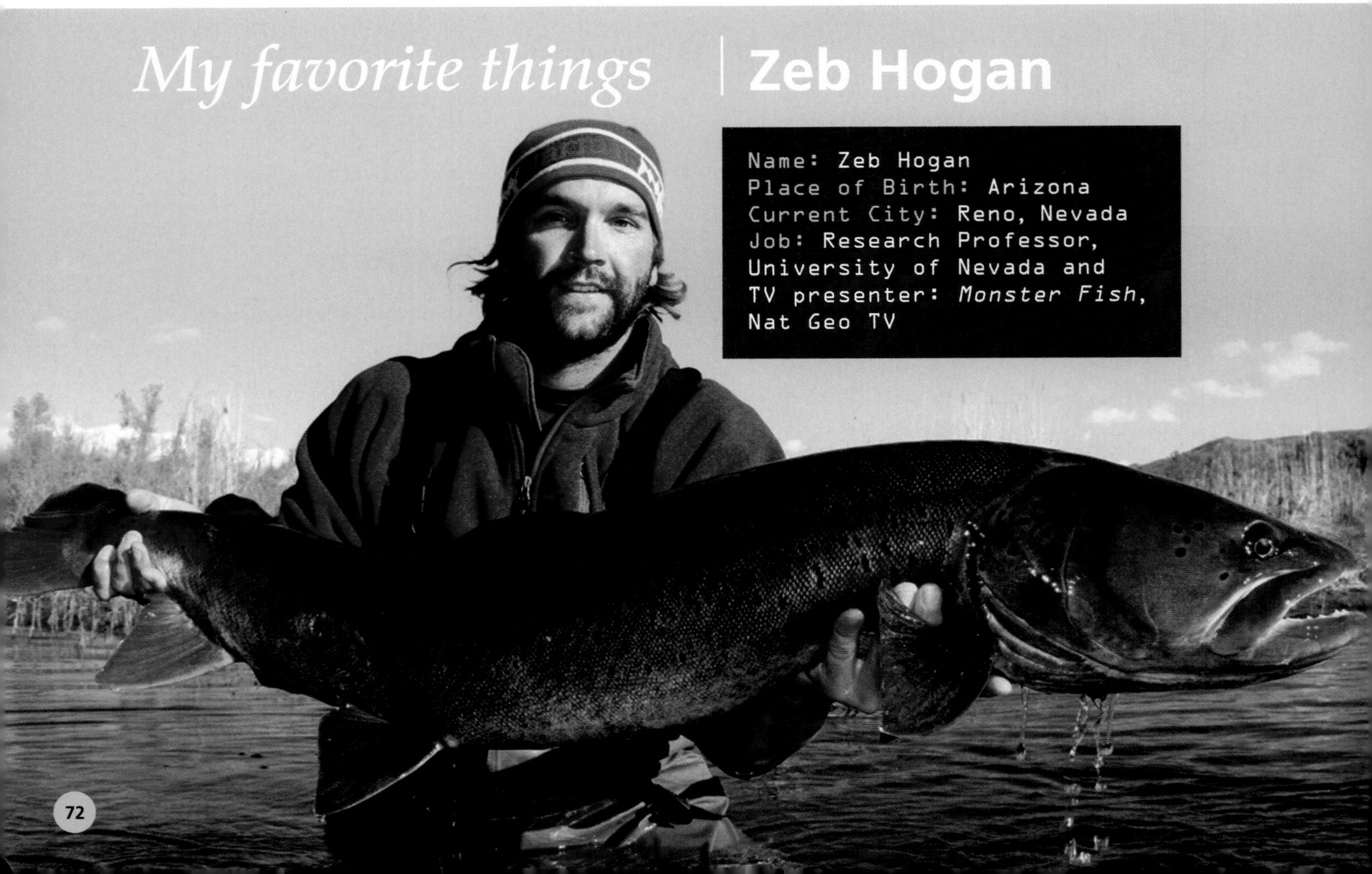

Name: Zeb Hogan
Place of Birth: Arizona
Current City: Reno, Nevada
Job: Research Professor, University of Nevada and TV presenter: *Monster Fish*, Nat Geo TV

Grammar *he/she + like*

5 Look at the grammar box. Then look at the article. What is the negative form of *likes*?

▶ HE/SHE + LIKE

He/She		**likes** **doesn't like**	fish. cold places.
Does	he/she	**like**	coffee?
Yes, No,	he/she	**does.** **doesn't.**	

(doesn't = does not)

For more information and practice, see page 165.

6 Look at the example. Write questions about Zeb Hogan.

Example:
like / fish? *Does he like fish?*

1 like / Botswana?
2 like / Arizona?
3 like / cold places?
4 like / hot places?
5 like / TV shows?

7 Work in pairs. Ask and answer the questions in Exercise 6 with *yes, no,* or *I don't know.*

Zeb Hogan likes fish. His passion is giant fish. He isn't a fisherman. He's a scientist. His job is to study and protect giant fish in different places around the world, like the Okavango Delta in Botswana. That's Zeb's favorite place. Zeb's from Arizona. It's a very hot, dry place. He doesn't like cold places, but he likes water. He loves swimming and scuba diving. Zeb's other passions are his friends, his family, and wildlife shows on TV.

8 Pronunciation *likes, doesn't like*

48 Listen to five sentences about Zeb Hogan and repeat them.

Speaking

9 Work in pairs. Look at the table.

Student A: Choose a person.

Student B: Ask *Does she like … ?* to discover the identity.

Take turns.

Does she like music?

No, she doesn't.

Does she like movies?

Yes, she does.

Is it Teresa?

Yes!

	Barbara	Diana	Stella	Teresa
(animals)	✓	✓	✗	✗
(books)	✗	✗	✓	✓
(movies)	✗	✓	✗	✓
(music)	✓	✗	✓	✗
(sports)	✗	✓	✗	✓
(TV)	✓	✗	✓	✗

6c In love with speed

Reading

1 Work in pairs. Look at the photos. Can you name famous sporting events with these things?

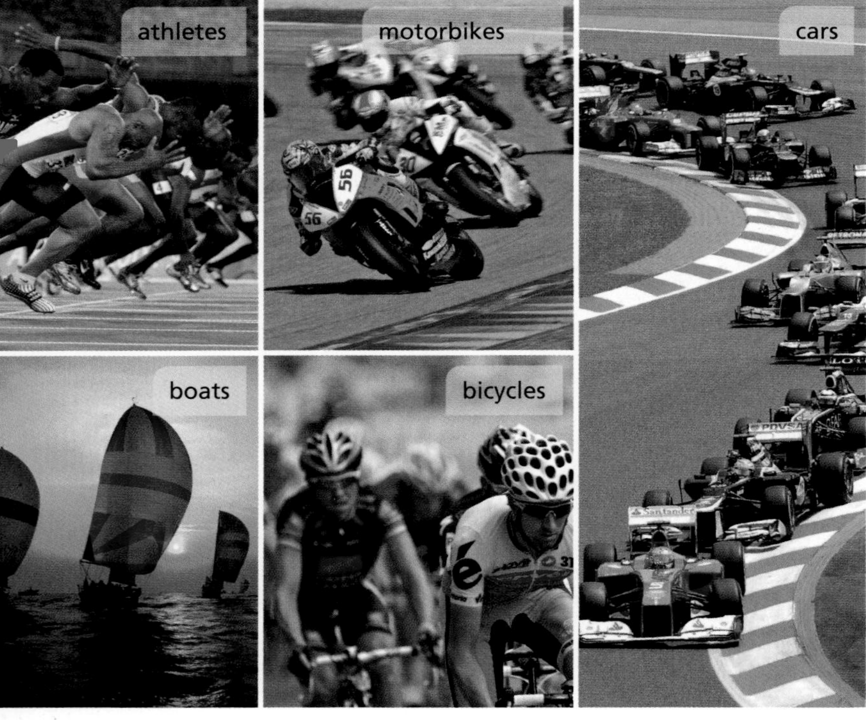

2 Look at your answers from Exercise 1. Answer the questions for each event.

1 Which city or country is the race in?
2 What is the prize?
3 Can you name any famous winners of the event?

3 Read the article on page 75. Find:

1 three types of racing
2 five countries
3 two types of prizes

4 Read the article again. Complete the sentences.

1 .... racing is popular in China.
2 .... racing is popular in Europe.
3 People in Qatar love .... racing.
4 .... can run at 40 miles per hour.
5 .... can fly 60 to 600 miles.

5 Match the comments from three people with the animal race.

1 "This sport is popular in Australia, but I don't like it."
2 "My birds are special to me. I like them a lot!"
3 "My brother is in this race. I can see him on his horse."

Grammar object pronouns

6 Look at the grammar box. Then look at the comments in Exercise 5. Find four object pronouns in the comments.

▶ OBJECT PRONOUNS

Subject pronoun	Object pronoun
I	me
you	you
he	him
she	her
it	it
we	us
you	you
they	them

For more information and practice, see page 165.

7 Choose the correct option.

1 That's my horse. I love *them / it*.
2 He's fantastic. I like *him / her* a lot.
3 Australians are great. I like *them / him*.
4 Where's your sister? I can't see *her / you*.
5 The *Tour de France* is a great race. I like *her / it*.

8 Word focus *it*

a Match 1–5 with a–e. Then underline *it* in the sentences.

1 What time is it?
2 Is it hot in your city today?
3 What's your favorite place?
4 What day is it?
5 Hello?

a Shanghai. I love it.
b It's ten o'clock.
c It's Monday.
d Hi, it's Susan.
e No, it's cold.

b Work in pairs. Ask and answer questions 1–4.

Speaking

9 Work in pairs. Ask and answer questions about international sporting events.

Student A: Turn to page 155.

Student B: Turn to page 159.

IN LOVE WITH SPEED

People love speed, racing, and winning. Read about our passion for races.

The Litang Horse Festival is in China. It's during the first week of August. The horses are small and fast. The races are over 180 miles. The prize is money or a special horse. People in China love this festival.

Camel racing is a popular sport in Qatar. A camel's top speed is about 40 miles per hour! They can run at 25 miles per hour over a long distance. Australians love camel racing too. One big race in Australia has prize money of $50,000.

Racing pigeons can fly from 60 to 600 miles. Pigeon races are popular in Belgium and in the United Kingdom. A racing pigeon's top speed is about 80 miles per hour. It was a sport at the Paris Olympic games in 1900!

festival (n) /ˈfestɪvəl/ a special day or celebration

6d Let's play ping pong

Vocabulary opinion adjectives

1 49 Listen to three conversations (1–3). Match the words from the conversations with the four opinion adjectives.

a Emily Blunt
b sports
c pasta
d pizza

2 Are the adjectives in Exercise 1 positive (+) or negative (–)? Write them in the table.

Positive +	Negative –
....	....
....	....

3 Pronunciation intonation

50 Listen and repeat.

4 Work in pairs. Add the names of four people or things to the list in Exercise 1. Tell your partner your opinion.

Basketball's boring.

Real life suggestions

5 49 Complete the conversations with the expressions for making and responding to SUGGESTIONS. Then listen again and check.

1
A: Let's watch TV tonight.
B: .... What's on?
A: A movie with Emily Blunt is on at eight o'clock.
B: Oh, ... She's fantastic.

2
A: ....
B: .... I don't like ping pong.
A: OK. .... ?
B: Sorry. Sports are boring.

3
A: Let's have spaghetti this weekend.
B: .... It's horrible.
A: .... How about pizza? Do you like pizza?
B: Yes, it's great.

▶ SUGGESTIONS

Let's play ping pong tomorrow.
That's a good idea.
I love her.
How about soccer?

No, thanks.
I don't like spaghetti.
OK.

6 Add three ideas to the table below.

Let's	play have watch	a movie soccer spaghetti pizza ping pong TV	tonight. tomorrow. this weekend.
How about		... ?	

7 Work in pairs. Take turns to make suggestions and respond with opinions.

8 Work in a group. Make suggestions and agree on an activity for this weekend.

6e A fantastic film

Writing a review

1 Read the reviews (1 and 2). Match the reviews with two of the pictures (a–c).

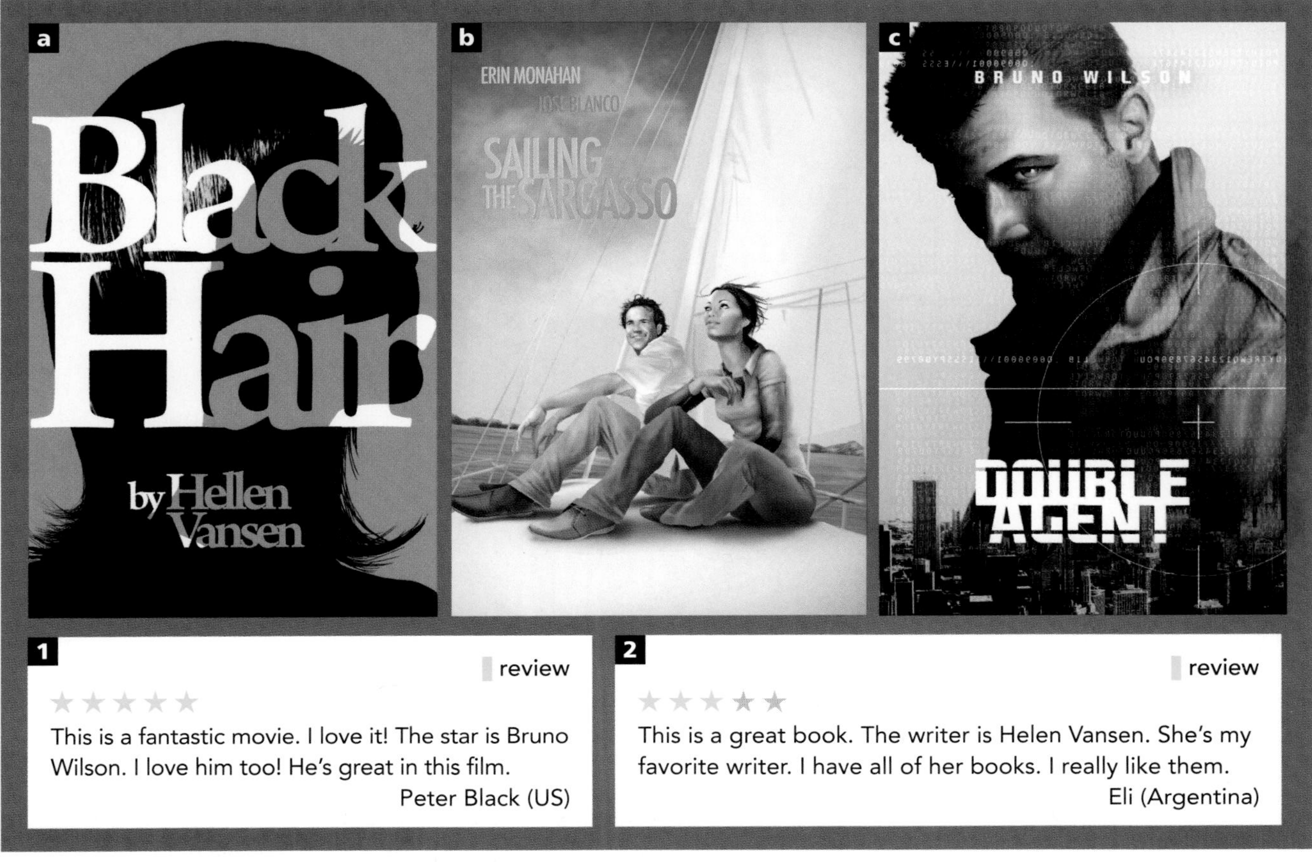

a
Black Hair
by Hellen Vansen
b
ERIN MONAHAN
JOSE BLANCO
SAILING THE SARGASSO
c
BRUNO WILSON
DOUBLE AGENT

1 review

★★★★★

This is a fantastic movie. I love it! The star is Bruno Wilson. I love him too! He's great in this film.

Peter Black (US)

2 review

★★★★★

This is a great book. The writer is Helen Vansen. She's my favorite writer. I have all of her books. I really like them.

Eli (Argentina)

2 Read the reviews again. Complete the tables.

Movie title	
Star	
Name of reviewer	
Reviewer's opinion	

Book title	
Writer	
Name of reviewer	
Reviewer's opinion	

3 Writing skill pronouns

a Use four of these pronouns to complete the review of movie b in Exercise 1.

he her him it she she them

This is a great movie. I love [1] .... ! The star is Erin Monahan. I love [2] .... [3] ....'s my favorite movie star! [4] ....'s fantastic in this movie.

b Complete these sentences with the correct pronoun.

1 "Do you like Bruno Wilson's movies?"
"Yes, I love ...."
2 Russell Crowe is in this movie. ....'s great.
3 "Meryl Streep is my favorite movie star."
"I don't like .... very much."
4 "I like Helen Vansen's books."
"I like .... too."
4 "This movie is boring."
"Oh! I like ...."
5 This is a good book. ....'s fantastic.

4 Write a review for a book or movie you like.

5 Check your review. Check the pronouns and the spelling.

6 Work in pairs. Exchange your reviews. Do you agree with your partner's opinion?

6f At the market

Video

At the Covered Market in Oxford

Before you watch

1 Look at the photos. Write the names with the market stalls.

> a cheese stall   a fish stall
> a fruit and vegetable stall

2 Look at the word box. Find four things you can buy at the stalls in Exercise 1.

3 Work in pairs. Say things you can buy at a market. Take turns. How many things can you say in 30 seconds?

While you watch

4 Watch the video and write the number (1–3) next to the question.

a Which stalls do you like?
b Is this your local market?
c Tell us what you don't like.

5 Work in pairs. What can you remember? How many things in your list from Exercise 3 are in the video?

6 Read the sentences. Then watch the video again and choose the correct option (a–c).

1 Jan Szafranski … .
  a likes the fruit and vegetable stall
  b likes the cheese stall
  c likes the fish stall

2 Amy Miller … .
  a doesn't like fruit
  b doesn't like vegetables
  c doesn't like meat

3 Richard Lewis … .
  a loves English cheese
  b loves French cheese
  c loves tomatoes

7 Watch the video again. Are the sentences true (T) or false (F)?

1 Richard's school is near the market.
2 Amy's favorite stall is the cheese stall.
3 Jan can cook fish.

8 What can you remember? Who says these sentences? Write the name of the person.

1 Yes, this is my local market. And it's really great.
2 My wife likes it, but I don't. It has bones. I don't like them.
3 I can't think—maybe tomatoes. I don't like them very much.
4 I'm a vegetarian.

After you watch

9 Work in pairs. Take turns to buy things from your partner.

Student A: You are in the market. Write your shopping list.

Student B: You have a stall in the market. Decide what you sell and the prices.

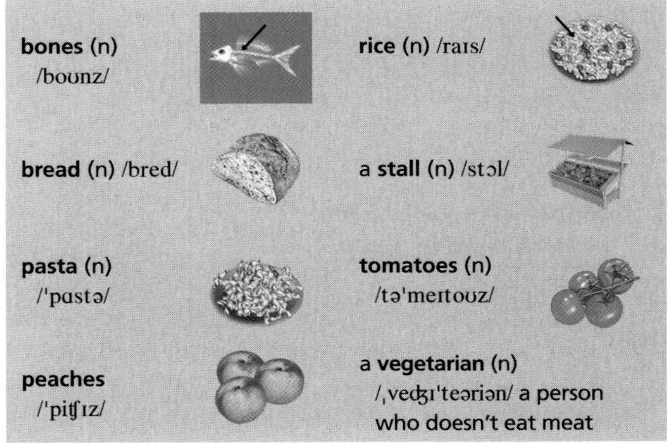

bones (n) /boʊnz/
rice (n) /raɪs/
bread (n) /bred/
a **stall** (n) /stɔl/
pasta (n) /'pɑstə/
tomatoes (n) /tə'meɪtoʊz/
peaches /'piʧɪz/
a **vegetarian** (n) /ˌveʤɪ'teəriən/ a person who doesn't eat meat

UNIT 6 REVIEW

Grammar

1 Complete the article about Kirk Allen with the correct form of ***like***.

Explore Travel

Kirk Allen is passionate about scuba diving. It's his job. He [1] ______ it very much. But [2] ______ cold water? [3] ______ boats? Read our interview with Kirk and find out.

Kirk, you are a professional scuba diver. Why?
Well, I [4] ______ swimming and scuba diving. And I love the ocean.

[5] ______ *the water?*
Yes and no. I [6] ______ cold water very much. It isn't very nice.

Is this your boat?
Yes, it is. I have three boats. I [7] ______ big boats. They're fantastic!

2 Complete the sentences with object pronouns.

1 Read the interview with Kirk Allen. Read the interview with ______ .
2 Kirk Allen loves the ocean. He loves ______ .
3 Kirk Allen likes big boats. He likes ______ .
4 Kirk Allen doesn't like cold water. He doesn't like ______ .

I CAN	
talk about likes and dislikes (*like*)	☐
use object pronouns correctly	☐

Vocabulary

3 Add the vowels and write the words. Then look at the shopping basket and mark (✓) the things.

1 chs ______
2 vgtbls ______
3 fsh ______
4 frt ______
5 rc ______
6 ggs ______
7 spghtt ______
8 chclt ______

4 Underline the odd one out in each group.

Practice
1 swimming pop jazz
2 comedies birds action movies
3 camels basketball fish
4 horses novels detective stories

5 How many examples can you find in Exercise 4 for these words?

1 music 3 animals 5 books
2 sports 4 movies

6 Choose the correct option.

1 I like Adele. She's *fantastic / horrible*.
2 I don't like pigeons. They're *great / horrible*.
3 I love jazz. It's *boring / great*.
4 "Do you like reality shows?"
"No, I don't. They're *boring / fantastic*."

I CAN	
talk about food	☐
talk about interests	☐
give positive and negative opinions (adjectives)	☐

Real life

7 Read the conversation. Choose the correct option.

A: Let's *have pizza / watch a movie / play tennis* tonight.
B: That's a good idea. What's on?
A: A movie with Will Smith.
B: Oh, *it's horrible / I don't like him / she's fantastic*.
A: How about Zoe Saldana? I have her new DVD.
B: *I don't like it. / OK. Great. / Yes, it's great.*

I CAN	
give my opinion	☐
make and respond to suggestions	☐

Speaking

8 Work in pairs. Practice the conversation in Exercise 7 with the other two options.

Unit 7 Different lives

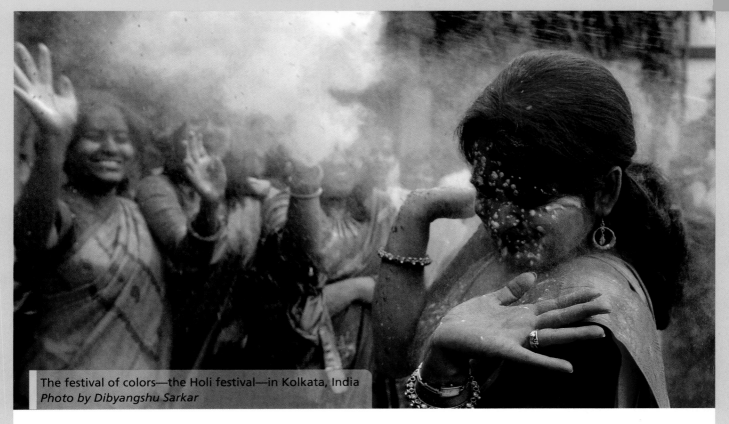

The festival of colors—the Holi festival—in Kolkata, India
Photo by Dibyangshu Sarkar

FEATURES

1 Look at the photo and the caption. Answer the questions.

1 Where are the people?
2 What is the celebration?

2 **51** Work in pairs. Listen to information about the Holi festival. Choose the correct option.

1 The Holi festival is in *December / March.*
2 It's a celebration of *new life / family life.*
3 The festival is one or two *days / weeks.*

3 The Holi festival is a celebration of spring. Look at these words for the four seasons. Listen and repeat them after your instructor.

spring summer fall/autumn winter

4 Work in pairs. Which months are the seasons in your country?

I'm from Peru. Winter is June, July, and August.

7a The Sami people

Reading

1 Look at the two photos. What season is it?

2 Look at the photos and read the captions. Find:

snow a sledge reindeer

3 Read the article about the Sami people. Find:

1 four countries
2 an animal
3 a language

The Sami people

By Jessica Benko
Photos by Franz Aberham

Henrik Gaup and his family are Sami. The Sami people live in Norway, Sweden, Finland, and Russia. They are the "people of the reindeer." Henrik Gaup is a traditional Sami. "I have five children," he says. "I teach my children about the reindeer. They don't study with books." Henrik and his family speak Sami, but many Sami children don't understand it. Reindeer are very important to the Sami people. In the Sami language the word for "a group of reindeer" is *eallu* and the word for "life" is *eallin*.

a Henrik Gaup and one of his reindeer

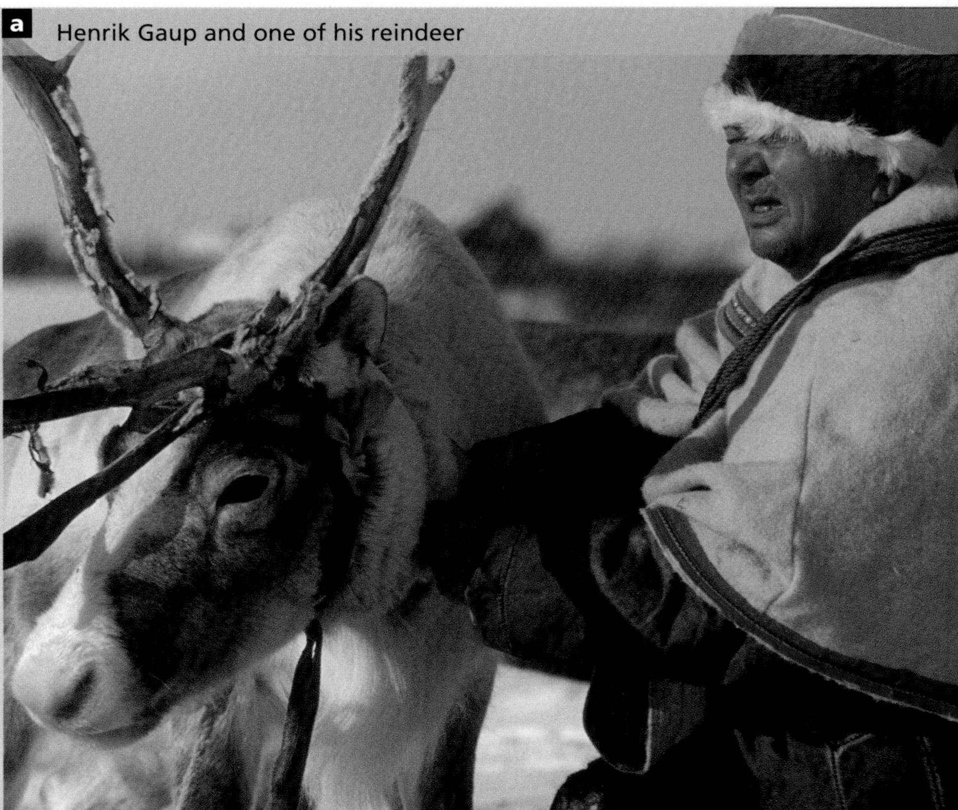

b Sami people at a winter camp

4 Underline these words in the article. Then complete the sentences with two of the words.

live have teach speak

1 The Sami people .... in Norway, Sweden, Finland, and Russia.
2 They .... the Sami language.

5 Use words from the box to write two sentences about yourself. Read your sentences to your partner.

Grammar simple present *I/you/we/they*

6 Look at the grammar box. Then look at this sentence. Choose the correct option. What is the negative form of the simple present?

Many Sami children *understand / don't understand* Sami.

▶ SIMPLE PRESENT *I/YOU/WE/YOU/THEY*	
I/You/We/You/They	**live** in Sweden. **don't study** with books.

For more information and practice, see page 165.

7 Read about the Sami people. Choose the correct option. Check your answers with your instructor.

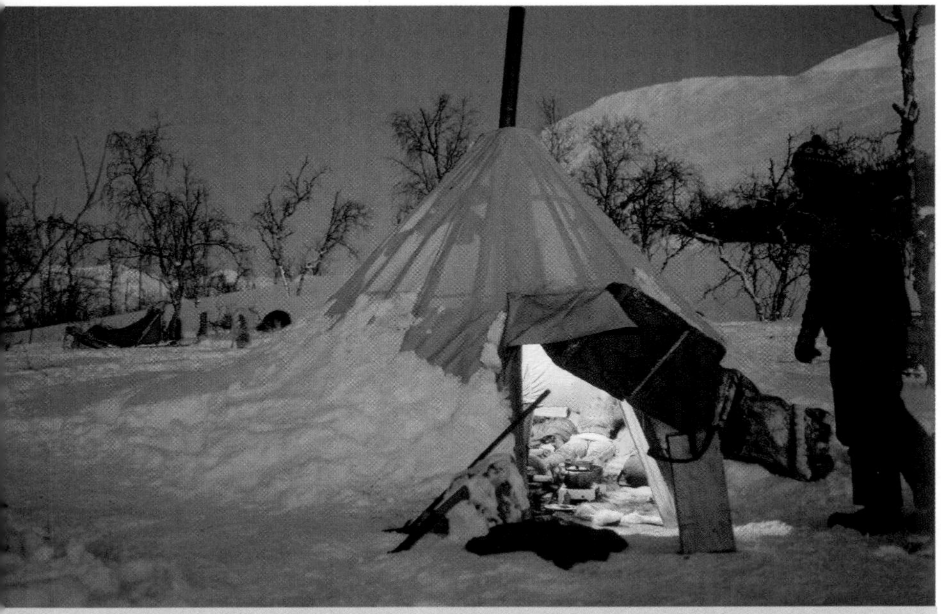

The traditional Sami [1] *live / understand* reindeer. In the summer, they [2] *have / live* in traditional tents. They [3] *have / study* tractors. Today many young Sami [4] *live / teach* in modern homes. They [5] *have / speak* television and the Internet. They [6] *don't speak / don't understand* traditional Sami life.

a **tent** /tent/ 

a **tractor** /ˈtræktə/ 

8 Pronunciation *don't*

a 52 Listen and repeat four sentences.

b Are you different from the traditional Sami? Write three sentences with *don't*. Read your sentences to your partner.

I don't live in Sweden.
They don't speak Spanish.

9 Are these sentences true for you? Change them so they are true.

1 I don't live in a house.
2 I don't have three children.
3 I speak four languages.
4 I don't understand French.
5 I teach English.
6 I study with books.

Speaking and writing

10 Work in pairs. Find three things you have in common. Write sentences with *We*. You can use these verbs.

have live speak study teach understand

I live in a house.

I live in an apartment.

I speak English.

I speak English too.

We both speak English.

7b School life

Vocabulary education

1 Match seven of these words with things and people in the photo.

board	book	classmate	classroom	college	pen
pencil	school	student	teacher	university	

2 Work in pairs. Look at the photo. Use some words from Exercise 1 to make sentences.

It isn't a university.

No, it's a school.

Kakenya Ntaiya is from Kenya. She's a Maasai. She is an unusual Maasai woman. She has a PhD from an American university. Now Kakenya is back in Kenya. She's a teacher. This is her school.

Maasai (n) /mɑ'saɪ/ people from a part of East Africa
unusual (adj) /ʌn'juʒuəl/ different, not usual
village (n) /'vɪlɪdʒ/ a very small town

School life in Kenya

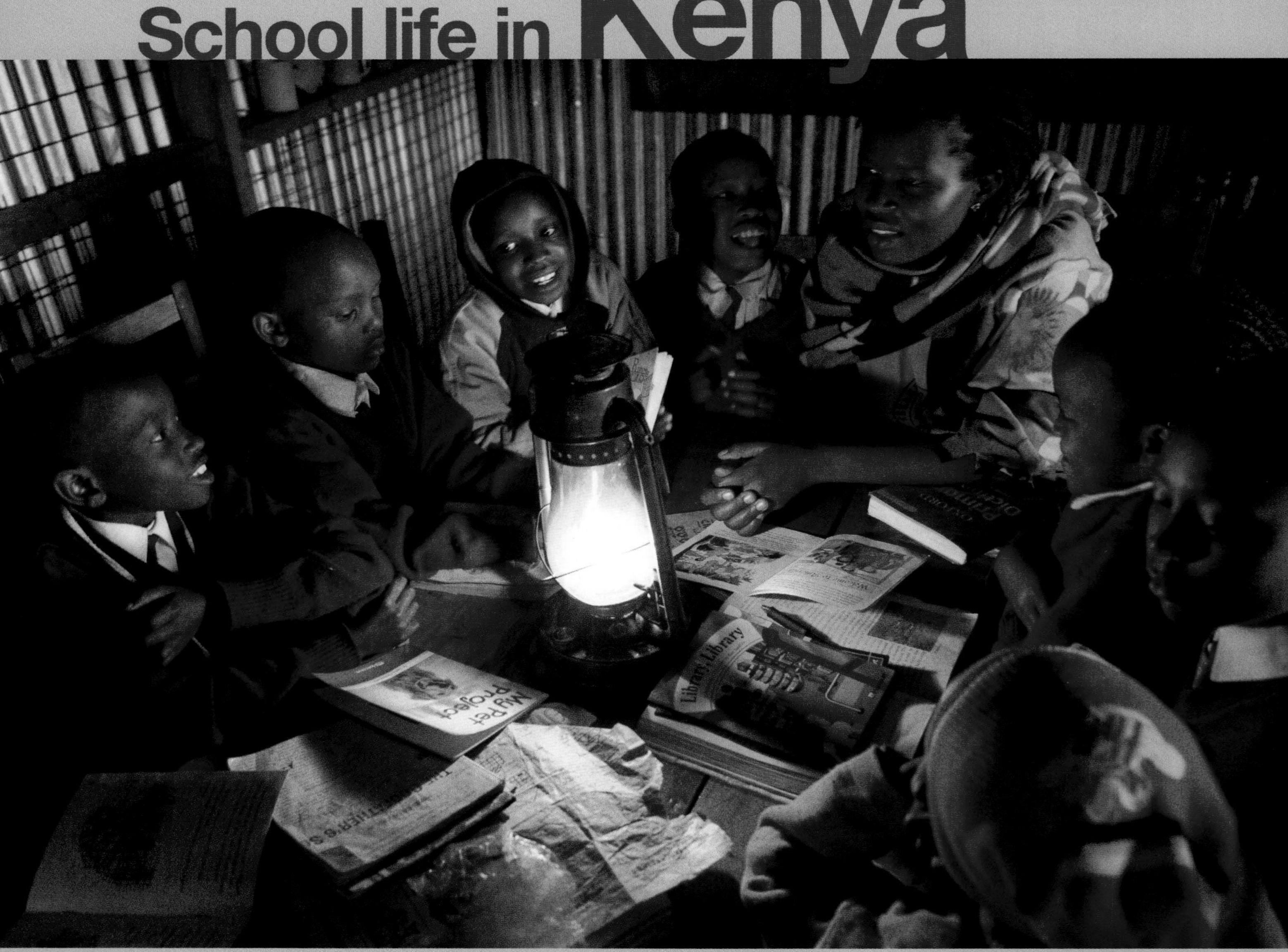

3 Use words from Exercise 1 to make true sentences.

1 I like my … 2 I have of lot of …
3 I study / don't study at a …

Reading and listening

4 Work in pairs. Read about Kakenya Ntaiya. Answer the questions.

1 Is she from America? 2 Is she a girl?
3 Is she a student?

5 **53** Listen to the interview with a teacher at the school. Match the questions (1–5) with the answers (a–e). Then listen again and check.

1 Do you work at Kakenya's school?
2 Do boys study at the school?
3 Do the girls live with their families?
4 Do they go home in the summer?
5 Do the girls learn English at the school?

a No, they don't. The school is for girls.
b No, they don't. They live at the school.
c Yes, they do. They go home to their villages.
d Yes, they do. And in the summer we teach extra classes in English too.
e Yes, I do. I teach there. We have five teachers.

6 Work in pairs. Do you think this school is unusual? Why? / Why not?

Grammar simple present questions *I/you/we/they*

7 Look at the grammar box. Then look at the questions in Exercise 5. Underline the question forms.

SIMPLE PRESENT QUESTIONS *I/YOU/WE/YOU/THEY*

Do	I/you/we/you/they	**study** English?
Yes, No,	I/you/we/you/they	**do.** **don't.**

For more information and practice, see page 165.

8 **54** Put the words in order to make questions. Then listen to an interview with a student and check. Write (✓) or (✗) for his answers.

1 study / you / at a college / do / ?
2 classes / do / have / you / every day / ?
3 like / you / do / your classes / ?
4 you / do / live / near your university / ?
5 do / with your family / live / you / ?
6 you / go home / for the summer / do / ?

9 **Pronunciation intonation in questions**

55 Listen to the questions from Exercise 8.

Work in pairs.

Student A: You are the interviewer.

Student B: You are Carl.

Ask and answer the questions. Take turns.

Writing and speaking

10 Prepare questions for a survey. Use these verbs. Choose an option for each question.

have like live study

1 .... with friends? / with classmates?
2 .... classes in the morning? / classes in the afternoon? / classes in the evening?
3 .... near your school? / near your college?
4 .... your book? / your classroom?

11 In pairs, ask and answer your questions.

Do you live with friends?

No, I don't. I live with my family.

7c A year in British Columbia

Vocabulary weather

1 Repeat these words after your instructor.

2 🔊 **56** Listen to people from four places. Write the number (1–4) next to the weather word.

3 🔊 **56** Listen again. Match the speaker with the country and the season.

	Country	Season
1	Australia	autumn (fall)
2	Canada	spring
3	Great Britain	summer
4	South Africa	winter

4 Work in pairs. Describe the weather for seasons in your country.

I'm from India. Winter is the dry season. It's hot and sunny.

Reading

5 Look at the photos on page 87 and find:

flowers ice leaves trees

6 Read the article on page 87. Match the paragraphs with the photos (a–d).

7 Underline the things people do in each season.

8 Do people in your country do the things in the article? Tell your partner.

We don't go skiing in the winter.

9 Word focus ***go***

a Look at these expressions with *go*. Find four of them in the article on page 87.

go to the beach go to work go home
go swimming go for walks

b Underline the option that is true for you.

1 I *go / don't go* to the beach in the summer.
2 I *go / don't go* swimming in the winter.
3 I *go / don't go* home in the evening.
4 I *go / don't go* to work every day.
5 I *go / don't go* for walks with my family.

Grammar simple present with question words

10 Look at the grammar box. Then look at the article. Find three of the question words from the grammar box in the article.

▶ SIMPLE PRESENT WITH QUESTION WORDS

What **Where** **Who** **Why** **When**	**do**	I/you/we/you/they/people	**do?** **go?** **go** with? **go** to the beach? **eat?**

For more information and practice, see page 165.

11 Complete the questions with question words.

1 .... do you go in the summer?
2 .... do you do in the fall?
3 .... do flowers open?
4 .... do you go cycling with?
5 .... do you like winter?

Speaking

12 Work in pairs. Ask and answer questions like these.

- Why / like … ?
- What / do?
- When / do … ?
- Where / go?
- Who / go with?

Why do you like winter?

I like cold weather.

a

b

c

d

A YEAR IN BRITISH COLUMBIA

By Chuck Spender

SUMMER

Where do people go in the summer?

Summer is a great time for a vacation here. The weather is hot and sunny. People go to the beach. I go to Vancouver Island with my family. We play summer sports and we go swimming in the lakes and rivers.

FALL

What do people do in the fall?

In autumn, classes start. Children go to school. Students go to college. People go to work. It's cloudy and rainy. Trees change color from green to brown. I think it's a beautiful season.

WINTER

Where do people go in winter?

In winter, it's cold, rainy, and snowy, too. A lot of people stay at home. They watch TV, read books, and cook winter food. Winter is my favorite season. I like winter sports. I go to the mountains. I go skiing and climbing. It's very cold!

SPRING

Why do people like spring?

For a lot of people, spring is their favorite season. It's cloudy and rainy, but it isn't cold. Flowers open, birds sing, and trees are green. People go cycling and running. They go for walks. I play golf with my friends.

7d What's the matter?

A bad vacation

Vocabulary problems

1 57 Look at the pictures and listen to seven people. Write the number (1–7) next to the picture.

2 Work in pairs. Say how you feel right now.

I'm hungry!

Real life problems

3 58 Listen to the conversation. Write the names (F = father, P = Paul, A = Anna).

1 .... is thirsty.
2 .... doesn't feel well.
3 .... is cold and wet.
4 .... is bored.

4 58 Listen again. Complete the mother's suggestions.

1 Why don't you have ....?
2 Why don't you eat ....?
3 Why don't you go ....?

PROBLEMS

What's the matter?
I'm hungry/thirsty/cold/tired/hot/wet/bored.
It's cold/wet/hot.
I don't feel well.
I don't like swimming.
I don't understand.
Why don't you have a cup of coffee?

5 Pronunciation sentence stress

59 Listen and repeat three sentences. Is *don't* stressed or unstressed?

6 Work in pairs. Look at the expressions for talking about PROBLEMS. Take turns to talk about problems and make suggestions.

What's the matter?

I'm bored.

Why don't you read a book?

7e Photography club members

Writing a profile

1 Read Omar's profile. Are the sentences true (T) or false (F)?

1 Omar is a student.
2 He's married.
3 He's in a photography club.

2 Writing skill paragraphs

a Read Omar's profile again. Write the number of the paragraph.

a interests: ....
b profession: ....
c family / friends: ....

b Read the profile information for Jenna. Number the paragraphs (a–c) in the correct order (1–3).

c Read the notes for Luther. Organize them into three paragraphs. Then write sentences with them.

> Luther
> animals
> a teacher
> engineering
> my wife and children
> photos

3 Make notes about yourself for a profile.

- professional information
- family / friends
- interests / organizations

4 Use your notes and write three paragraphs.

5 Check your profile. Check the paragraph order, the spelling, and the punctuation.

6 Work in pairs. Exchange profiles. Find two things you and your partner have in common.

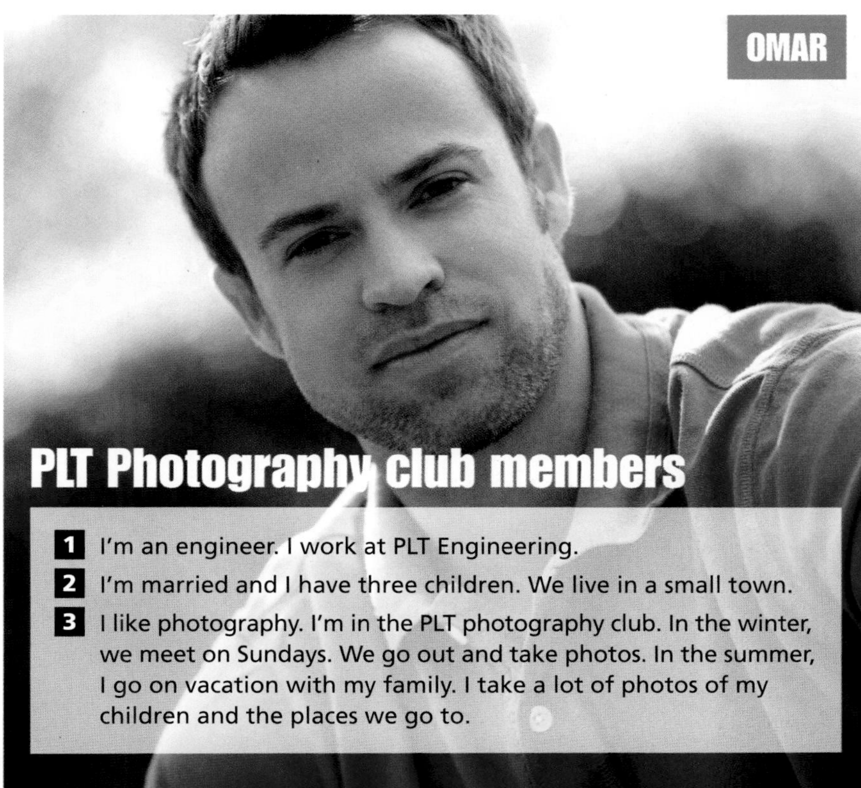

1 I'm an engineer. I work at PLT Engineering.
2 I'm married and I have three children. We live in a small town.
3 I like photography. I'm in the PLT photography club. In the winter, we meet on Sundays. We go out and take photos. In the summer, I go on vacation with my family. I take a lot of photos of my children and the places we go to.

a I live with three classmates. We live near our college.
b I like sports and photography. I take photos of sports people.
c I'm a student. I study engineering. In the summer, I work at PLT Engineering.

7f The people of the reindeer

Video

A Sami man with his reindeer

Before you watch

1 Work in pairs. Look at the photo on page 90. Answer the questions.

1 What kind of animals are they?
2 Who are the "people of the reindeer"?
3 Where are they from?

2 Work in pairs. What can you remember about the Sami people's lives? Are these sentences true (T) or false (F)?

1 They live in big cities.
2 They speak a traditional language.
3 They have modern homes.

While you watch

3 Watch the video and check your ideas from Exercise 1.

4 These things are in the video. Watch the video again and put the pictures in order.

a

a cup of coffee

b

a dog

c

a fire

d

snow *1*

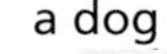

e

a tent

f

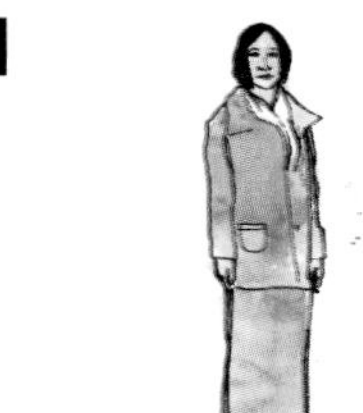

a woman

g

a young child

h

a young couple

5 Read these sentences about the Sami. Mark (✓) the things you can see in the video.

1 The Sami travel on tractors.
2 When they travel with the reindeer, the Sami cook their food on a fire.
3 Some young people wear traditional clothes.
4 Reindeer meat is a traditional Sami food.
5 Reindeer eat food under the snow.
6 The Sami people have dogs.

After you watch

6 Complete the paragraph with verbs. You can use the same verb more than once.

The Sami [1] .... in Norway, Sweden, Finland, and Russia. The reindeer [2] .... in spring. The Sami people [3] .... with them. On the journey, the people [4] .... in tents. These Sami people [5] .... traditional lives.

7 Work in pairs. Ask and answer questions with *when, where, what, who,* and *why* about Sami life. Take turns.

Student A: You are from a Sami family. Choose your age—young or old.

Student B: You are a journalist.

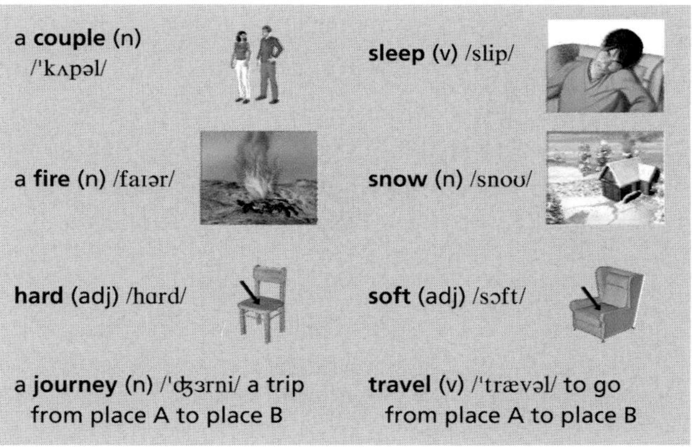

a **couple** (n) /ˈkʌpəl/

sleep (v) /slip/

a **fire** (n) /faɪər/

snow (n) /snoʊ/

hard (adj) /hɑrd/

soft (adj) /sɔft/

a **journey** (n) /ˈʤɜrni/ a trip from place A to place B

travel (v) /ˈtrævəl/ to go from place A to place B

UNIT 7 REVIEW

Grammar

1 Read about Cathy Gulpilil. Underline two places and circle two languages in the article.

Cathy Gulpilil and her husband Albert are from the Northern Territory of Australia. Now they live in Sydney. They have two children. Cathy and Albert teach at a college. They speak English and Yirram—their parents' language. Cathy's and Albert's parents live in the Northern Territory. Cathy and Albert's children understand Yirram, but they don't speak it.

2 Write the questions.

1 where / Cathy and Albert / live?
2 they / have / children?
3 where / they / teach?
4 they / speak / their parents' language?
5 their children /speak Yirram?

3 Work in pairs. Take turns.

Student A: You are Cathy or Albert Gulpilil.

Student B: Interview your partner. Use *you* and the questions in Exercise 2.

I CAN	
describe permanent states (simple present)	☐
ask and answer questions about habits (simple present)	☐

Vocabulary

4 Complete the words about education.

1 People: classmate, st _ _ _ _ _ , te _ _ _ _ _
2 Places: college, un _ _ _ _ _ _ _ _ , sc _ _ _ _ , cl _ _ _ _ _ _ _
3 Things: board, bo _ _ , pe _

5 Complete the sentences with these verbs.

have like live speak study

1 My friends ________ engineering in college.
2 I ________ in a small town.
3 Do you ________ Arabic?
4 My parents don't ________ a TV.
5 I ________ summer.

6 Complete the sentences with weather words.

1 It's ________ in Panama City.
2 It's ________ in Dubai.
3 It's ________ in Stockholm.
4 It's ________ in Kyoto.
5 It's ________ in Shanghai.

I CAN	
talk about education	☐
talk about people's lives	☐
talk about the weather	☐

Real life

7 Match words in A and B to make sentences. Then put the sentences in order to make a conversation.

	A	B
1	I'm	No thanks, ________ cold.
2	it's	the matter?
3	What's	eat this pizza?
4	Why don't you	hungry.

I CAN	
talk about problems	☐
make suggestions	☐

Speaking

8 Work in pairs. Write a conversation with these ideas. Take turns to start.

1 thirsty / cup of coffee
2 hot / drink of water
3 don't understand / use a dictionary
4 bored / go for a walk

Unit 8 Routines

Farmers and wild horses
Photo by Melissa Farlow

FEATURES

1 Work in pairs. Look at the photo. Where do you think this is?

2 **60** Read the sentences about the man in the photo. Which options are correct? Listen and check your ideas.

1 The job of the man in the photo is *in an office / outside*.
2 Farmers *use / don't use* cell phones.
3 They use *tractors / helicopters*.

3 Make true sentences about these jobs.

Artists Doctors Engineers Filmmakers Photographers Scientists Writers	work	outside. in laboratories. in offices. in studios. in hospitals. with people. with animals. with modern technology.

4 Work in pairs. Take turns choosing from Exercise 3.

I work in a hospital.

You're a doctor.

8a Day and night

Vocabulary routines

1 Match the sentences (1–7) with the pictures (a–g).

1 I get up at *six o'clock* . *f*
2 I have breakfast at ______ .
3 I start work at ______ .
4 I have lunch in a ______ .
5 I finish work at ______ .
6 I have dinner at ______ .
7 I go to bed at ______ .

2 What time do you do the activities in Exercise 1? Fill in the information.

3 In pairs, discuss your daily routines.

I get up at six o'clock.
Wow, that's early! I get up at nine!

Reading

4 Look at the photo. Where is it? What kind of class is this?

5 Read about one of the women in the photo. Are your routines similar?

DAY AND NIGHT

A writer in China

Chen Hong is from Shanghai. She's a writer. She gets up at six o'clock. She doesn't eat breakfast. She goes to an exercise class. It's on the Bund, near the river. It starts at 7:15 and it finishes at 7:45. Then Chen has breakfast. She starts work at 8:30. She works at home. At noon, she has lunch. She finishes work at 6:30 in the evening. At eight o'clock, she has dinner with her family. She goes to bed at 10:30. Chen Hong doesn't work every day, but she goes to her exercise class every day.

A morning exercise class on the Bund (riverside) in Shanghai

Grammar **simple present *he/she/it***

6 Look at the grammar box. Then underline the simple present verbs in the article about Chen Hong.

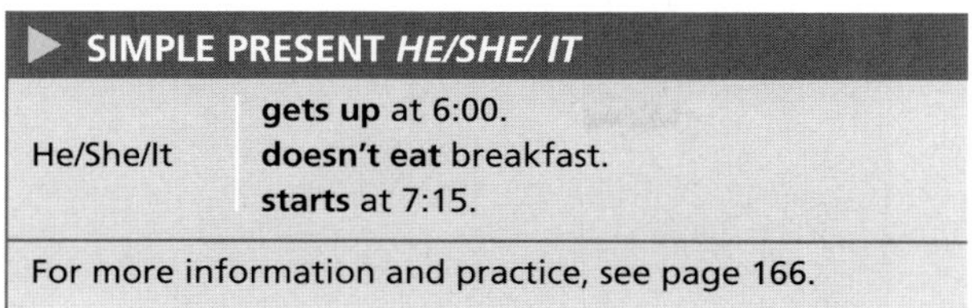

▶ SIMPLE PRESENT *HE/SHE/ IT*	
He/She/It	**gets up** at 6:00. **doesn't eat** breakfast. **starts** at 7:15.

For more information and practice, see page 166.

7 Complete the text about an astronomer with the correct form of the verbs. Use some verbs more than once.

finish get up go have not / work start work

An astronomer in Chile

Ronaldo Godoy is an astronomer. He [1] ______ at an observatory in Chile. Ronaldo [2] ______ work at nine o'clock at night. He [3] ______ work at 1:30 in the morning and he [4] ______ home. He [5] ______ to bed at two o'clock. He [6] ______ at 8:45 and [7] ______ breakfast with his family. Ronaldo [8] ______ on Monday and Wednesday. He [9] ______ every day.

Grammar **prepositions of time**

8 Look at the expressions in the grammar box. Underline similar expressions in the text in Exercise 7.

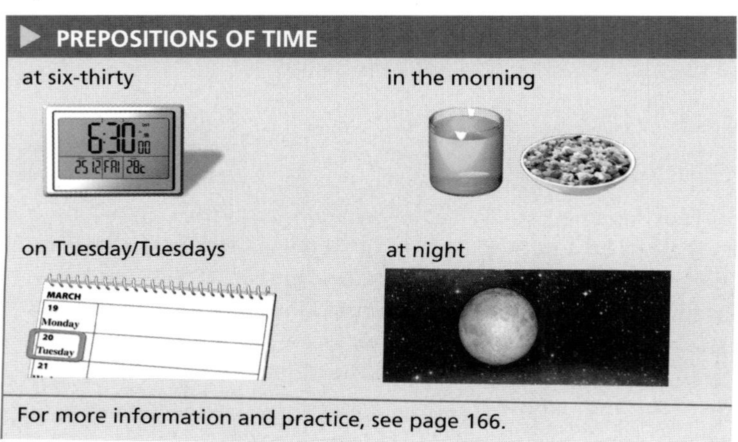

▶ PREPOSITIONS OF TIME

at six-thirty

in the morning

on Tuesday/Tuesdays

at night

For more information and practice, see page 166.

9 **Pronunciation *-s* and *-es* verbs**

a 61 Listen and repeat.

works starts finishes goes gets up

b 61 Listen again. Underline the verb with an extra syllable.

work	start	finish	go	get up
works	starts	finishes	goes	gets up

Speaking and writing

10 Work as a class. Ask questions. Find one name for each sentence. You have a time limit of five minutes.

Find a person in your class who …

gets up at six o'clock. ______

doesn't work. ______

has eggs for breakfast. ______

works in the evening. ______

doesn't eat lunch. ______

goes to bed after midnight. ______

starts work at nine o'clock. ______

gets up late on the weekend. ______

Do you get up at six o'clock, Issa?

No, I don't. I get up at 7:15.

Do you get up at six o'clock, Leonardo?

Yes, I do.

11 Write sentences with the names.

Leonardo gets up at six o'clock.

8b A typical day

Reading

1 Look at the photos (1 and 2) and the captions. Read the sentences and write A (archaeologists), G (geologists), or B (both).

1 They work on archaeological sites.
2 They work outside.
3 They study rocks.
4 They study old objects.

2 Work in pairs. What do you think is the daily routine of the people in the photos?

3 Read about a geologist and an archaeologist, and check your ideas from Exercise 2.

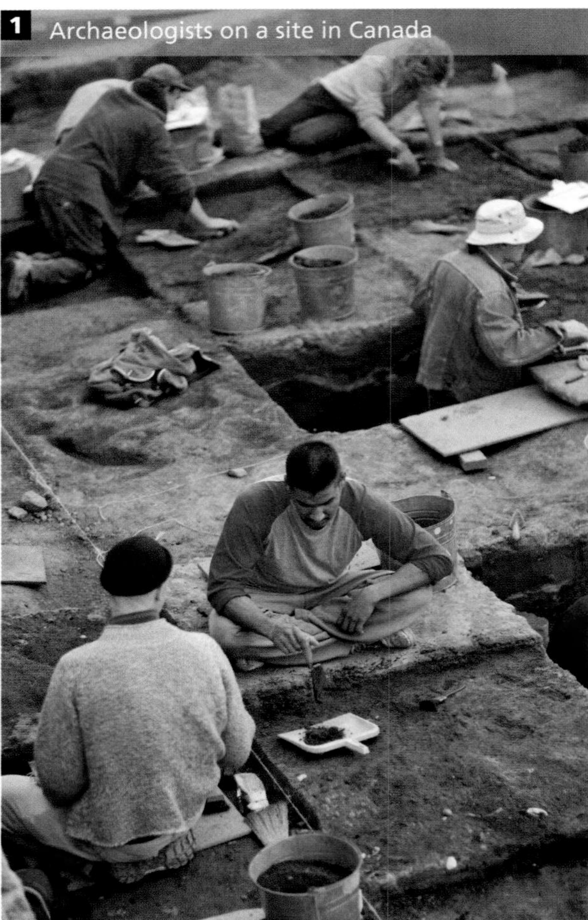
1 Archaeologists on a site in Canada

2 Geologists at work near the Azores, Atlantic Ocean

Cynthia Liutkus-Pierce

Geologist

Location: US

In the winter, Cynthia works in her university office in North Carolina. She gives lectures and she talks to her students every week. She often has meetings with other geologists. Every summer, she travels to Africa. She usually gets up and eats breakfast at six o'clock in the morning because it's very hot. She never works late. She goes to bed early, but she sometimes wakes up because the animals are noisy.

Julia Mayo Torne

Archaeologist

Location: Panama

Julia is from Panama. Her typical day changes with the seasons. In the dry season, Julia goes to her site. It's a good site and she usually finds objects every day. She often eats lunch there. In the evening, she always has coffee with her colleagues. They talk about their day. Then she reads before she goes to bed. In the rainy season, Julia returns to her laboratory. She studies the objects from the site, and writes articles and reports.

Grammar **frequency adverbs**

4 Look at the grammar box. Then look at the article. Underline the frequency adverbs.

▶ FREQUENCY ADVERBS

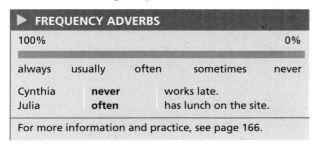

100%				0%
always	usually	often	sometimes	never

Cynthia	**never**	works late.
Julia	**often**	has lunch on the site.

For more information and practice, see page 166.

5 Rewrite the sentences with the adverb in the correct position.

1 Julia gets up early. (sometimes)
2 Julia has lunch with her colleagues. (always)
3 Cynthia goes to Africa in the summer. (always)
4 Julia reads novels. (usually)
5 Cynthia travels in the winter. (never)
6 Cynthia writes reports. (often)

6 Make the sentences in Exercise 5 true for you. Tell your partner.

Listening

7 **62** Listen and number the questions (1–6).

a Does she go to Africa every year?
b Does she work at this university? *1*
c What does she do?
d Does she give lectures?
e Where does Cynthia go?
f Does she teach languages?

8 **62** Listen again and answer the questions.

Grammar **simple present questions *he/she***

9 Look at the grammar box. Find two questions from Exercise 7.

▶ SIMPLE PRESENT QUESTIONS *HE/SHE*

What Where	**does**	he/she	**do?** **work?**	He/She's a geologist. He/She **works** in Africa.
	Does	he/she	**work** at this university?	
	Yes, No,	he/she	**does.** **doesn't.**	

For more information and practice, see page 166.

10 Put the words in order to make questions.

1 Julia / does / where / work / ?
2 meet / does / who / Cynthia / ?
3 Cynthia / children / teach / does / ?
4 Julia / like / does / coffee / ?
5 does / have lunch / where / Julia / ?
6 Cynthia / does / what time / get up / ?

11 Work in pairs. Ask and answer the questions.

Vocabulary **job activities**

12 Match a verb in A with words in B. Then underline three things that Cynthia does.

A	**B**
gives	articles / books
talks	late / at home
travels	lectures / talks
works	to different cities / countries / places
writes	to students / people / customers

13 Look at these jobs. Write sentences with the expressions in Exercise 12.

a journalist, a waiter, a businesswoman, a nurse, a receptionist, a salesperson

Speaking

14 Work in pairs. Tell your partner about your friends and family. Use the words in Exercise 13.

My brother travels for his job. He's a businessman.

15 Work in pairs. Ask your partner five questions about one of the people in Exercise 14.

Does your brother travel every week?

No, he doesn't. He travels every month.

8c Cats in crisis

Reading

1 Work in pairs. Match the animals in the photos (1–4) with the places (a–d).

a Africa and Asia
b Asia
c South America
d Africa

1
a jaguar

2
a leopard

3
a lion

4
a tiger

2 Mark the sentences as true (T) or false (F).

1 Tigers eat animals.
2 They sleep at night.
3 They hunt people.
4 Thailand has a lot of tigers.
5 Tigers live in forests.

3 Read the article and check your answers from Exercise 2.

4 Read the article again. Find these things.

1 one thing a tiger does at night
2 one thing Saksit Simcharoen does at night
3 two things Saksit Simcharoen does every month
4 one other thing he does in his job

5 Answer the questions.

1 How many wild tigers are in Asia today?
2 How many people work in the wildlife park?
3 How does Saksit study the tigers in the park?
4 How many tigers in the park have radio collars?
5 How often does Saksit write a report?

Grammar *How ... ?*

6 Look at the grammar box. Choose the correct option.

We use "how" to ask for *information / a "yes" or "no" answer*.

> **HOW ... ?**
>
> **How** does Saksit study the tigers in the park?
> **How many** people does Saskit work with?
> **How often** does Saksit write a report?
>
> For more information and practice, see page 166.

7 Put the words in order to make questions with *how*. Then work in pairs. Ask and answer the questions with your partner.

1 tigers / how many / in the park / are / ?
2 in the park / cameras / are / how many / ?
3 have / how often / a meeting / Saksit / does / ?
4 help / we / can / tiger conservation / how / ?

8 **Word focus *every***

a Look at the sentences. Which words can follow *every*?

1 Every month Saksit writes reports.
2 Does she go to Africa every year?
3 Does he travel every week?
4 Rosanna doesn't work every day.
5 I have a meeting every Tuesday.

b Write five sentences about yourself using *every*. Read your sentences to your partner. What do you have in common?

Speaking

9 Tigers are night animals. What about you? Are you a "morning person" or an "evening person"? Take a quiz.

Student A: Turn to page 155.

Student B: Turn to page 159.

CATS IN CRISIS

TIGERS, LIONS, LEOPARDS, AND JAGUARS ARE ALL "BIG CATS"... AND THEY ARE IN CRISIS!

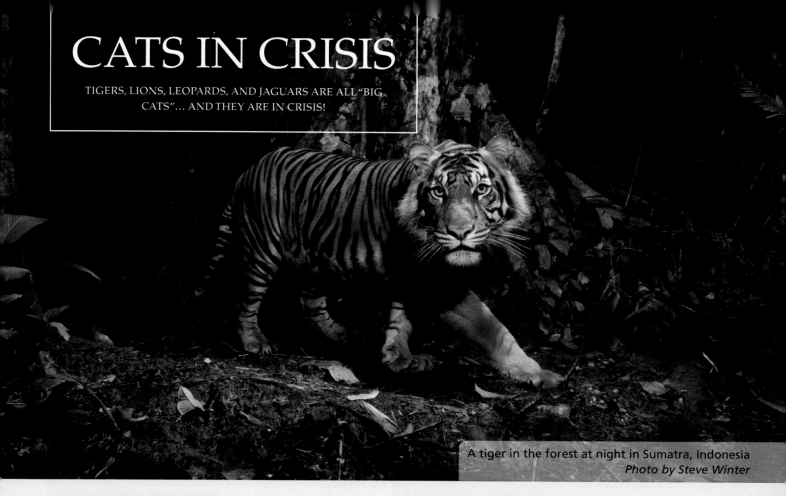

A tiger in the forest at night in Sumatra, Indonesia
Photo by Steve Winter

Tigers

number of wild tigers
in 1900 – 100,000
in 2010 – 3,500

Tigers live in many places in Asia, from very cold mountains in the Himalayas to very hot areas. They usually live in places without people. Tigers eat other animals. They hunt at night. In places without people, tigers also hunt in the day. They usually kill wild animals, but they sometimes kill domestic animals. Tigers are in crisis because people move into their areas and sometimes kill them.

A team in Thailand studies a tiger.

Tiger conservation

tigers in Huai Kha Khaeng Wildlife Park
in 1980 – 20
in 2010 – 60

Saksit Simcharoen works at the Huai Kha Khaeng Wildlife Park in Thailand. The park is a tiger conservation area. About sixty tigers live there. Saksit works with 170 people in the park. He goes into the forest at night. He doesn't see many tigers, but the park has 180 automatic cameras. They take photos of tigers. Saksit checks the cameras. About eight of the tigers in the park have radio collars. Every month Saksit writes reports about the tigers in the area and meets with his colleagues. Saksit loves his job because the tigers in the park are not in crisis.

automatic (adj) /ˌɔtəˈmætɪk/ without a human operator
conservation (n) /ˌkɑnsərˈveɪʃən/ protection
crisis (n) /ˈkraɪsɪs/ a difficult or dangerous time
domestic (adj) /dəˈmestɪk/ not wild

a radio collar (n) /ˈreɪdioʊ ˌkɑlər/

8d One moment, please

Real life on the phone

1 63 Listen to three phone calls (1–3). Match the number of the conversation to the person.

a Mrs. Jackson
b Ed Carr
c Mr. Watts

2 64 Look at the photos. Then listen to two of the phone calls again. Mark (✓) the reasons the callers can't speak to the persons.

3 Look at the expressions for ON THE PHONE. Write caller (C) or receptionist (R).

ON THE PHONE

Good morning, / Hello, PJ International.
May I help you?
Yes, can I speak to Ed Carr, please?
Yes, one moment, please.
I'm sorry. He's/She's in a meeting.
OK. Thank you. / Thanks.
I'll call back later.

4 Complete the conversation with the expressions.

R: ______________, City College.
______________?
C: Yes, ______________
Mrs. Jackson, please?
R: ______________.
She's out of the office at the moment.
C: OK, thank you. ______________
______________.

5 **Pronunciation /s/ and /z/**

65 Listen to these words. Is the s like *this* or *is*? Listen again and repeat.

please he's yes Fridays
works thanks

6 Work in pairs. Practice phone calls. Use the ideas in the photos.

works from home on Fridays

out of the office

on vacation

with a customer

doesn't work in the afternoons

in a meeting

8e My new job

Writing an email

1 Read Vijay's email about his new job in a call center. Complete the email with seven of these words.

classmates	colleagues	evening	job
morning	office	phone calls	tasks

2 Who do you think the email is to?

a his boss b his friend c his colleague

Hi!

Here I am at my new [1] ______ ! It's good! The [2] ______ opens at 8:00 a.m. I usually arrive at about 7:45 and I have coffee with my [3] ______ . They're great. We have a meeting every [4] ______ and the boss gives us our [5] ______ for the day. I usually make about 40 [6] ______ a day. I finish early on Fridays. Let's meet for lunch. How about next week?

Vijay

3 Writing skill spelling: double letters

a Look at the email again. Underline the words with double letters.

b Complete the words with the letter. How many words have double letters?

1 ar______ist (t)
2 busine______man (s)
3 cla______es (s)
4 co______ege (l)
5 di______erent (f)
6 di______icult (f)
7 di______er (n)
8 m______t (e)
9 su______er (m)
10 w______kend (e)

c Complete the email from a student with words from Exercises 1 and 3b.

Hi!

Here I am at my new [1] ______ ! It's good! I have [2] ______ every day except Wednesday. My courses aren't [3] ______ . I usually write about two essays a week. I often go out with my [4] ______ in the evenings. Let's [5] ______ and play tennis. How about next [6] ______ ?

Jim

4 Write an email to a friend. Include a suggestion to meet.

5 Work in pairs. Exchange emails. Check the spelling. Reply to your partner's email.

8f The elephants of Samburu

Video

An elephant at night in Samburu National Reserve

Before you watch

1 Work in pairs. Look at the photo and the caption. Where does this elephant live?

2 Read about Samburu. Answer the questions.

1 Where is the Samburu National Reserve?
2 What does the organization Save the Elephants do?
3 How does Google Earth help Save the Elephants?

> The Samburu National Reserve is in Kenya. Lions, leopards, elephants, and buffalo live in the reserve. The reserve is the home of the elephant conservation organization Save the Elephants. It works in four African countries: Kenya, Mali, Gabon, and South Africa. Save the Elephants works with Google Earth to follow elephants with GPS collars.

3 Work in pairs. How much do you know about elephants? Choose the option you think is correct.

1 Elephants live *in family groups / alone*.
2 Elephants *like / don't like* water.
3 Elephants eat *plants / animals*.
4 Elephants *hunt / sleep* at night.

While you watch

4 Watch the video. Check your answers above.

5 Choose the correct option (a–c).

1 Nick Nichols
  a is a photographer for National Geographic.
  b is a student.
  c works for Save the Elephants.

2 Daniel Lentipo
  a is a photographer for National Geographic.
  b is a student.
  c works for Save the Elephants.

3 Daniel teaches Nick how to
  a take photos of the elephants.
  b identify individual elephants.
  c follow elephants.

4 Nick and Daniel follow the elephants for
  a four hours a day.
  b eight hours a day.
  c ten hours a day.

5 Elephants put their trunks up
  a at night.
  b to greet other elephants.
  c when they are thirsty.

6 Watch the video again. Write three things:

1 the elephants do every day.
2 Nick and Daniel do every day.

After you watch

7 Read about Nick and Daniel's work routine. Complete the text with these verbs.

drive	get up	start	study
work	work	take	

Nick Nichols [1] ______ for National Geographic. Daniel Lentipo is the Chief Research Assistant at the Samburu National Reserve. Nick and Daniel [2] ______ early every day. They [3] ______ work early. Daniel [4] ______ the jeep and he [5] ______ the elephants. Nick [6] ______ photos of the elephants. Nick and Daniel sometimes [7] ______ at night. Nick's photos of sleeping elephants are very unusual.

8 Work in pairs.

Student A: You are a photographer.

Student B. You are a journalist.

Prepare answers to these questions. Then take turns to ask and answer the questions.

- Who do you work for?
- Where do you work?
- Where do you travel to in your job?
- What do you take photos of / write about?
- What's a typical day like in your job?

call (v) /kɔl/ to make a noise

identify (v) /aɪ'dentɪˌfaɪ/ to find

follow (v) /'fɑloʊ/ to travel behind a person or animal

an **individual** (n) /ˌɪndɪ'vɪdʒuəl/ one person or animal

gentle (adj) /'dʒent(ə)l/ kind

a **jeep** (n) /dʒip/

greet (v) /grit/ to say "hello"

lie down (v) /'laɪ 'daʊn/

a **hand** (n) /'hænd/

sleep (v) /slip/

a **bath** (n) /'bæθ/

a **trunk** (n) /trʌŋk/

UNIT 8 REVIEW

Grammar

1 Read about Joel Murray. Write eight sentences with the underlined words. Use *he*.

Hi. I'm Joel. I'm 46. I'm a truck driver. [1] I have a new job. In my new job, [2] I drive from New Mexico to Arizona every week. That's about 1,500 miles. [3] I work Monday to Friday. [4] I start work at six o'clock. [5] I don't have breakfast, but [6] I eat a snack in my truck. [7] I have lunch in a restaurant with other drivers. [8] I work late.

2 Rewrite sentences 3, 6, and 8 with these adverbs:

3 usually 6 sometimes 8 often

3 Complete the sentences with prepositions.

1 Joel drives to Arizona ________ Mondays.
2 He doesn't work ________ the evening.
3 He finishes work ________ 4:30 p.m.
4 He takes a vacation ________ August.

4 Complete the questions with three of these expressions. Then answer the questions.

How many	How much	How often	How old

1 ________ is Joel?
2 ________ miles does he drive every week?
3 ________ does Joel work late?

I CAN	
say what people do every day (simple present)	☐
say when people do things (prepositions of time)	☐
say how often people do things (frequency adverbs)	☐
use *how* correctly	☐

Vocabulary

5 Match a verb from A with a word from B.

A	B
finish	breakfast
get up	early
go	to bed
have	work

6 Work in pairs. Ask and answer questions about your day with the expressions from Exercise 5.

7 Complete the sentences with these verbs.

talk	travel	work	write

1 Journalists ________ articles.
2 Businessmen ________ to different countries.
3 Salespeople ________ to customers.
4 Waiters ________ late.

I CAN	
talk about routines	☐
talk about job activities	☐

Real life

8 Put the phone conversation in order.

a Hello.
b Oh. Well, can I speak to her assistant?
c Yes, can I speak to Ms. Becker, please?
d Can I help you?
e I'm sorry. She's on vacation this week.
f Good morning, Sports Unlimited. *1*
g OK. Thank you.
h Yes, one moment please.

I CAN	
say why people can't answer a phone call	☐
make phone calls	☐

Speaking

9 Work in pairs. Take turns.

Student A: You have a new job as a driver.

Student B: Ask your friend about his/her new job. Use the ideas below.

what / do?	what time / start?
where / work?	how often / work late?
how many days / work?	you / like the job?

Unit 9 Travel

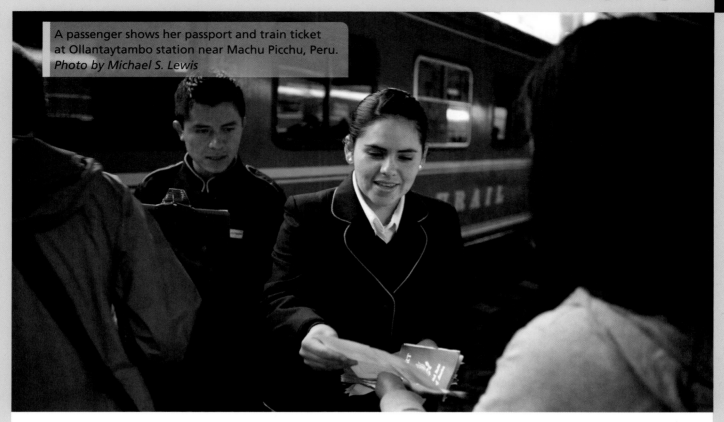

A passenger shows her passport and train ticket at Ollantaytambo station near Machu Picchu, Peru. *Photo by Michael S. Lewis*

FEATURES

1 Work in pairs. Look at the photo. Who does the woman work for (a–c)? Who are the other people?

a a bus company b a train company c an airline

2 **66** Listen to four people talk about travel. Write the number of the speaker (1–4) next to the picture.

by boat

by bus

by plane

by train

3 **66** Listen again and complete the table.

	Where do they go?	When?
1	....	*every week*
2	....	....
3	....	....
4	....	....

4 Work in pairs. Ask and answer questions about travel with *where, when,* and *how*?

Where do you go?

I travel to Cairo.

9a Travel essentials

Vocabulary clothes

1 Look at the photos. Repeat the words after your instructor.

a coat

a pair of sandals

a jacket

a T-shirt

a pair of boots

a hat

a skirt

a pair of jeans

a blouse

a dress

a pair of shoes

a shirt

a pair of pants

a scarf

a pair of shorts

a sweater

2 Work in pairs. Look at the people in your class. Match clothes with names.

A white shirt and a jacket.

Ramon?

Yes.

3 Work in pairs. Talk about your clothes. What do you usually wear … ?

- to work
- to class
- on the weekend
- on vacation

Reading

4 Read the article. Underline the clothes.

5 Read the article again. What does Kate always take with her? What about her sister and her husband?

6 What do you always take? Tell your partner.

I'm a travel writer. I usually travel alone, but my family sometimes comes with me. It's difficult because they always have a lot of bags. Look at this photo of our trip to Ecuador. There are eight people and there are about fifteen bags! In my sister's bags there are three jackets, four or five sweaters, seven pairs of pants, and two dresses. There are six or seven books, too. She never travels without books. In my husband's bag there's a pair of boots, a pair of shoes, and a pair of sandals! And his maps. My husband loves maps and he always takes them on trips.

When I travel alone, I take a very small suitcase. There's a pocket for my travel documents and inside there are two parts, one for clothes and one for my laptop. I never travel without my laptop! That's it!

Grammar *there is/are*

7 Look at the grammar box. Then look at the article. Underline the sentences with *there's* and *there are*.

▶ THERE IS/ARE

There's	a	laptop	in my suitcase.
There are	two some	parts clothes	

(there's = there is)

For more information and practice, see page 166.

8 Make sentences about things in Kate's bags in the photo. Use the words below.

There's There are	a camera. a laptop. three scarves. two shirts. a pair of shoes. a skirt. some T-shirts.

9 Pronunciation *there is/are*

67 Listen and repeat the sentences from Exercise 8. Pay attention to the stress.

Speaking and writing

10 Imagine you travel a lot. Choose three countries to complete the sentences. Write a list of the things you pack in your suitcase for each trip.

1 I travel to .... for my job.
2 I go to .... on my vacation.
3 I go to .... to visit my family.

11 Work in pairs. Tell your partner where you go and what's in your suitcase.

I often travel to Singapore. In my suitcase today, there's a pair of shoes …

9b Places to stay

Listening

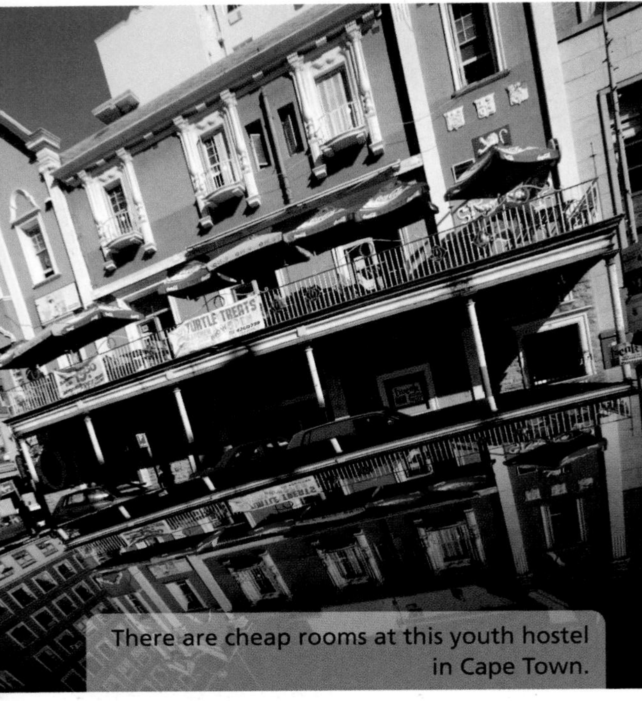
There are cheap rooms at this youth hostel in Cape Town.

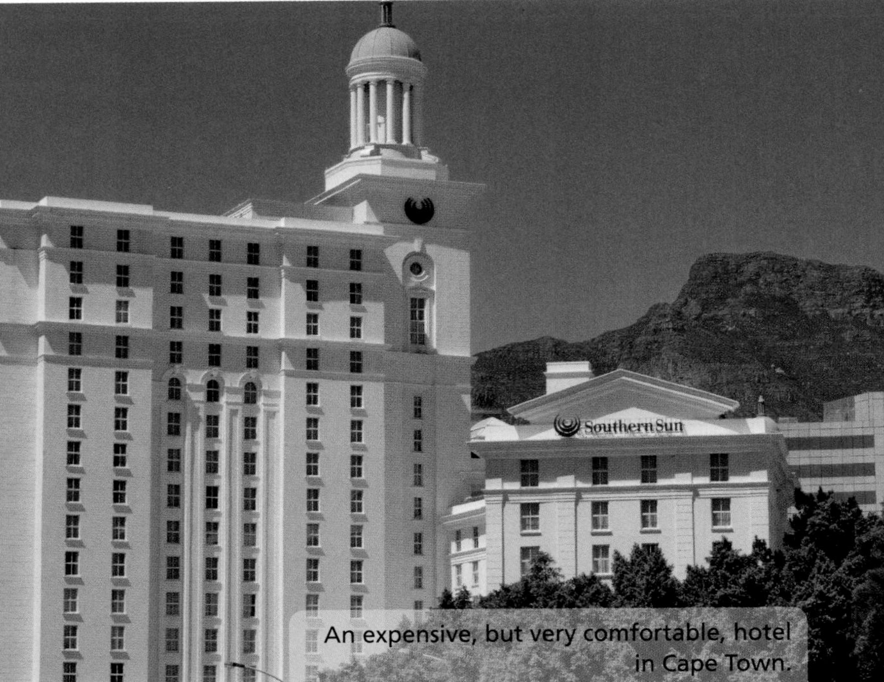

An expensive, but very comfortable, hotel in Cape Town.

1 Look at the photos. Which people stay in these two places?

business travelers	families
students	young couples

2 68 Listen. Then read Luke's questions and underline the words he uses.

1 Are there any hotels near the *airport / beach*?
2 Is there a youth hostel *downtown / near the airport*?
3 Is there *a bus / a train* to downtown?

3 68 Listen again. Are the sentences true (T) or false (F)?

1 There's a youth hostel near the airport.
2 There are some cheap hotels near the airport.
3 There's a train to downtown.

Grammar *there is/are* negative and question forms

4 Look at the sentences and questions in the grammar box. When do we use *any*?

▶ *THERE IS/ARE* NEGATIVE AND QUESTION FORMS		
There **isn't**	a train.	
There **aren't**	**any** cheap hotels.	
Is there	a youth hostel?	Yes, there **is**. No, there **isn't**.
Are there	**any** hotels?	Yes, there **are**. No, there **aren't**.

For more information and practice, see page 166.

5 Work in pairs. Tell your partner the name of your hometown or a place you know. Write questions about your partner's town. Use *Is there a/an … ? / Are there any … ?*

airport nice beach cheap restaurants good hotels tourist attractions youth hostels	in near	the city/town downtown

6 Work in pairs. Ask and answer your questions from Exercise 5.

Are there any good hotels near downtown?

No, there aren't.

Vocabulary **furniture**

7 **69** Look at the photos (1–12). Then listen and repeat the words. Write the words with the photos.

armchair	bathtub	bed	chair	desk	fridge
lamp	shower	sofa	table	TV	closet

1 ....

2 ....

3 ....

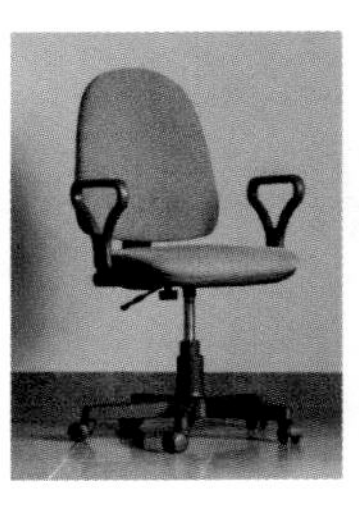

4 ....

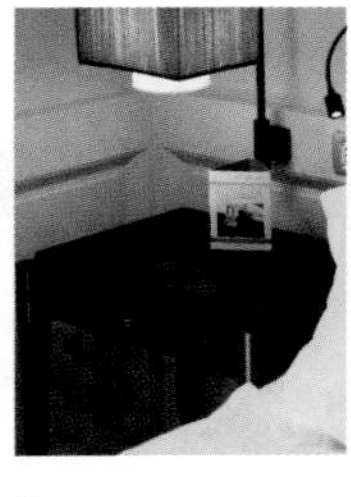

5 ....

6 ....

7 ....

8 ....

9 ....

10 ....

11 ....

12 ....

8 Work in pairs. Which things are there usually in a hotel room?

There's a bed, ...

9 **70** Listen to the conversation. Mark (✓) the furniture in Exercise 7 that you hear.

10 **70** Listen again. Which room (a or b) is it?

a

b

Speaking

11 Work in pairs. You are in a hotel. Ask and answer questions about your hotel room.

Student A: Turn to page 156.

Student B: Turn to page 160.

9c Across a continent

Reading

1 Work in pairs. Look at the map and the photos on page 111. What things do you think you can see or do on a trip across Russia?

2 Read the article on page 111 and check your ideas from Exercise 1. Then find the places in the article on the map.

3 Are the sentences true (T) or false (F)?

1 There's a road from Moscow to Vladivostok.
2 There are two trains every day from Moscow to Vladivostok.
3 You can't sleep on the train.
4 You can leave the train and stay in hotels.
5 There aren't any towns near Lake Baikal.
6 The Trans-Siberian Highway is only for trucks.

4 Work in pairs. Is this the kind of trip you like? What do you like?

I love trips to different countries.

I like to vacation on the beach.

Vocabulary travel

5 Match a verb in A with words in B. Check your answers in the article.

A	B
travel	a bus
leave	an ice cave
book	from east to west
use	home
stay	in hotels
visit	in Vladivostock
take	Moscow
drive	your tickets
arrive	a travel agent
fly	your car

6 Complete the sentences with verbs from Exercise 5.

1 "What time does your plane ________ ?" "At 8:40 in the morning."
2 We don't ________ in expensive hotels.
3 I usually ________ my tickets with a travel agent.
4 A boat ________ Vladivostok for Japan every week.
5 Let's ________ a bus from the airport.
6 "Is there an airport in Irkutsk? Can you ________ there?" "Yes, there is."

7 Word focus *take*

a Look at these expressions with *take*. Find one of the expressions in the article on page 111.

take a bus   take a photo   take a suitcase

b Work in pairs. Ask and answer the questions.

1 How many suitcases do you take when you travel?
2 Do you usually take photos when you are on vacation?
3 Do you often take a taxi / a bus / a train / a plane? Where to?

Grammar imperative forms

8 Look at these sentences from the article. Are the words in **bold** nouns or verbs?

IMPERATIVE FORMS

Book your tickets in advance.
Don't wait until you arrive.
(don't = do not)

For more information and practice, see page 167.

9 Complete these sentences from the article with the missing verb.

1 ________ non-stop in seven days.
2 ________ in hotels.
3 ________ sightseeing in the big cities.
4 ________ the new Trans-Siberian Highway.
5 ________ your car.

Writing and speaking

10 Work in pairs. Write five tips for travelers in your country or a country you know. Think of reasons for the tips.

Don't travel by bus.

11 Work in groups of four. Discuss your travel tips. Ask follow-up questions.

Don't travel by bus.

Why?

The buses are very slow.

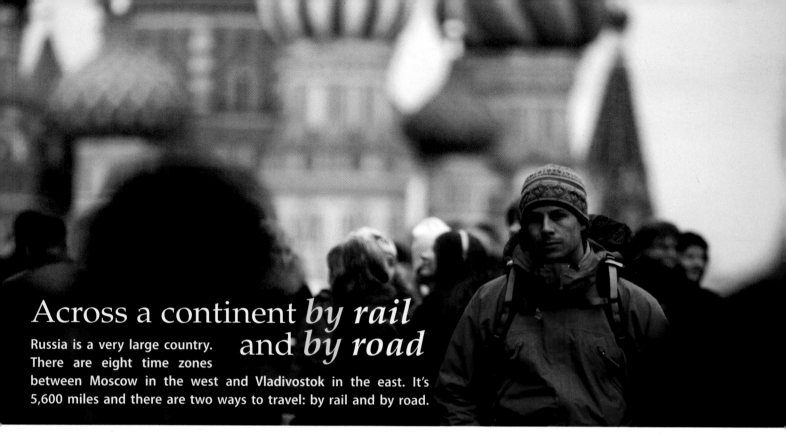

Across a continent *by rail* and *by road*

Russia is a very large country. There are eight time zones between Moscow in the west and Vladivostok in the east. It's 5,600 miles and there are two ways to travel: by rail and by road.

BY RAIL: **THE TRANS-SIBERIAN RAILWAY**

Trains leave Moscow almost every day. Book your tickets in advance—don't wait until you arrive in Moscow. You can book online or use a travel agent. There are two options:

Travel non-stop in seven days. You sleep and eat on the train. You can talk to other passengers, learn some words in Russian, and enjoy the views. The train travels through amazing mountains, beautiful forests, and strange deserts.

Stop on the way and stay in hotels. Go sightseeing in the big cities. In Novosibirsk, the main city in Siberia, there are museums, art galleries, theaters, and a famous opera house. Or visit the Kungur Ice Cave near Perm. From the towns of Irkutsk or Ulan-Ude, you can take a bus or train to Lake Baikal, a UNESCO World Heritage site. Lake Baikal is 395 miles long and there are only four or five towns near it. The lake is a great place for sports activities. Diving, hiking, and horseback riding are all popular.

BY ROAD: **THE TRANS-SIBERIAN HIGHWAY**

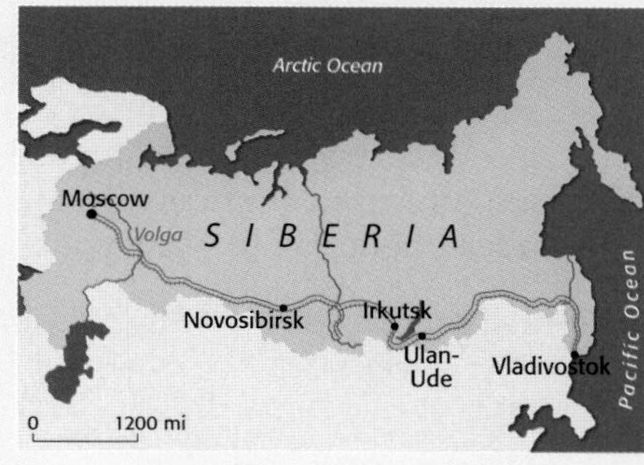

Are you adventurous? Then take the new Trans-Siberian Highway. Drive your car or, for the trip of a lifetime, hitchhike with Russian drivers in their cars and trucks.

And when you finally arrive in Vladivostock, you can fly home or continue your trip. There's a boat to Japan every week.

adventurous (adj) /əd'ventʃərəs/ an *adventurous* person likes danger
(do it) **in advance** (exp) /ɪn əd'væns/ to do one thing before another thing
hitchhike (v) /'hɪtʃˌhaɪk/ to ask a stranger for a ride
lifetime (n) /'laɪfˌtaɪm/ all of your life

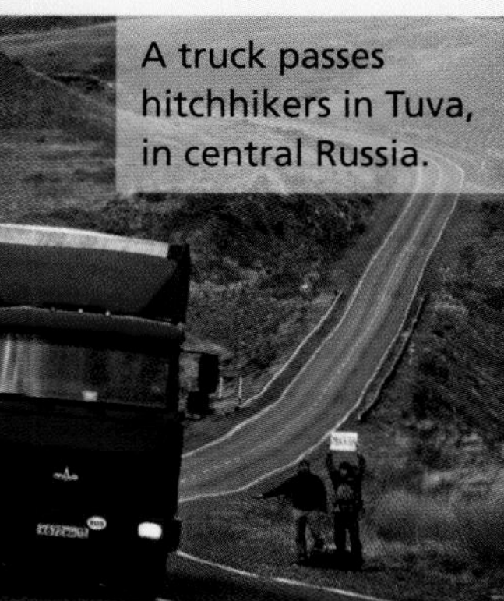

A truck passes hitchhikers in Tuva, in central Russia.

9d At the hotel

Vocabulary hotel services

1 Match the hotel services (1–5) in the brochure with the explanations (a–e).

Guest services – numbers

1	room service	101
2	wake-up call	110
3	business center	109
4	laundry	111
5	medical service	112

THE MARLIN HOTEL

a a doctor or nurse
b something to eat in your hotel room
c a service to wash or clean your clothes
d a room with computers, printers, and Internet
e a telephone call to wake you

2 Which services do you think business travelers use? And tourists?

Real life requests

3 71 Read part of a conversation between a hotel guest and a receptionist. Match a guest's requests (1–4) with the receptionist's responses (a–d). Then listen and check your answers.

1 I'd like a wake-up call at 7:30, please.
2 I'd like to have dinner in my room this evening.
3 I'd like to use the Internet.
4 Is there a bank near the hotel?

a Yes, there's one on this street.
b In the morning? Certainly, sir.
c No problem, sir. There's wi-fi in all the rooms.
d Of course. There's a menu in your room.

4 71 Listen again and answer the questions.

1 What's the guest's room number?
2 Where's the menu?
3 Where's the bank?

REQUESTS

I'd like a wake-up call at 7:30, **please.**
I'd like to get room service.
I'd like to book a taxi.
Certainly, sir/ma'am.
Of course.

5 Pronunciation *I'd like*

a 72 Listen and repeat three of the sentences.

b Work in pairs. Practice these requests. Use *I'd like a …* or *I'd like to … .*

breakfast in my room
a wake-up call
use the Internet
see a doctor

I'd like breakfast in my room.

Certainly.

6 Work in pairs.

Student A: You are a hotel guest. Make two requests and/or ask for information.

Student B: You are the hotel receptionist. Respond to the requests and/or answer the questions.

Take turns. Use the ideas in Exercise 5b and those below.

room service
book a table in the restaurant
stay an extra night
make an international phone call
a bus stop / subway station near the hotel

9e A great place for a weekend

Writing travel advice

1 Read the advice and answer the questions.

1 What's the name of the city?
2 How can you travel there?
3 Where can you eat?
4 What can you eat?
5 What can you see?
6 What can you do?

2 Read the advice again. Underline four tips.

3 **Writing skill *because***

a Look at the sentence from the text. Find more sentences with *because*.

Lisbon is a great place for a vacation ***because*** *there is a lot to see and do.*

b Rewrite these sentences with *because*.

1 Go in spring. It's very hot in summer.
2 Travel by bus. It's cheap.
3 Book your hotel in advance. It's a very popular place.

4 Make notes about a place you know. Use the questions in Exercise 1. Then write two or three paragraphs of advice for travelers to the place. Include at least one tip.

5 Check your advice. Check the spelling, the punctuation, and the verbs.

6 Work in pairs. Exchange advice. Is your partner's place a good place to travel to?

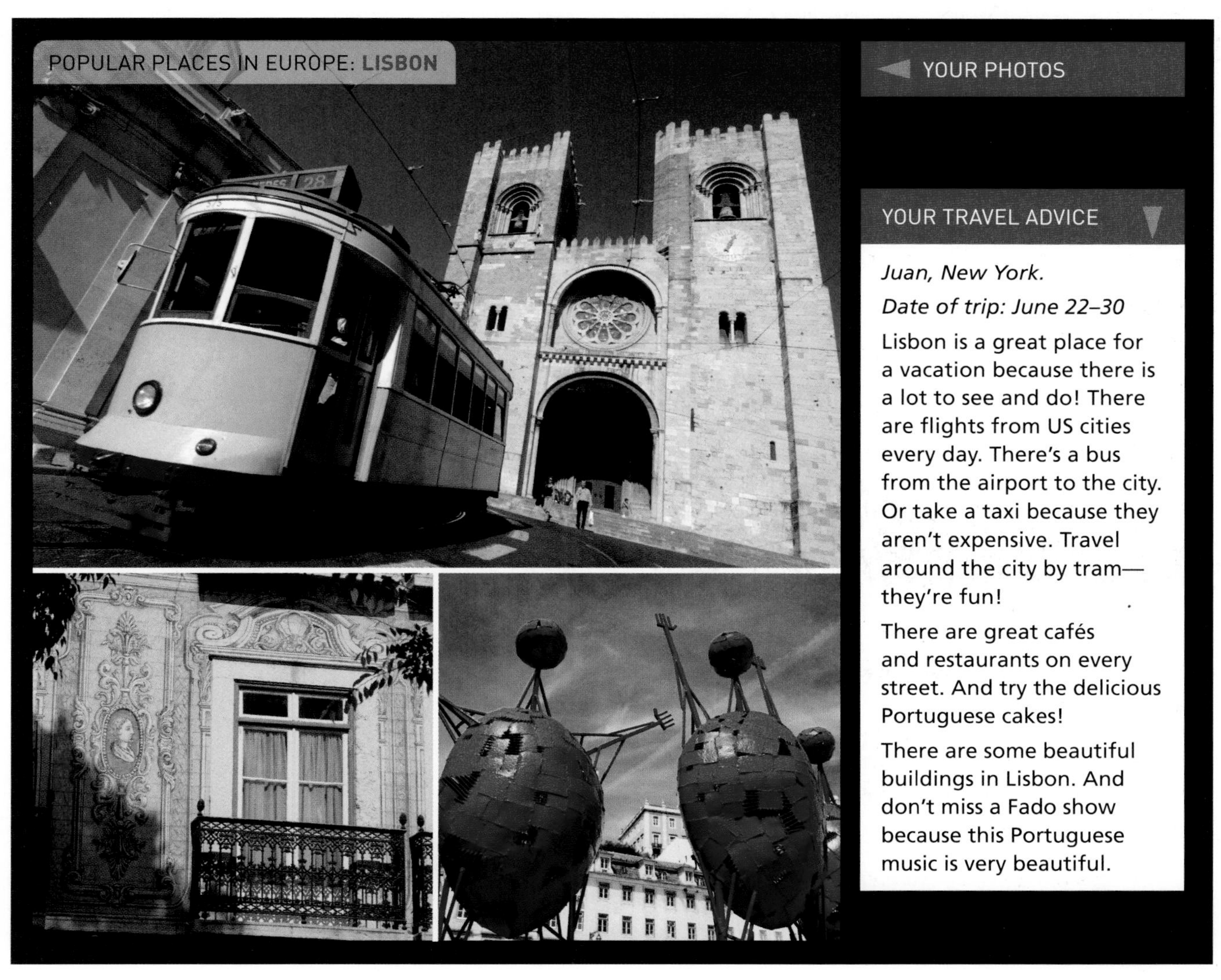

YOUR PHOTOS

YOUR TRAVEL ADVICE

Juan, New York.

Date of trip: June 22–30

Lisbon is a great place for a vacation because there is a lot to see and do! There are flights from US cities every day. There's a bus from the airport to the city. Or take a taxi because they aren't expensive. Travel around the city by tram—they're fun!

There are great cafés and restaurants on every street. And try the delicious Portuguese cakes!

There are some beautiful buildings in Lisbon. And don't miss a Fado show because this Portuguese music is very beautiful.

9f Along the Inca Road

Video

A woman walks along an ancient Inca road.

Before you watch

1 The Inca road goes through Ecuador, Peru, Bolivia, Chile, and Argentina. How old is it? Choose the correct option (a–c).

a 50 years old b 500 years old
c 5,000 years old

2 Work in pairs. Read the introduction to the video. What things do you think you can see or do on a trip along the Inca Road?

Along the Inca Road

Karin Muller is an American adventurer and writer. She is on a trip through South America to explore the cultures and people along the Inca Road. She travels more than 3,000 miles through four countries. Her adventure begins in Ecuador.

While you watch

3 Watch the video and mark (✓) what you see.

a plane	a truck
a donkey	a bus
a camel	a sheep
a helicopter	a horse
a bicycle	a llama
a canoe	a train

4 Watch the video again. Choose the correct option or options (a–c).

1 Where does Karin start her trip?
 a in the United States
 b in Peru
 c in Ecuador

2 What can you buy at the village market?
 a animals b snacks c vegetables

3 Where does Karin walk on day 1?
 a across a desert
 b along a beach
 c through mountains

4 How does Karin travel?
 a hitchhiking b by train c on foot

5 Who does Karin meet?
 a farmers b passengers c tourists

5 Watch the video again. Mark these sentences true (T) or false (F).

1 There's a young boy at the market.
2 There are three fish on Karin's plate.
3 The tent is orange and blue.
4 There's a woman on the road when Karin hitchhikes.
5 There's a man in a blue shirt at the bus stop.
6 On the beach, Karin wears a hat.

After you watch

6 Match the two parts of the sentences about Karin.

1 She goes canoeing	a a lot of people.
2 She rides	b across sand dunes.
3 She walks	c in a river.
4 She meets	d in the back of a truck.

7 Work in pairs. Have two conversations:

1 At the market food stall

Student A: You are Karin. Ask about the food.

Student B: You are the stall holder.

What's this? *It's fish.*

2 Meeting people on a trip

Student A: You are the helicopter pilot.

Student B: You are Karin.

Hi. I'm … . Nice to meet you. *Hello. …*

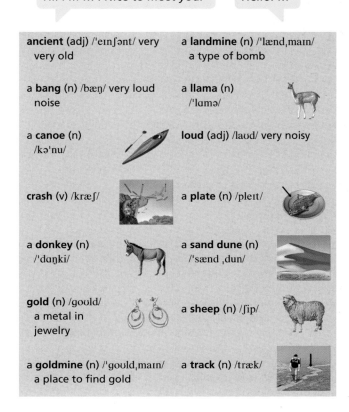

ancient (adj) /ˈeɪnʃənt/ very very old

a bang (n) /bæŋ/ very loud noise

a canoe (n) /kəˈnu/

crash (v) /kræʃ/

a donkey (n) /ˈdɑŋki/

gold (n) /goʊld/ a metal in jewelry

a goldmine (n) /ˈgoʊldˌmaɪn/ a place to find gold

a landmine (n) /ˈlændˌmaɪn/ a type of bomb

a llama (n) /ˈlɑmə/

loud (adj) /laʊd/ very noisy

a plate (n) /pleɪt/

a sand dune (n) /ˈsænd ˌdun/

a sheep (n) /ʃip/

a track (n) /træk/

UNIT 9 REVIEW

Grammar

1 Look at the photo. Write questions with ***is there / are there***?

1 ________ a map?
2 ________ books?
3 ________ tickets?
4 ________ a passport?

2 Work in pairs. Ask and answer the questions in Exercise 1. Take turns.

3 Are these sentences true (T) or false (F)? Change the false sentences so they are true.

1 There isn't a map.
2 There's a bottle of water.
3 There are some books.
4 There isn't a pair of boots.

4 Put the words in order.

1 late / be / don't
2 moment / a / wait
3 night / travel / don't / at
4 cafés / try / local / the
5 stay / hotel / this / don't / in

I CAN	
use *there is* and *there are* correctly	☐
give instructions (imperative forms)	☐

Vocabulary

5 Read the sentences. Which item doesn't belong?

1 In cold weather, I wear *a pair of sandals / a coat / a pair of boots / a hat*.
2 In hot weather, I wear *a T-shirt / a pair of sandals / a skirt / a jacket*.
3 At home, I wear *a sweater / a scarf / a pair of jeans / a top*.
4 In the office, I wear *a pair of pants / a T-shirt / a shirt / a pair of shoes*.

6 Match the two columns to make sentences.

1 There's a tourist information brochure
2 Is there one bed
3 You can put these bottles
4 There's an armchair,
5 Is there a shower

a on the table.
b or two?
c in the bathroom?
d in the fridge.
e but there isn't a sofa.

7 Complete the sentences with the verbs.

arrives book leaves stay take visit

1 We usually ________ our tickets online.
2 The train ________ in Kyoto at midnight.
3 We can ________ a bus to the airport.
4 Our plane ________ Kyoto at 10:20.
5 We often ________ in cheap hotels.
6 We usually ________ the museums.

I CAN	
talk about clothes	☐
talk about furniture	☐
talk about travel	☐
talk about hotel services	☐

Real life

8 Complete the requests (1–4) in a hotel. Then match the requests with the responses (a–d).

breakfast room service stay use

1 I'd like to ________ the Internet.
2 I'd like ________ at 7:30 a.m., please.
3 I'd like to ________ an extra night.
4 I'd like ________ .

a The restaurant opens at 7:00 a.m.
b Of course. The number is 101.
c Certainly, sir. What's your name?
d Of course. There's wi-fi in your room.

I CAN	
make and respond to requests	☐
ask for and give information	☐

Speaking

9 Work in groups. You work in your town's tourist information center. What is there for visitors to do and to see? List at least six things and say where they are.

Unit 10 History

Invention of color television.
Photo by Willard Culver

FEATURES

1 Work in pairs. Do you know this invention? What does it do?

2 73 Can you match the invention with the years? Listen and check your answers.

Year	Invention
1950	Blu-ray discs
1963	color television
1973	digital cameras
1975	digital television
1993	cell phones
1995	MP3 players
2006	video recorders

3 Work in pairs. Choose and write five years in a list. Dictate them to your partner. Then compare your lists.

10a Explorers

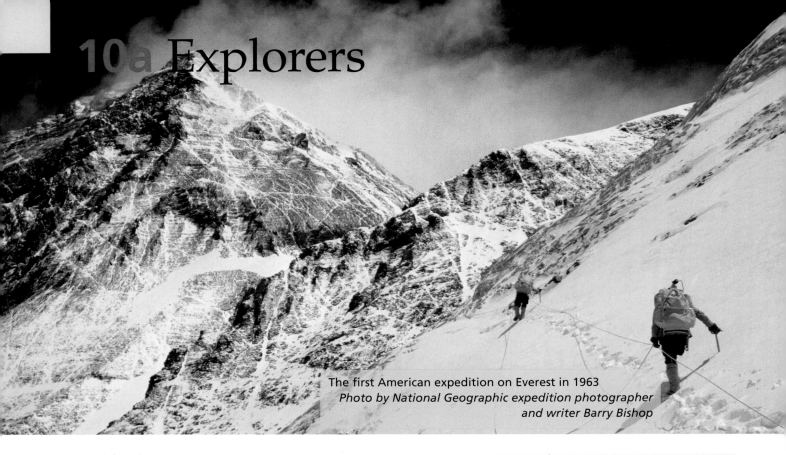

The first American expedition on Everest in 1963
Photo by National Geographic expedition photographer and writer Barry Bishop

Reading and listening

1 Look at the photo of the mountaineers. Where are they? Read the caption and check your answer.

2 Complete the quiz. Check your answers with your instructor.

captain (n) /ˈkæptɪn/ a leader or commander
expedition (n) /ˌekspəˈdɪʃən/ a trip with scientists and/or explorers
North Pole (n) /ˈnɔrθ ˈpoʊl/
South Pole (n) /ˈsaʊθ ˈpoʊl/
around the world (exp) /əˈraʊnd ðə ˈwɜrld/
space (n) /speɪs/

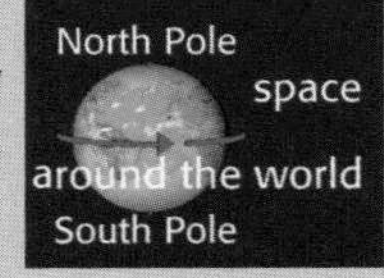

Ferdinand Magellan

Yuri Gagarin

Roald Amundsen

Junko Tabei

Ann Bancroft

Valentina Tereshkova

Explorers Quiz: historical moments

Do you know these famous explorers?

- The first expedition around the world was from 1519 to 1522. The expedition captain was ________.
- The first successful South Pole expedition was in 1911. The expedition leader was ________.
- The first man in space was ________. The first woman in space was ________. They were both from Russia.
- On May 16, 1975, ________ was the first woman to reach the top of Everest.
- The first woman to reach the North Pole was ________ on May 1, 1986.

3 74 Listen. Then match the texts with four of the people from the quiz.

1 She was born in **1939**. She was in a team of Japanese mountaineers. They were all women.

2 He was born in **1480**. He was Portuguese, but he was an explorer for the Spanish king Carlos I.

3 She was born in the United States on **September 29, 1955**. She was the leader of an expedition to the South Pole in **1993**. The expedition was all women.

4 He was from Norway and he was born on **July 16, 1872**. His father was a sea captain.

Grammar *was/were*

4 Look at the past forms of *be* in the grammar box. Underline these forms in the texts in Exercise 3.

WAS/WERE

I/He/She/It	**was**	born in 1480. an explorer.
You/We/You/They	**were**	explorers. from Russia.

For more information and practice, see page 167.

5 Pronunciation *was/were* weak forms

a 75 Listen and repeat.

b Complete the sentences. Read them to your partner. What do you have in common?

1 I .... born in .... [place].
2 My father .... born in .... [year].
3 My mother .... born in .... [year].

6 Complete the paragraphs with *was* and *were*.

Yuri Gagarin [1] .... born in 1934. His parents [2] .... farmers. From 1955 to 1961, he [3] .... a pilot. The first space rockets [4] .... small and so the first people in space [5] .... small too. Gagarin [6] .... a small man—five foot and one inch (1.57 m).

Valentina Tereshkova [7] .... born in 1937 in central Russia. Her parents [8] .... from Belarus. She [9] .... a factory worker. After their trips into space, on April 12, 1961, and June 16, 1963, Gagarin and Tereshkova [10] .... famous all over the world.

Vocabulary **dates**

7 Look at the table. Complete it with information from the quiz.

Important dates in exploration

.... 1st, ...	first woman at the North Pole
June 2nd, 1953	news of first men on Everest
November 3rd, 1957	Sputnik II into space
October 4th, 1957	Sputnik I into space
5th / 6th / 7th / 8th / 9th / 10th / 11th	
April 12th, 1961	first man in space
December 13th, 1972	last man on the Moon
December 14th, 1911	first people at the South Pole
15th	
.... 16th, ...	first woman on Everest
17th / 18th / 19th	
July 20th, 1969	first men on the Moon

8 76 Listen and repeat the ordinal numbers.

9 77 Say these ordinal numbers. Then listen and check.

21st	22nd	23rd	24th	25th	26th
27th	28th	29th	30th	31st	

Speaking

10 Work in pairs. What are three important dates in your country?

September 16th is Independence Day.

11 Work in pairs.

Student A: Dictate five important dates from your past to your partner.

Student B: Say the dates.

Student A: Say why the dates are important.

the first of September 1990

It was my first day of school.

10b Heroes

Reading and listening

1 Work in pairs. Look at the photos of the people. What do you know about them?

Who's this?

I'm not sure. I think he's an athlete.

2 Read the information about the radio show *Heroes*. Answer the questions.

1 When is the show on the radio?
2 What do the people on the show talk about?
3 Who is on the show today?
4 Who were their heroes?

David Attenborough

107.1 WFNX 7:30 p.m. March 13–18

Heroes

Who is a hero?

In this program, we talk to people about their heroes. Today we hear about Aneta's hero, the Olympic champion Michael Johnson. Joe's hero wasn't happy in his first job, but is now the television star David Attenborough. We also talk to Clare. Her heroes weren't famous, but they were important to her. They were her teachers at college.

Peter and Rose Harvey

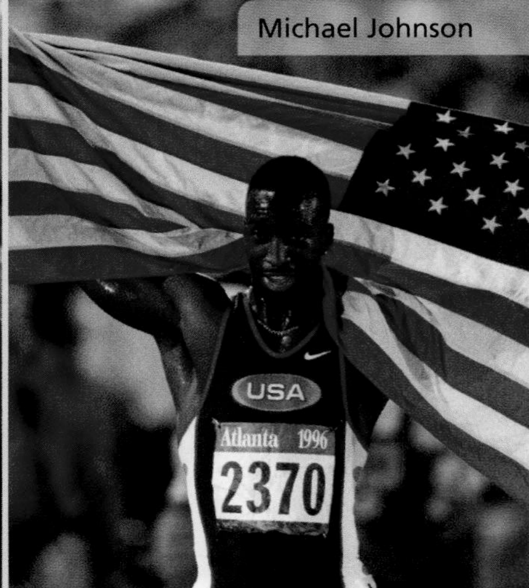

Michael Johnson

3 78 Complete the sentences with these words. Then listen to the show and check.

art eight first funny great interesting

1 He was a .... athlete.
2 He was the world champion .... times.
3 His .... job was with books.
4 All his shows were really ....
5 Mrs. Harvey was my .... teacher.
6 She was very ....

4 78 Listen again. Choose the correct answer.

1 Was he the Olympic champion?
Yes, he was. / No, he wasn't.

2 Were you good at sports in school?
Yes, I was. / No, I wasn't.

3 Was it his first job?
Yes, it was. / No, it wasn't.

4 Were you born then?
Yes, I was. / No, I wasn't.

5 Were they good teachers?
Yes, they were. / No, they weren't.

5 What can you remember? Write Aneta, Joe, or Clare.

1 ....'s heroes weren't famous.
2 .... was on the basketball team at school.
3 ....'s favorite show was *Life on Earth*.

Grammar *was/were* negative and question forms

6 Look at the grammar box. How do we make the negative and question forms of *was* and *were*?

▶ *WAS/WERE* NEGATIVE AND QUESTION FORMS

I/He/She/It		**wasn't**	happy. famous.	
You/ We/You /They		**weren't**		
Was	I/he/she/it		happy? famous?	Yes, I/he/she/it **was**. No, I/he/she/it **wasn't**.
Were	you/we/ you/ they			Yes, you/we/you/they **were**. No, you/we/you/they **weren't**.

For more information and practice, see page 167.

7 Pronunciation **strong forms**

a 79 Listen and repeat.

1 Was he the Olympic champion?
Yes, he was.

2 Was it his first job?
No, it wasn't.

3 Were they good teachers?
Yes, they were.

b 79 Listen again. Are the underlined words weak or strong?

8 Write questions with *was* or *were*.

1 Michael Johnson / on TV / ?
2 your hero / David Attenborough / ?
3 your parents / famous / ?
4 you / happy at school / ?
5 your teachers / friendly / ?
6 you / good at sports / ?

9 Work in pairs. Think about when you were young. Ask and answer the questions in Exercise 8.

Vocabulary describing people

10 Work in pairs. Think of a person you both know for each word.

famous friendly good
happy interesting nice

Speaking

11 Write the answers to these questions about two heroes from your past.

- Who was he/she?
- Was he/she on television? famous? a teacher? a … ?
- Why was he/she your hero?

12 Work in groups. Write the names from Exercise 11 on pieces of paper. Mix them. Take turns to read a name. Ask and answer the questions about the names.

Who was Jill Roberts?

She was my first boss.

10c The first Americans

Reading

1 Mark these sentences as true (T) or false (F).

1 The Inca Empire was in North America.
2 The Maya people were from Central America.
3 The Aztecs were from Peru.
4 The Sioux people were from South America.

2 Read the first paragraph of the article. Check your answers from Exercise 1.

3 Read the rest of the article. Answer the questions.

1 Who was Tupac Amaru?
2 Where were the Apache people from?
3 When was Geronimo born?
4 Why was Geronimo famous?

4 Who were the leaders in your country's history?

Vocabulary **time expressions**

5 Underline these words and expressions in the article. Do they use verbs in the present or past form?

today   ago   at that time   now

6 Complete the sentences with words and expressions from Exercise 5. In two sentences, more than one word is possible.

1 About two hundred years .... Geronimo was born.
2 .... people know the name "Geronimo."
3 .... the Maya people live in Mexico.
4 .... , the Native Americans and the USA were at war.

7 **Word focus *first***

a Look at the sentences. Is *first* a date (D) or a number (N)?

1 The first man in space was Yuri Gagarin.
2 Why was the first of May, 1986, important?
3 The first American expedition to Everest was in 1963.

b Work in pairs. Ask and answer the questions.

1 Who was your first best friend?
2 When was your first day of school?
3 Where was your first job?
4 Who was your first boss?

Speaking

8 Look at these people. Are they from North America or South America?

George Washington

Tupac Amaru

Hillary Clinton

Pocahontas

Simón Bolívar

Robert E. Lee

9 Now work in two pairs in a group of four. Talk about famous Americans.

Pair A: Turn to page 156.

Pair B: Turn to page 160.

THE FIRST AMERICANS

Geronimo: Apache hero
June 16, 1829 – February 17, 1909

Today there are 23 countries in North, Central, and South America. But five hundred years ago, a large area of South America, including Peru, was part of the Inca Empire. In Central America and Mexico, the Maya people were important. The Aztec empire also ruled in Mexico. In North America, there were different groups in different areas, for example, the Apache, Navajo, and Sioux. Today the name for these different groups is Native Americans. The leaders of these people are still famous today; for example, the last Inca leader Tupac Amaru, the Aztec emperor Moctezuma, and the Apache war hero, Geronimo.

The Apache people were from the south and west of North America. Geronimo was the grandson of an important Apache leader. He was born on June 16, 1829. When Geronimo was a young man, there was a war between Mexico and the US, and the Native Americans. At that time, his family's land was part of Mexico. Now, it's part of the US.

Geronimo was an Apache war hero. From 1886 until 1909 he was a prisoner of war. But he was also a famous celebrity. He was with President Theodore Roosevelt on March 4, 1905, his first day as president.

celebrity (n) /sɪˈlebrɪti/ a person famous in their lifetime
land (n) /lænd/ area or nation
war (n) /wɔr/ conflict. For example: World War I, 1914–1918.

10d I'm sorry

Vocabulary activities

1 Match the photos (a–f) with the words.

At nine o'clock yesterday I was … .

1	asleep	4	in traffic
2	at home	5	sick
3	busy	6	on the phone

a

b

c

d
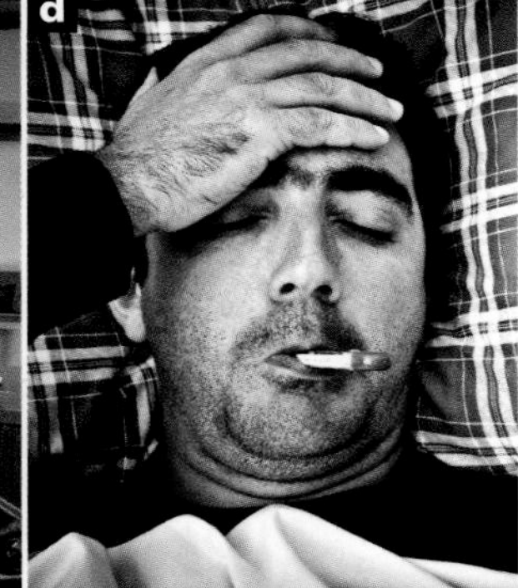

e

f

2 Work in pairs. Ask and answer questions.

Were you at home at nine o'clock yesterday?

Yes, I was.

Real life apologizing

3 80 Listen to three conversations. Write the number of the conversation (1–3) next to the places.

a in a café   b in a classroom   c in an office

4 80 Listen again. Complete the conversations with expressions for APOLOGIZING.

1
S: Hi, I'm sorry I'm late. [1] ....
T: That's OK. Take a seat.

2
R: Umm, the meeting was at 2:30. Where were you?
C: Oh, I'm sorry. [2] ....
R: [3] .... It wasn't an important meeting.

3
A: So, what about yesterday? We were at your house at ten o'clock. Where were you?
B: I'm very sorry. [4] ....
We were at my sister's house!
A: It's OK. [5] ....

▶ APOLOGIZING

I'm (very) sorry.	We weren't at home.
I'm sorry I'm late.	It's OK.
The bus was late.	That's OK.
I was (very) busy.	Don't worry.

5 Pronunciation sentence stress

a 81 Listen and repeat these sentences. Underline the word with the main stress.

1 I'm sorry I'm late.
2 The bus was late.
3 I was very busy.
4 We weren't at home.

b Work in pairs. Practice the conversations.

6 Work in pairs. Practice the conversations again. Use the vocabulary in Exercise 1.

Hello.

Hi, I'm sorry I'm late. I was in traffic.

That's OK.

10e Childhood memories

Writing a blog

1 Work in pairs. Ask and answer the questions.

1 Do you read blogs? What about?
2 Do you write a blog? What about?

2 Answer the questions.

1 When and where was Tyler born?
2 Where was his family's house?
3 What was his favorite toy?
4 Who were his friends?

3 What information does he give about these things?

1 his parents and family
2 his house
3 his toys
4 his friends

4 Writing skill *when*

a Complete these sentences from the blog.

1 When I was a child, ...
2 When I was ten, ...

b Find two more sentences with *when*.

c Rewrite these sentences as one sentence with *when*. Don't forget the comma.

1 My parents were young. They weren't rich.
2 My father was a student. He was poor.
3 I was a child. I was happy.
4 I was three. My sister was born.

5 Make notes about your childhood. Answer the questions in Exercise 2 for yourself. Make notes about the things in Exercise 3.

6 Use your notes and write two or three paragraphs about your childhood memories. Include a sentence with *When*.

7 Check your blog. Check the spelling, the punctuation, and the verbs.

8 Work in pairs. Exchange blogs. Find one surprising thing in your partner's blog. Ask two questions about his or her childhood.

MY CHILDHOOD MEMORIES

Tyler Sanford

I was born on July 4, 1990, in Texas. My parents were teachers. When I was a child, we weren't rich. Our house was in a small town. It wasn't a big house. My family was small: me, my parents, and my grandfather. My grandfather was old. He was kind and funny. But when he wasn't well, he wasn't happy.

I remember my favorite toy. It was a helicopter. It was a present from my grandfather. And I remember my first bicycle. It was red and it was fantastic. My friend Jack's bike was blue. When I was ten, my best friends were Jack and Nathan. They were in my class at school. We were bored at school. But when we were on vacation, it was great. We were typical boys!

10f The space race
Video

The first American in space

Before you watch

1 Work in pairs. What do you know about the space race? Discuss.

2 Work in pairs. How many astronauts can you name? Where were they from?

While you watch

3 Watch the video without sound. How many times do you see these things?

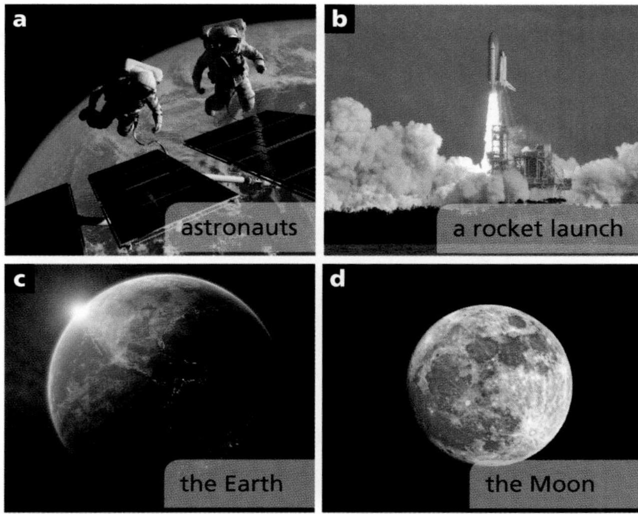

4 Watch the video. Check your answers from Exercise 1.

5 Work in pairs. Match the dates with the events.

Date	Event
1957	fire on Apollo 1
April 12, 1961	men on the Moon
May 5, 1961	Sputnik in space
February 20, 1962	the first American in space
January 27, 1967	the first person in space
July 20, 1969	the first American to orbit the Earth

6 Watch the first part of the video again and check your answers from Exercise 5.

7 Work in pairs. Check your memory. Take turns to ask and answer these questions.

1 Who was president of the United States in 1961?
2 Who was Alan Shepard?
3 What was Sputnik?
4 What was the Mercury program?
5 Who was John Glenn?
6 What was the Apollo program?

8 Watch the second part of the video. Answer the questions.

1 What were *Challenger* and *Columbia*?
2 Which countries send astronauts to the International Space Station?

After you watch

9 Complete the sentences with *was, wasn't, were,* or *weren't*.

1 The Soviet Union and the United States .... in a space race.
2 Sputnik .... part of the Soviet Union's space program.
3 Alan Shepard, John Glenn, and Gus Grissom .... part of the Mercury program.
4 On January 27, 1967, there .... a fire on Apollo 1.
5 The first men on the Moon .... Russian.

10 Work in groups. Write a list of five important events in the last ten years. Ask and answer the questions about the events.

- What was the date of the event?
- Where were you?
- Who were you with?

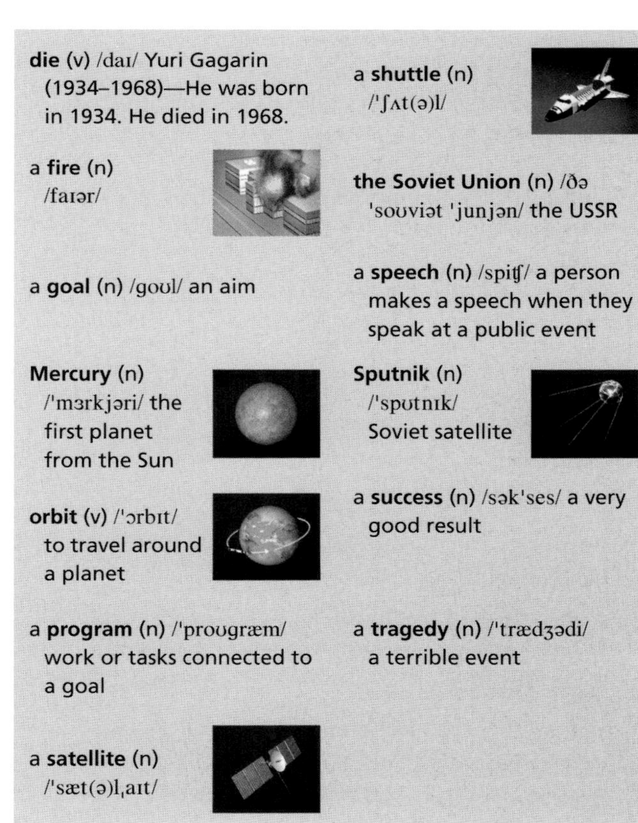

die (v) /daɪ/ Yuri Gagarin (1934–1968)—He was born in 1934. He died in 1968.

a **fire** (n) /faɪər/

a **goal** (n) /goʊl/ an aim

Mercury (n) /ˈmɜrkjəri/ the first planet from the Sun

orbit (v) /ˈɔrbɪt/ to travel around a planet

a **program** (n) /ˈproʊgræm/ work or tasks connected to a goal

a **satellite** (n) /ˈsæt(ə)lˌaɪt/

a **shuttle** (n) /ˈʃʌt(ə)l/

the Soviet Union (n) /ðə ˈsoʊviət ˈjunjən/ the USSR

a **speech** (n) /spitʃ/ a person makes a speech when they speak at a public event

Sputnik (n) /ˈspʊtnɪk/ Soviet satellite

a **success** (n) /səkˈses/ a very good result

a **tragedy** (n) /ˈtrædʒədi/ a terrible event

UNIT 10 REVIEW

Grammar

1 Complete the article about Bradley Wiggins with *was* or *wasn't*.

Bradley Wiggins: the first British winner of the *Tour de France*

Bradley Wiggins [1] ________ the first British winner of the *Tour de France*, but he [2] ________ born in Great Britain. He [3] ________ born in Belgium. His mother [4] ________ English, but his father [5] ________ ; he [6] ________ Australian. His father [7] ________ a professional cyclist. Wiggins won his first medal at the Olympic Games in 2000 when he [8] ________ 20 years old. He [9] ________ the winner of the 2012 *Tour de France*.

2 Complete the sentences about the *Tour de France* with *was* or *were*.

1 The first race ________ in 1903.
2 The cyclists in 1903 ________ from France, Italy, Germany, and Belgium.
3 The first winner five times in a row (1991–1995) ________ Miguel Indurain, a Spanish cyclist.
4 From 2006 to 2009, the winners ________ from Spain.
5 In 2011, the winner ________ Australian.

3 Complete the questions about Bradley Wiggins with *was* or *were*.

1 Where and when / he born?
2 Where / his parents from?
3 What / his father's job?
4 How old / Wiggins in 2000?

4 Work in pairs. Ask and answer the questions in Exercise 3. Take turns.

I CAN	
talk about the past (*was/were*)	☐
say when people did things (time expressions)	☐

Vocabulary

5 Complete the sentences with ordinal numbers.

1 The ________ person in a race is the winner.
2 The person in ________ place gets a bronze medal.
3 May is the ________ month of the year.
4 August is the ________ month of the year.
5 October is the ________ month of the year.
6 The year ends on the ________ of December.

6 Complete the sentences with these words.

in in of on the

1 I was born ________ the third ________ June.
2 My sister was born ________ 1987.
3 My wife was born on ________ 27th of September.
4 My son was born ________ April.

7 Choose the correct option.

1 My first boss was very *nice / great*.
2 My sister is always *happy / famous*.
3 This TV presenter is very *great / interesting*.
4 Bradley Wiggins is a *famous / interesting* cyclist.
5 I wasn't always *good / nice* at sports.
6 My math teacher at school was nice and *fantastic / friendly*.

I CAN	
say dates	☐
describe people (adjectives)	☐
talk about activities	☐

Real life

8 Put the conversation in order.

a Don't worry. Are you OK now?
b Hello, Carolyn. *1*
c Hi. Where were you this morning?
d Oh! I'm sorry. I was sick.
e The boss was here at nine o'clock.
f Why?
g Yes, thank you.

I CAN	
say where I was at different times	☐
make and accept apologies	☐

Speaking

9 Work in pairs. Choose two famous people. Prepare questions for an interview with these people.

10 Ask and answer your questions. Take turns.

Unit 11 Discovery

Photo by Tim Laman

FEATURES

1 Work in pairs. Look at the photo. What can you name?

2 Work in pairs. Which of the captions (a–c) matches the photo? Why?

a An unusual campsite in the forests of Papua New Guinea.
b Police find a mystery object in a river in Papua New Guinea.
c A scientist discovers new plants in the forests of Papua New Guinea.

3 **82** Listen and check your ideas from Exercise 2.

4 **82** Listen again and complete the sentences.

1 A large ________ of these discoveries are in Indonesia.
2 Scientists in Papua New Guinea usually find about two new plants or animals every ________ .
3 Scientists sometimes arrive and leave by ________ .

5 Work in pairs. Can you name six animals and plants from your country?

11a The mystery of "Ötzi the Iceman"

Reading

1 Read the article about an unusual discovery. Answer the questions.

1 Where were the tourists from?
2 Where were they in September 1991?
3 Where was the body?
4 What kind of investigation was it?

2 Read the article again. Underline the past forms in the article. Then write the verbs next to the past forms.

1 was/were	*be*	~~be~~
2 went	....	find
3 found	....	go
4 took	....	have
5 had	....	take

Grammar irregular simple past verbs

3 Look at the grammar box. Then choose the correct option.

There is *only one / more than one* simple past form for each verb.

▶ IRREGULAR SIMPLE PAST VERBS	
I/You He/She/It We/You/They	**went** for a walk. **found** a body.

For more information and practice, see page 167.

4 Complete the sentences with these irregular simple past verbs.

found had took went

1 The German tourists .... to the police station.
2 The police .... some arrows near the body.
3 The person .... unusual shoes.
4 Scientists .... the body to a museum of archeology in Italy.

PART 1: THE DISCOVERY

The mystery of "Ötzi the Iceman"

THE DISCOVERY In September 1991, two German tourists were on vacation in the Austrian Alps.

They went for a walk and they found a body in the ice. The body was very old. It wasn't the body of a mountaineer. The police took it to the University of Innsbruck in Austria.

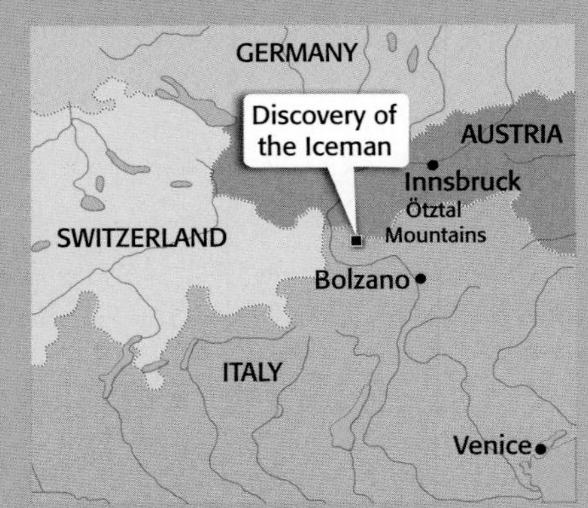

This body was a mystery. Was it a man or a woman? Who was he or she? The person had an unusual knife and a bag with arrows. Where was he or she from? How old was the body? There were many questions. But this wasn't a police investigation. It was a scientific investigation.

Listening

5 83 Listen to part 2 of the Iceman's story: the investigation. Underline any information that is different.

1 The police started their investigation.
2 Scientists called the body "Ötzi."
3 He was about 65 years old.
4 He lived 10,000 years ago.

6 83 Match the sentence parts. Then listen again and check.

1 The scientists studied	from the north of Italy.
2 They finished	Ötzi.
3 Ötzi was	the body.
4 He walked	their report.
5 An arrow killed	to the mountains.

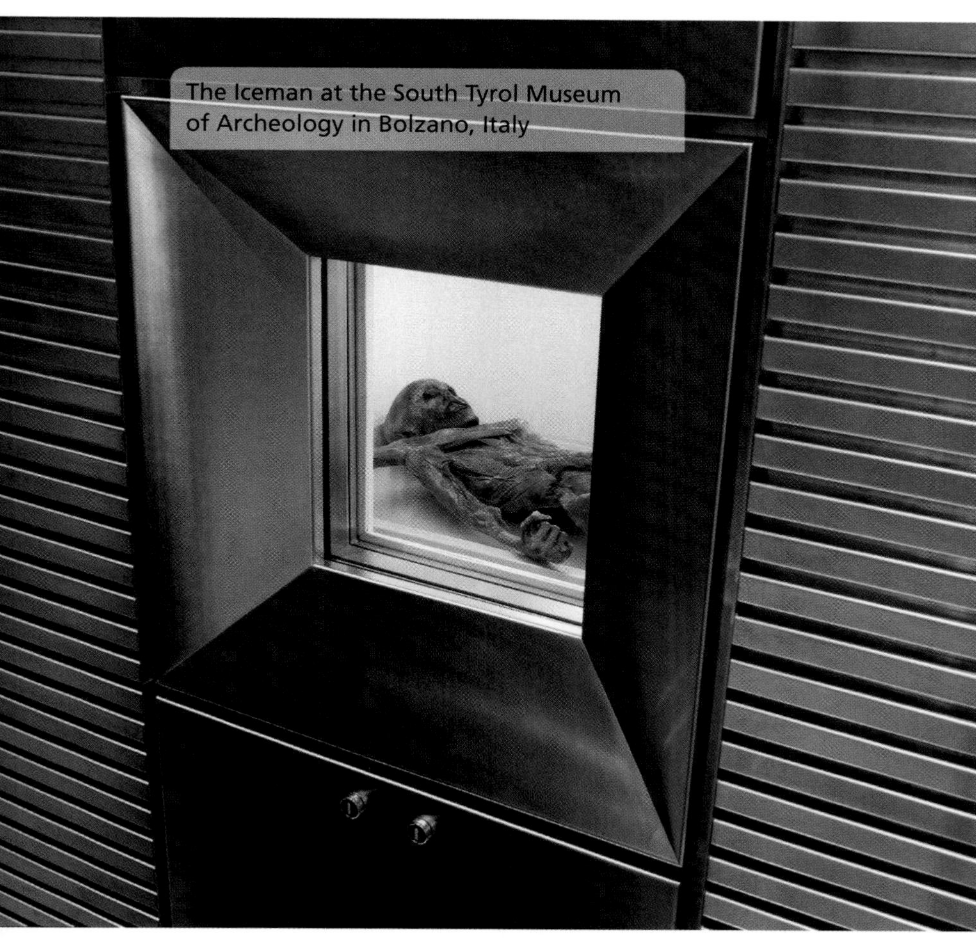
The Iceman at the South Tyrol Museum of Archeology in Bolzano, Italy

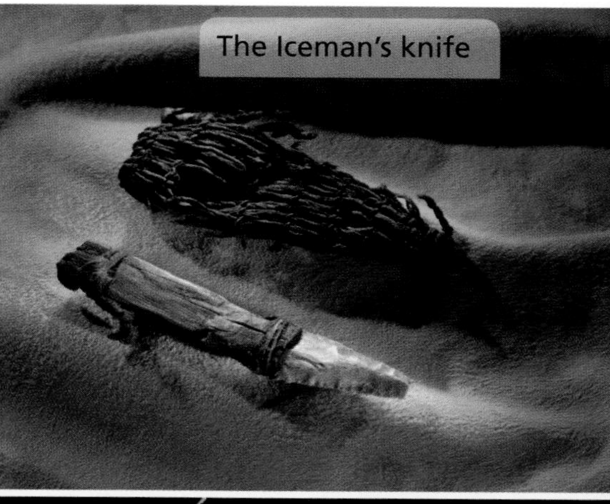
The Iceman's knife

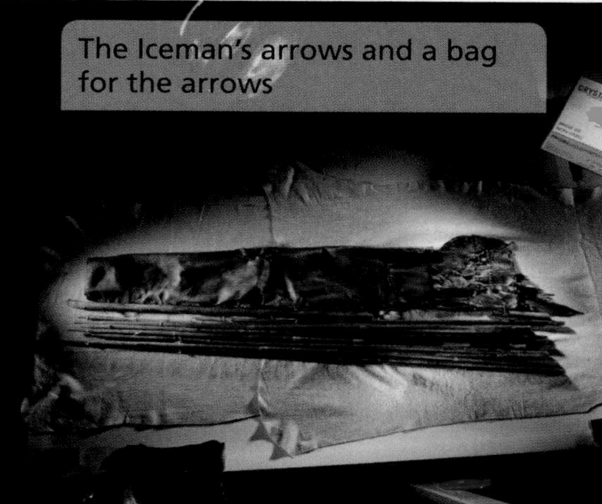
The Iceman's arrows and a bag for the arrows

Grammar regular simple past verbs

7 Look at the grammar box. What do we add to verbs to make the regular simple past form?

▶ REGULAR SIMPLE PAST VERBS

I/You	**studied** the body.
He/She/It	**called** him Ötzi.
We/You/They	**finished** their report.

For more information and practice, see page 167.

8 Pronunciation *-ed* verbs

84 Listen and repeat the infinitive and simple past form of these verbs. Which verb has an extra syllable?

1	call	called	5	kill	killed
2	die	died	6	live	lived
3	discover	discovered	7	start	started
4	finish	finished	8	study	studied

9 Write true sentences with this information.

Albert Einstein	died	from Germany.
Dian Fossey	lived	gorillas in Africa.
John Lennon	studied	in 1980.
Marie Curie	was	in North America.
The Apache people	went	to the university in Paris.

10 Complete the sentences. Use the simple past form of the verb.

1 My grandmother .... (have) six children.
2 She .... (die) in 1998.
3 My grandfather .... (study) with Albert Einstein.
4 My father .... (go) to Cuba.
5 I .... (live) in Italy last year.

Writing and speaking

11 Write sentences about you and your family with the verbs in Exercise 10. Write one false sentence.

My parents went to the South Pole in 2009.

12 Read your sentences to your partner. Can you guess the false sentence?

My parents went to the South Pole in 2009.

I think that's false!

11b Adventurers in action

Reading and listening

1 Read the article and answer the questions.

1 How old is Alastair Humphreys?
2 Where does he live?
3 What's his job?
4 How does he travel on his adventures?

2 Underline the simple past forms of these verbs in the article.

have go leave see meet make

3 85 Listen to an interview with Jamie, a Twitter follower of Alastair. Put the sentences in order.

a His friend made a video.
b He went swimming.
c They posted the video online.
d He watched a video.
e He drove to a lake.

4 85 Can you remember? Why did Jamie go to the lake? Listen again and check.

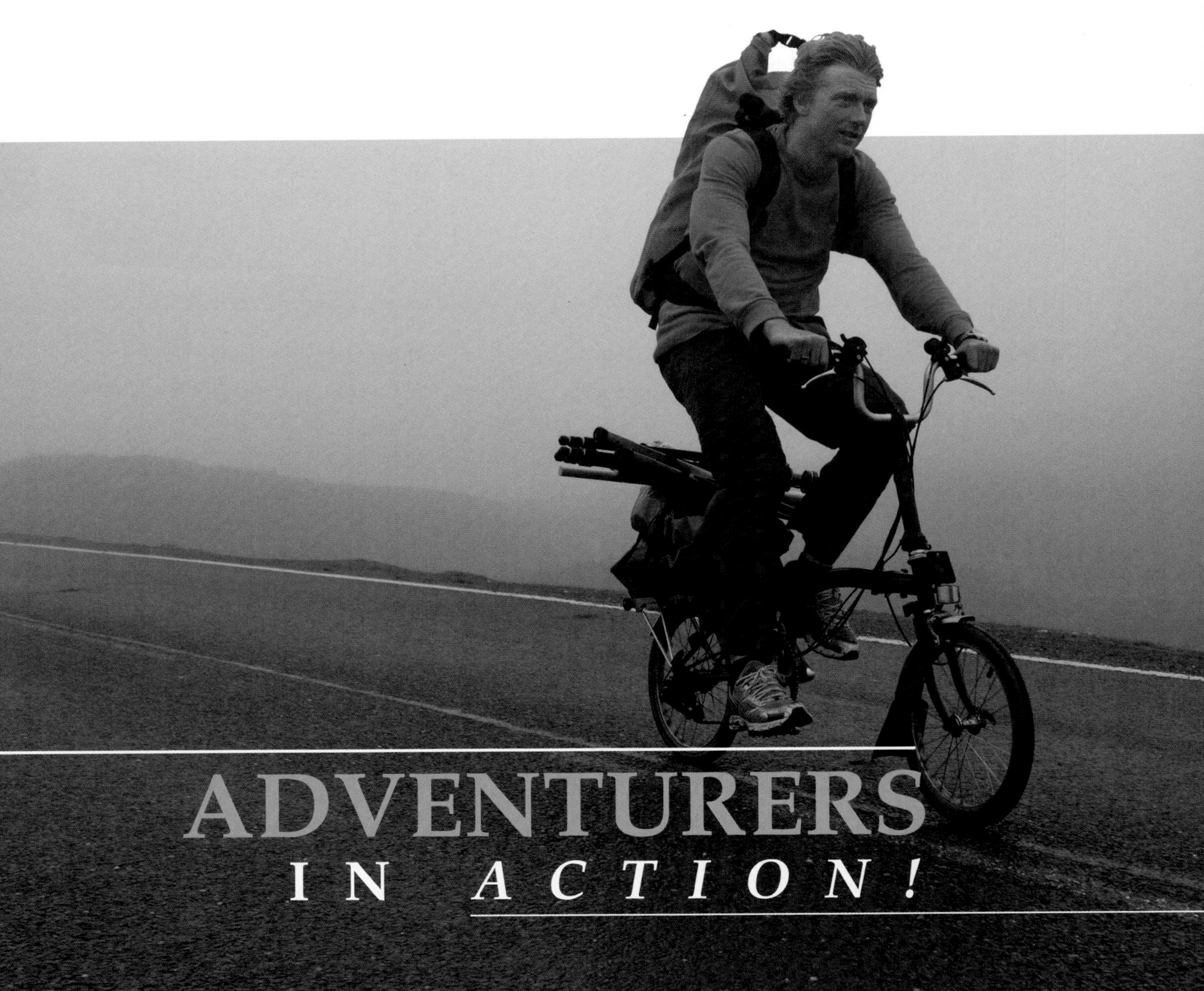

5 Pronunciation *did you ... ?*

86 Listen and repeat these questions from the interview.

1 Did you watch Alastair's videos?
2 Did you like it?
3 Did you make a video too?

Grammar simple past negative and question forms

6 Look at the grammar box. Which auxiliary verb do we use to make questions and negatives in the simple past?

SIMPLE PAST NEGATIVE AND QUESTION FORMS

I/You/He/She/It We/You/They		didn't	leave the UK.
Did	I/you/he/she/it we/you/they	walk?	Yes, I/you/he/she/it/we/you/they **did**. No, I/you/he/she/it/we/you/they **didn't**.

For more information and practice, see page 168.

After ten years of international adventures, last year Alastair Humphreys stayed in the UK. He had a different kind of adventure: a "local adventure." We asked him about it.

Tell us about your last adventure. Did you go to a dangerous place?

No, I didn't. I went around London on the M25 highway.

Did you drive?

No, I walked. I left my house in London in January. It was cold and it was snowy. It wasn't easy, but I saw some beautiful new places. And I met interesting people. It was a local adventure.

And then what did you do?

I had one or two more local adventures and I made videos about them. People around the world watched the videos. They liked my ideas and they went on local adventures too.

ALASTAIR HUMPHREYS

DISCOVER YOUR LOCAL AREA
Age: 35
Home: London
Profession: Writer and adventurer

ADVENTURES:
2001–2005: bike trip around the world
2008: *Marathon des Sables*
2009: walking trip across India
2010: walking trip across Iceland

7 Look at the example. Then write questions about Alastair.

Example:
bike / around the world two years ago?

Did he bike around the world two years ago?

1 run / a marathon in 2008?
2 walk across India / in 2009?
3 go to Iceland / last year?
4 drive around the M25 / last year?
5 make videos / in 2006?

8 Work in pairs. Ask and answer the questions in Exercise 7.

Did he bike around the world two years ago?

No, he didn't.

9 Write sentences about Alastair with the information in Exercise 7.

He walked across Iceland in 2010.

Writing and speaking

10 Prepare a survey about last year. Write questions with these ideas.

- go on vacation
Did you go on vacation last year?
- stay in a hotel
- make a video
- leave your job
- drive to an interesting place
- meet an old friend
- send a message on Twitter

11 Work as a class. Find one name for each question.

Did you go on vacation last year?

Yes, I did. I went to Cairo.

12 Write sentences with the names.

José went to Cairo last year.

11c Discovering Madagascar

Reading

1 Look at the photos on page 135 and find:

an animal   a plant   rocks

2 Work in pairs. Which things in the photos do these adjectives describe?

beautiful   dangerous   fantastic
interesting   unusual

3 Read the article and answer the questions.

1 When did the writer go to Madagascar?
2 Who did he go with?
3 Why did they go to Madagascar?
4 What did they see there?

4 Read the last paragraph of the article again. Complete the sentences.

1 The writer fell on a ________ .
2 He cut his ________ .
3 He went to ________ .
4 A nurse cleaned his ________ .
5 She asked him a ________ .

5 Work in pairs. What did the nurse think about the trip? Do you agree with her?

Grammar simple past with question words

6 Look at the grammar box. Which question words are in Exercise 3?

▶ **SIMPLE PAST WITH QUESTION WORDS**

What Where When Why Who	did	I/you/he/she/it we/you/they	do? go? arrive? fall? meet?

For more information and practice, see page 168.

7 Complete the questions with the correct *wh-* word.

1 ________ did he cut?
2 ________ did he go?
3 ________ did he see there?
4 ________ did she say?

8 Work in pairs. Ask and answer the questions in Exercise 7.

9 **Word focus *with***

a Look at the pictures. Find and complete these two sentences from the article.

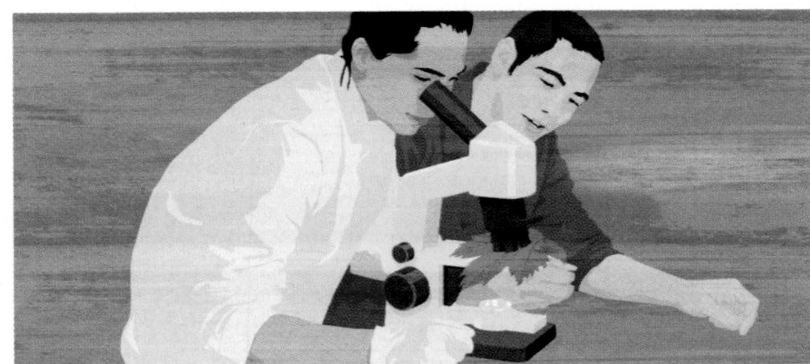

1 I was with a ________ .

2 We saw unusual white lemurs with ________ .

b Match the two parts of the sentences.

1 I booked my tickets with   a animals.
2 You can hitchhike with   b a travel agent.
3 Vets work with   c my friends.
4 We saw a bird with   d Russian drivers.
5 I had lunch with   e unusual colors.

Speaking

10 Work in pairs. Tell Neil Shea's story with these verbs. Take turns to say a sentence. You can use some verbs more than once.

arrived   cleaned   cut   fell
saw   traveled   walked   went

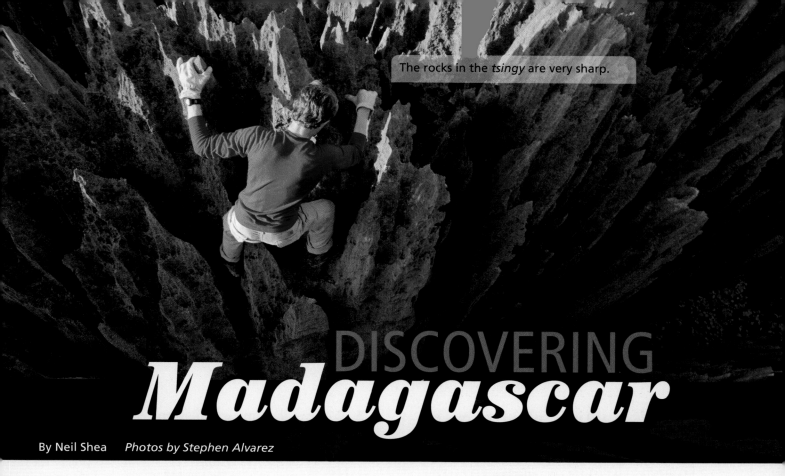

The rocks in the *tsingy* are very sharp.

DISCOVERING Madagascar

By Neil Shea *Photos by Stephen Alvarez*

Madagascar is a fantastic place. About 90 percent of the animals and plants there live only in Madagascar. Scientists love it! There are some very unusual animals and plants in Madagascar's Tsingy de Bemaraha national park, but it's a dangerous place. The rocks—the "tsingy"—in the park are very sharp. Neil Shea reports.

I arrived in Madagascar in March, at the end of the rainy season. I was with a biologist and a photographer. We wanted to find some new species. We traveled to the park with our guide and after five days, we finally arrived there.

We walked through the *tsingy*. The rocks cut our clothes and our shoes. It was dangerous, but we saw hundreds of animals and plants. We saw beautiful birds and unusual white lemurs with red eyes. They didn't have any problems on the *tsingy* rocks!

One afternoon, I fell on a rock. I cut my leg. The cut was very deep. It took two days to reach the hospital. The nurse cleaned my leg. "I have a question. Why did you go to the *tsingy*?" she asked. Then she said, "It's very dangerous. I think you are a little crazy." She didn't understand us. The *tsingy* is a natural paradise.

crazy (adj) /ˈkreɪzi/ not sensible

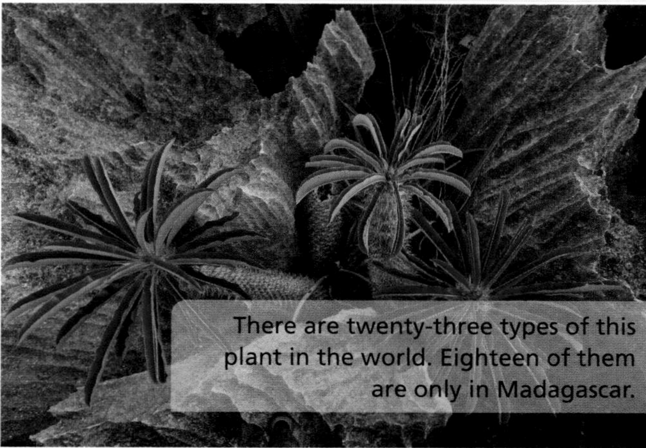

There are twenty-three types of this plant in the world. Eighteen of them are only in Madagascar.

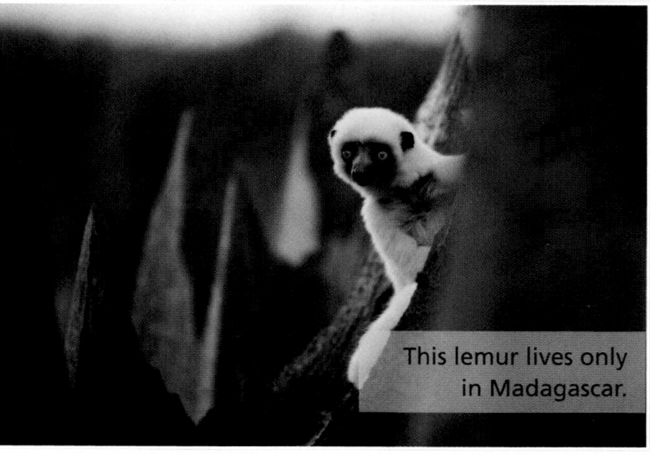

This lemur lives only in Madagascar.

11d Did you have a good time?

Real life talking about the past

1 In pairs, look at the photo. What can you see?

2 87 Listen to three conversations. Write the number of the conversation (1–3).

The people …
a went out to eat.
b were in Sydney.
c didn't have a vacation.

3 87 Listen again and answer the questions for the conversations.

1 Did they stay at home?
2 Did they go swimming?
3 Did they pay for dinner?

TALKING ABOUT THE PAST

Did you have a good vacation last year?
Did you have a good time in Sydney last week?
Did you have a nice dinner last night?
Why not?
There was a shark in the ocean!
We didn't go swimming.
It was delicious.

4 Pronunciation *didn't*

88 Listen to three sentences from the conversations and repeat them.

5 Vocabulary time expressions

Which of these expressions did you hear in the conversations?

on Friday	last week	last year
last night	last weekend	yesterday

6 Work in pairs. Say one thing you did at each time in Exercise 5.

I had a nice dinner on Friday.

7 Work in pairs. Practice the conversations on page 174.

8 Work in pairs. First, choose an event for each time. Then take turns to ask and answer questions about the events. Say one thing you didn't do.

a day at the beach	last month
a vacation	last night
a party	last week
a trip	yesterday

Hi. Did you have a good day at the beach yesterday?

No, I didn't go.

Why not?

It was very cold!

11e Thank you!

Writing an email

1 Work in pairs. Look at the photo. What's the situation?

2 Read the email. Choose the correct option (a–c).

a Lili, Bibia, and Mark went on vacation together.
b Bibia and Mark visited Lili.
c Lili visited Bibia and Mark.

> Dear Lili,
>
> Thank you for a fantastic weekend! It was great to see you and we had a fantastic time.
>
> On the way home we had a little adventure (see photo)! We got home late, but it was OK.
>
> Thanks again. Talk to you soon!
>
> Love,
> Bibia and Mark

3 Read the parts of an email (a–c). Which part completes the email to Lili?

a We missed the plane (!), but we found a hotel and stayed there for the night.

b We got lost! We didn't have a map so we went on the wrong road!

c We had a problem with the car! We called my dad. After an hour, he came and helped us.

4 Writing skill expressions in emails

a Write S or E next to the expressions we use to start (S) or end (E) an email.

All the best,	Hi
Best wishes,	Love,
Dear	Regards,

b Complete this email from Toni to Celia with expressions from Exercise 4a.

> 1 ....
>
> Thanks for your help yesterday. I found my car keys when I got home!
>
> See you soon.
>
> 2 ....

5 Work in pairs. Each person choose one of these situations. Tell your partner how you helped him/her.

- You helped him/her when he/she lost his/her phone.
- You helped him/her when he/she didn't have any money.
- You sent him/her some photos.
- He/She had dinner at your house.

6 Write a "thank you" email to your friend for his/her help in the situation in Exercise 5.

7 Exchange emails with your friend. Ask a follow-up question about your friend's email.

11f Perfumes from Madagascar

Video

An unusual plant in the Madagascan forest

Before you watch

1 Work in pairs. Answer the questions.

1 What perfumes do you know or use?
2 Where do perfumes come from?

2 Work in pairs. Do you think these sentences about Madagascar are true (T) or false (F)?

1 Madagascar is an island.
2 There are some unusual plants in the forests.
3 It's an interesting place for scientists.
4 It's easy to travel into the forests by car.

While you watch

3 Watch the video without sound. Mark (✓) the things you see.

a forest	a laboratory
scientists	a store
flowers	some fruit
a river	some animals
a balloon	the ocean

4 Watch the video with sound. Then choose the correct summary (a or b).

a Some scientists discovered a new flower.
They made a new perfume.
They sold the perfume in Madagascar.

b Some scientists went to Madagascar.
They looked for plants and flowers.
One of the scientists found two new plants.

5 Read the sentences. Then watch the video again. Are the sentences true (T) or false (F)?

1 The scientists are from Switzerland.
2 They make perfumes.
3 Their laboratory is in Madagascar.
4 They found plants with black fruit.
5 Willi Grab didn't like the taste of the fruit.

6 Work in pairs. Which option(s) (a–c) are true?

1 The scientists went to Madagascar...
   a because there are a lot of interesting plants.
   b because they go there every year.
   c because they wanted to find new plants.

2 They saw...
   a some interesting animals.
   b some beautiful flowers.
   c some unusual fruits.

After you watch

7 Match the two parts of the sentences.

1 The scientists went to Madagascar
2 They traveled into
3 Then they flew in
4 They looked for
5 They cut the fruits and
6 They studied the new scents
7 Last year, this scientist found two

a a balloon.
b in the laboratory.
c interesting flowers and fruits.
d the forest by boat.
e they tasted them.
f last year.
g new plants.

8 Work in pairs. Take turns. Read the sentences in Exercise 7.

Student A: Read the first part of the first sentence.

Student B: Read the second part of the first sentence.

9 Work in pairs. Take turns.

Student A: You are a scientist. You went to Madagascar.

Student B: You are a journalist.

Ask and answer questions with *when, where, what, who,* and *why* about the trip to Madagascar.

acidic (adj) /ə'sɪdɪk/ Lemons taste acidic.

a **balloon** (n) /bə'lun/

a **chemist** (n) /'kemɪst/ a type of scientist

close (adj) /kloʊs/ similar

earthy (adj) /'ɜrθi/ similar to soil or earth

a **flower** (n) /'flaʊər/

juicy (adj) /'dʒusi/ with a lot of juice

man-made (adj) /'mæn'meɪd/ the opposite of natural; made by people

a **scent** (n) /sent/ a natural perfume

stephanotis (n) /ˌstefə'noʊtɪs/ a type of flower

taste (v) /teɪst/ to try or eat a small part of some food

watery (adj) /'wɔtəri/ with a lot of water

UNIT 11 REVIEW

Grammar

1 Complete the blog with the simple past forms of the verbs.

Field notes

A blog by National Geographic Expeditions

Last month, I was with a group of people on a boat. We 1 ________ (be) in Alaska. Justin Hofman, a scuba diver, 2 ________ (be) in the water. He 3 ________ (have) a camera. He 4 ________ (take) pictures underwater. He 5 ________ (send) video pictures to us on the boat. It was very exciting! We 6 ________ (see) beautiful animals and plants. There was an audio connection too. Justin 7 ________ (talk) about the animals and plants and we 8 ________ (ask) him questions. It was a great experience.

Posted by Carly

2 Read the blog again. Are the sentences true (T) or false (F)? Change the verb to the negative form to make the false sentences true.

1 Carly went to Canada.
2 She was on a bus.
3 Justin Hofman took photos.
4 Carly saw interesting things.

3 Read Carly's answers. Write the questions.

1 No, I didn't go in the water.
2 Yes, I had a great time.
3 No, I didn't take any photos.
4 I went with my friends.

4 Work in pairs. You were on the boat in the photo. Ask and answer questions with these words.

1 Where / go?
2 When / get there?
3 What / see?
4 Who / talk to?
5 Why / go?

I CAN	
talk about the past (irregular and regular simple past verbs)	☐
ask and answer questions about the past (question words)	☐

Vocabulary

5 Complete the sentences with six of these verbs.

cleaned	cut	drove	fell	finished	found
made	met	paid	sent	swam	took

Yesterday

1 I ________ breakfast.
2 I ________ my room.
3 I ________ to a café.
4 I ________ my friend Alex.
5 He ________ a photo of us.
6 I ________ for lunch.

6 Write true sentences for you with six of the verbs from Exercise 5 and time expressions.

Last night / weekend / week / month / year
On Monday / Tuesday, etc.

7 Work in pairs. Read your sentences.

I CAN	
talk about people's lives	☐
say when people did things	☐

Real life

8 Read the conversation and choose the best option.

A: Did you have *a good day at the beach / a nice dinner / a good vacation* last night?
B: No, I didn't.
A: Oh? Why not?
B: The food was delicious, but my friend *missed the plane / saw a shark in the water / cut her hand with her knife*!
A: Oh no!

I CAN	
talk about the past	☐
give reasons for events in the past	☐

Speaking

9 Work in pairs. Practice the conversation in Exercise 8 with the other two options.

Unit 12 The weekend

A group of women in Chengdu, China
Photo by Cary Wolinsky

FEATURES

1 Work in pairs. Look at the photo of women on their day off work. What days do you work or study?

2 **89** Work in pairs. Look at the photo again and discuss the questions. Then listen and check your ideas.

1 Which day of the week do you think is the women's day off?
2 What do you think they usually do on their day off?
3 Which days do you think are the weekend in China?

3 **89** Listen again. Write the weekend days for these countries. What about your country?

Oman: .... , ...
Egypt: .... , ...

4 Work in pairs. What do you do on the weekend? Do you stay at home, do you go out, or do you work?

I work on Saturday, and on Sunday I stay home.

12a At home

Vocabulary rooms in a house

1 Look at the things (1–5) there are in different rooms. Write the rooms next to the things. Check your answers with your instructor.

bathroom bedroom dining room ~~kitchen~~ living room

1 a fridge, an oven *kitchen*
2 a chair, a table ....
3 an armchair, a sofa ....
4 a bed, a closet ....
5 a bathtub, a shower, a toilet ....

2 Work in pairs. Tell your partner one thing about each room in your home.

We don't have a dining room. We eat in the kitchen.

My kitchen is very small.

HOME LIFE
PHOTO PROJECT

We asked our readers to take photos of the important things in their homes. This week, we show Ayu Malik's photos. It's Saturday at her home in Sumatra, Indonesia.

1

2

3

4

5
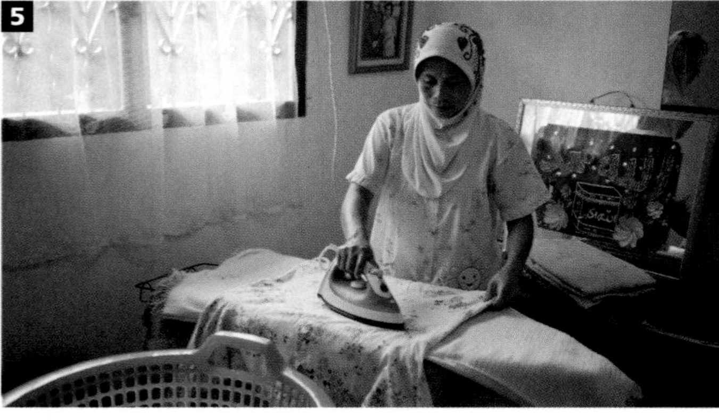

6

Listening

3 Look at the photos (1–6) of a family at home in Indonesia. Which rooms are the people in?

4 **90** Match the sentences with the photos. Then listen and check.

a They're drinking coffee.
b He's playing a computer game with his son.
c He's bathing his daughter.
d They're washing their bikes.
e She's making lunch.
f She's ironing.

5 **90** Listen again and say who the people are. Write next to the sentences in Exercise 4.

Example:
a They're drinking coffee.
Ayu's father and his friend

Grammar **present continuous**

6 Look at the grammar box. Then look at the sentences in Exercise 4. Which auxiliary verb do we use to make the present continuous?

▶ PRESENT CONTINUOUS AFFIRMATIVE and NEGATIVE

I	**am (not)**	**sitting** on the floor.
You/We/They	**are (not)**	**making** lunch.
He/She/It	**is (not)**	**ironing**.

For more information and practice, see page 168.

7 Complete the sentences about the photos on page 142.

1 *Ayu's mother* is cooking.
2 .... are smiling.
3 .... are sitting on mats.
4 .... is lying on the sofa.
5 .... is standing alone.
6 .... is wearing shorts.

8 Write true sentences about the photos. Use the negative form when necessary.

1 Ayu's mother /eat
Ayu's mother isn't eating.
2 Amir / play with his daughter
3 Ayu's father and his friend / read a book
4 Amir's brother / watch TV
5 Ayu's sister / do homework
6 Ayu's brother / wash his cars

9 Look at these questions from the conversation with Ayu Malik. Which photos are the questions about?

a What's she making?
b Are they sitting outside or inside?
c What are they doing?
d Are they reading?

10 Work in pairs. Ask and answer the questions in Exercise 9.

▶ PRESENT CONTINUOUS QUESTIONS and SHORT ANSWERS

(What)	**Am**	I	**reading?** **doing?**
	Are	you/we/you/they	
	Is	he/she/it	
	Yes, **I am**. No, **I'm not**. Yes, **he/she/it is**. No, **he/she/it isn't**. Yes, **you/we/you/they are**. No, **you/we/you/they aren't**.		

For more information and practice, see page 168.

11 Look at the photo below. Write questions. Then ask and answer the questions with your partner.

Example:
children / watch TV?
Are the children watching TV?

1 boy / lie on the sofa?
2 man / sit on a chair?
3 women / wear scarves?
4 girls/ sit on the floor?

Speaking

12 Work in groups. Show some of your photos to the group. Take turns to ask and answer questions.

Who's that?
That's my cousin and her husband.
What are they doing?
They're singing.

12b Next weekend

Vocabulary weekend activities

1 Look at the photo. Where are the people? What are they doing?

2 Read the *On the weekend* questionnaire. Are the activities at home (H) or out of the home (O)?

3 Work in pairs. Complete the questionnaire. Are your weekends similar or different?

I never get up late on the weekend.

I sometimes get up late.

On the weekend

How often do you do these weekend activities? Always? Sometimes? Never?

	me	my partner
get up late		
go out to eat		
go for a walk		
go shopping		
go to the movies		
go to a museum		
meet friends		
play soccer		
read the newspaper		
visit family		

A busy shopping center on a typical Saturday

Listening

4 91 Look at the information about three events. Then listen to a conversation between friends. Mark (✓) the events they talk about.

5 91 Listen again. Answer the questions.

1 When is Lauren going shopping?
2 Why is she going shopping?
3 Who is giving a talk at the museum?
4 What is Alex doing on Sunday?

6 **Pronunciation *going* and *doing***

92 Listen to five sentences from the conversation. Notice the /w/ sound in *going* and *doing*. Repeat the sentences.

Grammar **present continuous with future time expressions**

7 Look at the sentences from the conversation in Exercise 4 in the grammar box. Are the speakers talking about now or a time in the future?

> **▶ PRESENT CONTINUOUS WITH FUTURE TIME EXPRESSIONS**
>
> What are you doing **this weekend**?
> Sports Gear is having a sale **tomorrow**.
> She's giving a talk about her trip **on Sunday evening**.
>
> For more information and practice, see page 168.

8 Look at the information for City Hall in Exercise 4. Write the conversation between Alex and Oscar.

A: What / you / do / this weekend?
O: *I'm not sure.* My sister / come / tomorrow.
A: she / stay the weekend?
O: *Yes, she is.* We / go / to a party on Saturday.
A: *Does she like music?* The West Country Folk Band / play at City Hall on Sunday.
O: *OK. Great!*

Speaking

9 Write activities for this weekend.

Saturday	
MORNING	
AFTERNOON	
EVENING	
Sunday	
MORNING	
AFTERNOON	
EVENING	

10 Work in pairs. Ask and answer questions about next weekend. Are you doing the same things?

What are you doing on Saturday morning?

I'm going shopping with my sister. What about you?

12c A different kind of weekend

Reading

1 Look at the photos on page 147. Answer the questions.

1 What do you think the people are doing?
2 Where do you think they are?
3 Is there anything unusual about them?

2 Read the article and check your ideas from Exercise 1.

3 Read the article again. Are the sentences true (T) or false (F)?

1 Joel Connor works for free on the weekend.
2 He's a builder.
3 He's building a house for his family.
4 He works with his friends.
5 He's coming to Greensburg next weekend.

4 Look at the photos on page 147. Complete the sentences.

1 Joel is moving a large ....
2 .... are working on the roof.
3 Jill Eller is standing near ....
4 Jill's holding a part of ....

5 Match a verb in A with words in B. Check your answers in the article.

A	B
build	people
help	a house
know	a project
start	people
work	in an office

Grammar tense review

6 Look at these four sentences from the article. Underline the verbs. Then write past (P), present (PR), or future (F) next to the sentences.

1 Joel Connor works in an office in Kansas.
2 The community started a project.
3 Jill is standing near her new house.
4 Next weekend, Joel is moving to a different project.

7 Add these expressions to the sentences.

In this photo
From Monday to Friday
Last year

1 .... , Joel Connor works in an office.
2 .... , the community started a project.
3 .... , Jill is standing near her new house.

8 **Word focus *do***

a Match the questions (1–5) with the answers (a–e).

1 What do you do?
2 What are you doing?
3 What do you usually do on the weekend?
4 What did you do on the weekend?
5 What are you doing on the weekend?

a I'm going to a concert with a friend.
b I'm a builder.
c I visited my cousin in Miami.
d I'm making lunch.
e I meet my friends.

b The verb *do* is a main verb and an auxiliary verb. Look at the questions. Underline the main verbs and circle the auxiliary verbs.

c Work in pairs. Ask and answer the questions in Exercise 8a.

What do you do?

I'm a ...

Speaking

9 Work in groups. Plan a special weekend for a person you all know. Then tell the class.

Next weekend is our special weekend for Tracey. On Saturday morning, we're all going shopping. Then Tracey is having a beauty makeover.

A different kind of weekend

Joel Connor works in an office in Kansas. His job is a typical nine-to-five, Monday-to-Friday job, but on the weekend, he does something different. He does volunteer work. He helps different organizations and people for free. Every weekend, there's a new project. This weekend, Joel is helping to build a house. You can see him in the photo. He's moving a large blue panel. It's part of a wall. Joel isn't a professional builder, but the other people are volunteers too.

These "weekend builders" are from the small town of Greensburg in Kansas. A year ago, a tornado hit their town. After the tornado, the community started a project to build new homes. The project is for 30 new homes. They have help from a building company and the volunteers.

"I heard about the tornado and the new project. I knew some people in Greensburg so I wanted to help," Joel says. His friends are here this weekend too. They're on the roof. They're working with Jill and Scott Eller. Jill and Scott are building their new house. Jill (right) is standing near her new house. She's holding a part of the new wall. They're making the house "tornado-resistant." That's why it has an unusual shape.

The Ellers' house is almost ready, so next weekend, Joel is moving to a different project. Why does he volunteer? "I have time, I can help people, I make friends, and it's fun! So why not?" he says.

tornado /n/ /tɔr'neɪdoʊ/ a very windy storm
tornado-resistant /n/ /tɔr'neɪdoʊ rɪˌzɪstənt/ a tornado can't hurt this

12d Would you like a brochure?

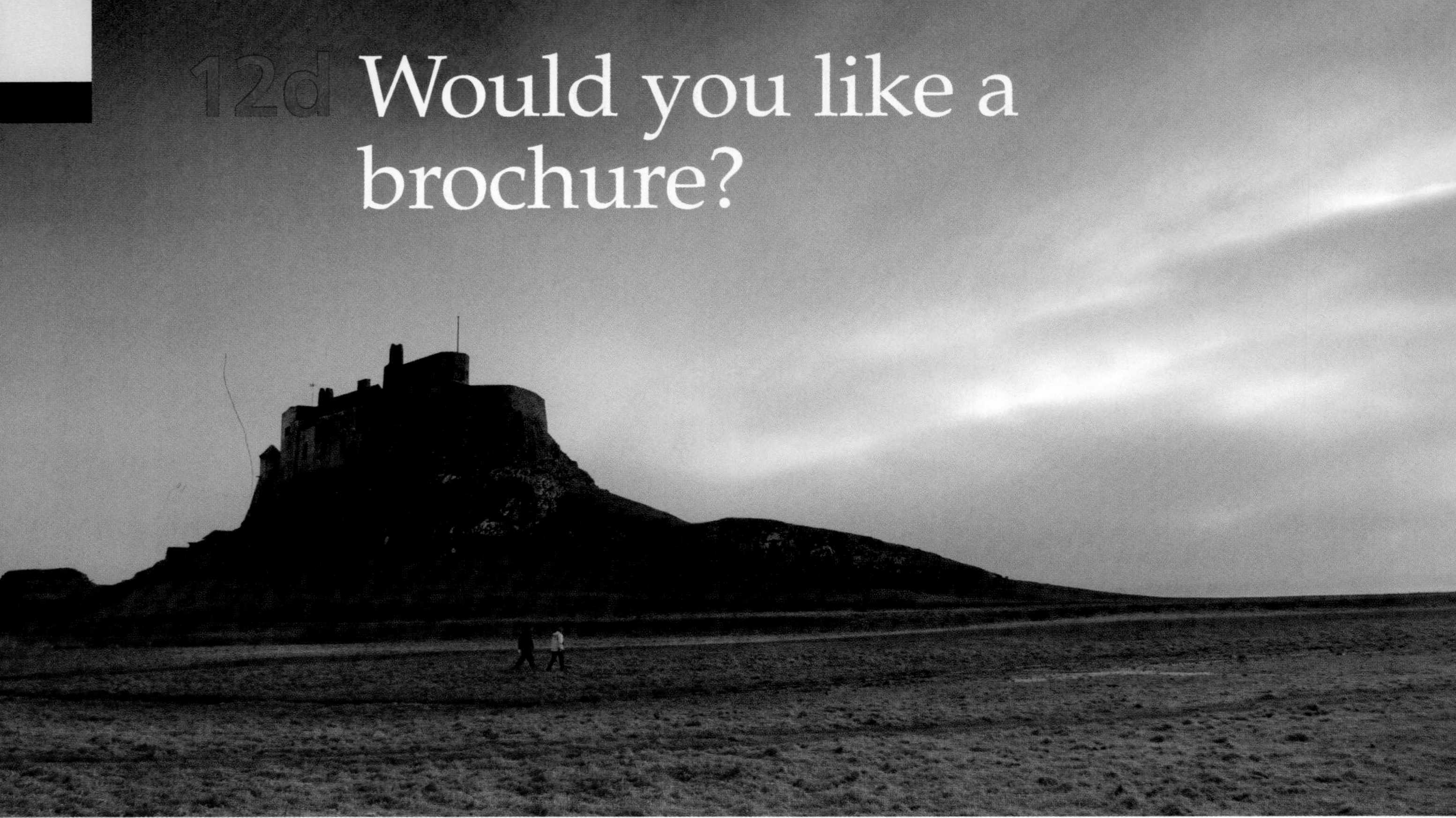

Vocabulary weekend trips

1 Complete the sentences. There is one extra word.

brochure court exhibition museum round-trip ticket

1 You look at pictures in an ....
2 You play tennis on a ....
3 You read a ....
4 You buy a .... to go to a place and come back.

Real life buying tickets

2 93 Listen to three conversations (a–c). Match the number of tickets with the place and the price.

Number of tickets	Place	Price
a four	a castle	16 dollars
b three	a museum	10 dollars
c two	a tennis court	34 dollars

3 93 Listen again. Are the sentences true (T) or false (F)?

a 1 There are four children.
2 They get a brochure in French.

b 3 They buy one-way tickets.
4 They are going to the castle and gardens.

c 5 People are playing on all the tennis courts.
6 They buy a ticket for two hours.

4 Pronunciation *would you ... ?*

a 94 Look at the expressions for BUYING TICKETS. Listen and repeat.

b Work in pairs. Ask and answer questions with *Would you like ... ?*

a single ticket
to play soccer
a drink
to go to the museum

▶ BUYING TICKETS

Four tickets to the museum, please.
Three round-trip tickets to Lindisfarne, please.
Would you like a brochure?
Would you like it in English?
Would you like to buy the tickets now?

5 Work in pairs. Look at the audioscript on page 174. Practice the conversations.

6 Work in pairs. Buy and sell tickets.

Student A: Turn to page 156.

Student B: Turn to page 160.

12e Join us for lunch

Writing an invitation

1 Read the invitation. Answer the questions.

1 Why are Estefania and Tim celebrating?
2 How are they celebrating?
3 When and where is it?
4 What do you think *RSVP* means?

2 Read the replies to the invitation. How many people are coming to the party?

1

Estefania, thank you for the lunch invitation. My sister is arriving from Canada that day, so I can't come! Yoko

2

Today at 6:51 PM Pete:

Hi Tim. Thanks for the invitation. I'm coming!

3

Hi Estefania. We'd like to come to lunch, but Bill has swim class. Can we come late? Is that OK?

Maya and Steve

4

Dear Estefania and Tim

Thank you very much for your invitation. We had a great time when we saw you last year. We are traveling on April 4, so we can't make it this time. Sorry!

Dani and Eve

5

Hi Stef and Tim

Thank you for the invitation. I'd like to come. Why don't I bring a cake? See you on April 4!

Gabi

ESTEFANIA AND TIM ARE MOVING!

PLEASE JOIN US FOR LUNCH

ON SUNDAY APRIL 4 AT 2 P.M.

OUR NEW ADDRESS IS 3 FORD STREET
CHULA VISTA

RSVP STEF@ROUNDHOUSE.NET

3 Writing skill spelling: verb endings

a Read the invitation and the replies again. Write the forms of the verbs.

1 move ....
2 arrive ....
3 come ....
4 swim ....
5 travel ....

b How does the spelling of these verbs change in the present continuous?

c Complete the table. Spell the verbs correctly.

	Present continuous	Simple present (*he/she/it*)	Simple past
do	*doing*	*does*	*did*
drive			
fly			
lie			
make			
see			
sit			
smile			
study			

4 Write an invitation to an event like a party. Check the spelling.

5 Exchange invitations with somone in your class. Read your classmate's invitation. Can you go to this event? Write a reply. If you can't go, give a reason. Give the reply to your classmate.

12f Saturday morning in São Tomé

Video

This fisherman doesn't work on Saturdays.

Before you watch

1 Work in pairs. Ask and answer these questions.

1 Can you play a musical instrument?
2 Can you paint or draw?
3 Do you go fishing?
4 Can you swim?

2 Work in pairs. What do these people do on the weekend? Write true sentences.

People	Activities
	do homework.
Children	give concerts.
Farmers	go to school.
Fishermen	go to the market.
Musicians	meet friends.
Salespeople	play music.
	rest.

3 Work in pairs. What do the people in Exercise 2 do on the weekend in your country?

4 São Tomé is the captial of São Tomé and Principe. How many islands are there in the country?

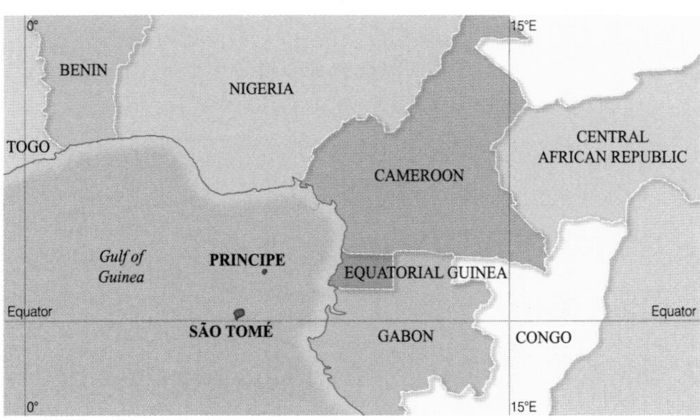

While you watch

5 These things are in the video. Watch the video again and put the pictures in order.

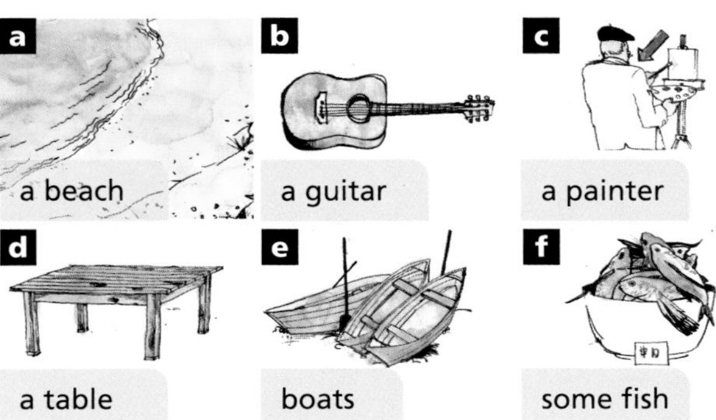

6 Watch the video again and write down one thing about each person.

1 Oswaldo Santos 2 Guillerme 3 Nezo

7 Work in pairs. Compare your answers from Exercise 6.

8 Watch the video again and answer the questions.

1 Who is playing in the water?
2 Who is resting in a boat?
3 Who is buying fish?
4 Who is playing the guitar?
5 Who is singing?
6 Who is painting?

9 Work in pairs. Ask and answer the questions in Exercise 8. Do you agree?

After you watch

10 Complete the text with these words.

art colors concert guitar life music musician painters people song

Oswaldo is a [1] ____________ . He's in a group called *Grupo Tempo*. He plays the [2] ____________ , he sings, and he writes [3] ____________ .

Oswaldo, Guillerme, and Nezo are playing a new [4] ____________ . They're giving a [5] ____________ next week.

Guillerme and Nezo are [6] ____________ too. They paint things from local life: the [7] ____________ , the [8] ____________ , and the animals. Their music and [9] ____________ is about [10] ____________ in São Tomé.

11 Work in pairs. Make notes about musicians or artists you like. Tell your partner about them.

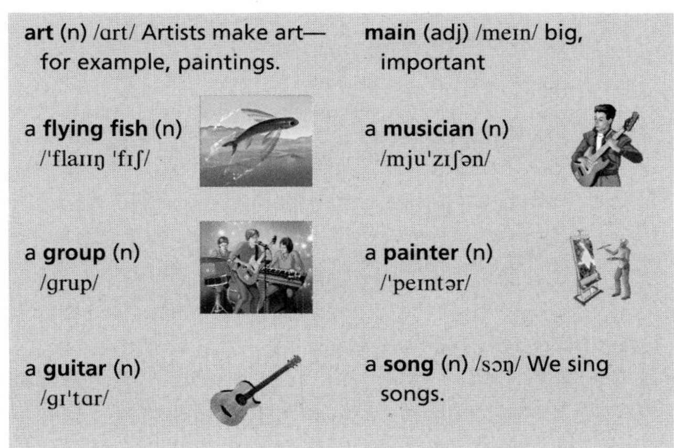

art (n) /ɑrt/ Artists make art—for example, paintings.

main (adj) /meɪn/ big, important

a **flying fish** (n) /ˈflaɪɪŋ ˈfɪʃ/

a **musician** (n) /mjuˈzɪʃən/

a **group** (n) /grup/

a **painter** (n) /ˈpeɪntər/

a **guitar** (n) /gɪˈtɑr/

a **song** (n) /sɔŋ/ We sing songs.

UNIT 12 REVIEW

Grammar

1 Look at the photo of people at a bus stop in Santiago, Chile. Match the words (1–4) with the people (a–d) in the photo. Then write sentences with the present continuous.

1 wear / a brown jacket
2 hold / some books
3 talk / to her friend
4 walk / to the bus stop

2 Complete the paragraph about the photo with the correct form of the present continuous.

It's Friday evening in Santiago. These people [1] __________ (stand) at a bus stop. There's a bus and its doors [2] __________ (open), but the people [3] __________ (not get) on it. They [4] __________ (wait) for different buses. Some of the people [5] __________ (go) home. They [6] __________ (think) about the weekend. Some [7] __________ (not go) home. They [8] __________ (take) the bus to work.

3 Put the words in the conversation in order.

A: *Oh hello.* you / what / doing /are / ?
B: office / I / leaving / the / am / .
A: *Really?* late / is / it / .
B: *I know.* this / working / we / late / are / week / .
A: *OK.* to / coming / you / tomorrow / the beach / are / ?
B: *I don't know.* are / going / time / you / what / ?
A: leaving / at /are /eleven o'clock / we / .
B: friend / is / coming / your / ?
A: *Yes, he is.*
B: *OK. Great.*

I CAN	
talk about now (present continuous)	☐
talk about the future (present continuous with future time expressions)	☐
use the simple present, present continuous, and simple past correctly	☐

Vocabulary

4 Work in pairs. Ask and answer questions about the rooms where people do these things. Use these words.

1 cook?
2 sleep?
3 take a shower?
4 watch TV?
5 eat?
6 read?

5 Match a verb from A with words from B.

A	B
get up	to a concert
go	family
have	soccer
meet	friends
play	late
read	the newspaper
visit	a party

6 Work in pairs. Tell your partner what you usually do on the weekend. Do you do similar things?

I CAN	
talk about rooms in a house	☐
talk about weekend activities	☐

Real life

7 Match the requests (1–4) with the responses (a–d).

1 A round-trip ticket to Oxford.
2 Three tickets for the concert, please.
3 Two tickets for Cinema One, please.
4 Two tickets for the museum, please.

a Two adults? That's twenty-four dollars, please.
b Here you are. Would you like an audio guide?
c Are you coming back today?
d Would you like to sit upstairs or downstairs?

I CAN	
buy tickets	☐
talk about weekend trips	☐

Speaking

8 Work in pairs. Tell your partner about your plans. What are you doing next weekend/week/month?

2

UNIT 1a, Exercise 15, page 11

Student A

1 Listen to your partner. Write the jobs.

a .... b ....

c .... d ....

2 Spell these jobs to your partner.

e driver

f artist

g photographer

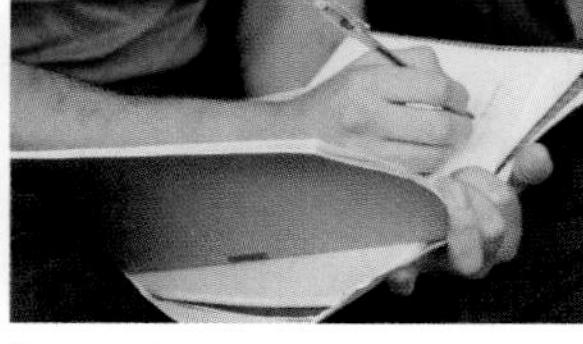

h writer

UNIT 2b, Exercise 13, page 25

Student A

1 Look at the photo. You are on vacation in Oman. Look at the sentences (1–4) and choose an option. Then have a telephone conversation with your friend (Student B) about your vacation.

1 You're *OK / happy*.
2 It's *hot / cold*.
3 The beach is *nice / beautiful*.
4 Your hotel is *nice / OK*.

2 Your friend (Student B) is on vacation. Prepare questions with these words. Then have a telephone conversation with Student B.

1 where?
2 OK?
3 cold?
4 city / beautiful?
5 hotel / nice?

Wone you are
are you OK
It cold the city

UNIT 3b, Exercise 9, page 37

Student A

1 Look at the information about photo A. Answer your partner's questions about this photo.

Ivan
Miroslava
in Russia
Miroslava's sister
Ivan's 23 and Miroslava's 21

A

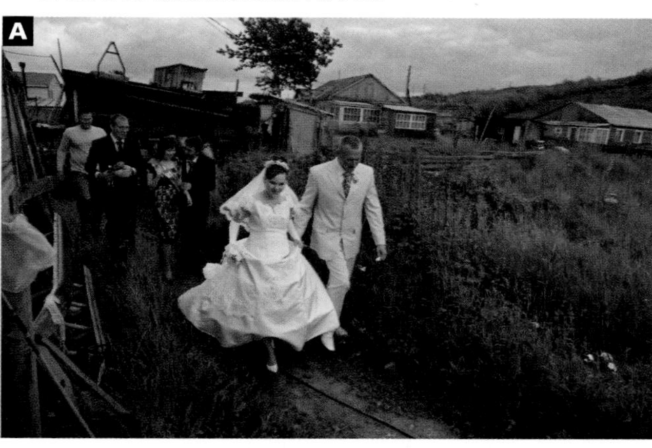

2 Look at photo B. Ask your partner about this photo. Ask questions with ***who, where, what,*** and ***how old***.

B

UNIT 4b, Exercise 10, page 49

Student A

1 Look at the information about photo A. Answer your partner's questions about this tower.

- The Space Needle tower
- It's in Seattle in the United States.
- It's open every day of the year.
- It's a symbol of Seattle. It's in Hollywood movies, for example, *Sleepless in Seattle*.

2 Look at photo B. Ask your partner about this tower. Ask the questions on page 49.

UNIT 5c, Exercise 7, page 62

Student A

1 Tell your partner about this microwave oven. Use ***can*** and ***has***.

shopping_online.com

EasyCook Microwave

Product features:
cook and heat food ✓
3 power options ✓
make cakes ✗
digital clock ✓
buy online ✓

2 Listen to your partner. Make notes (1–5) about this microwave oven.

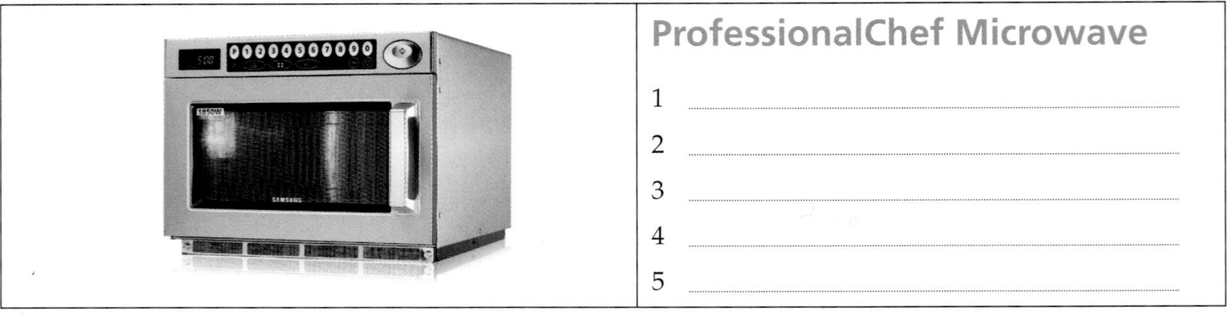

ProfessionalChef Microwave

1 ....
2 ....
3 ....
4 ....
5 ....

3 Look at the two microwave ovens. Do you think they are cheap or expensive?

UNIT 6c, Exercise 9, page 74

Student A

1 Look at the photos and the information about sports events 1 and 3. Ask your partner five questions about events 2 and 4. Complete the information. You get 5 points if you identify the event after one question, 4 points if you ask two questions, etc.

	1 Wimbledon	2	3 the Dakar Rally	4 ....
1 Where?	London	....	South America	....
2 When?	June and July	....	January	....
3 What kind of event?	a competition	....	a race	....
4 Prize?	money	....	–	....
5 Sport?	tennis	....	motor sport	....

2 Look at the information about Wimbledon and the Dakar Rally. Answer your partner's questions.

UNIT 8c, Exercise 9, page 98

Student A

Write the questions (1–3) and choose your answers.

Then ask your partner the questions. Write your partner's answers and check the results on page 157.

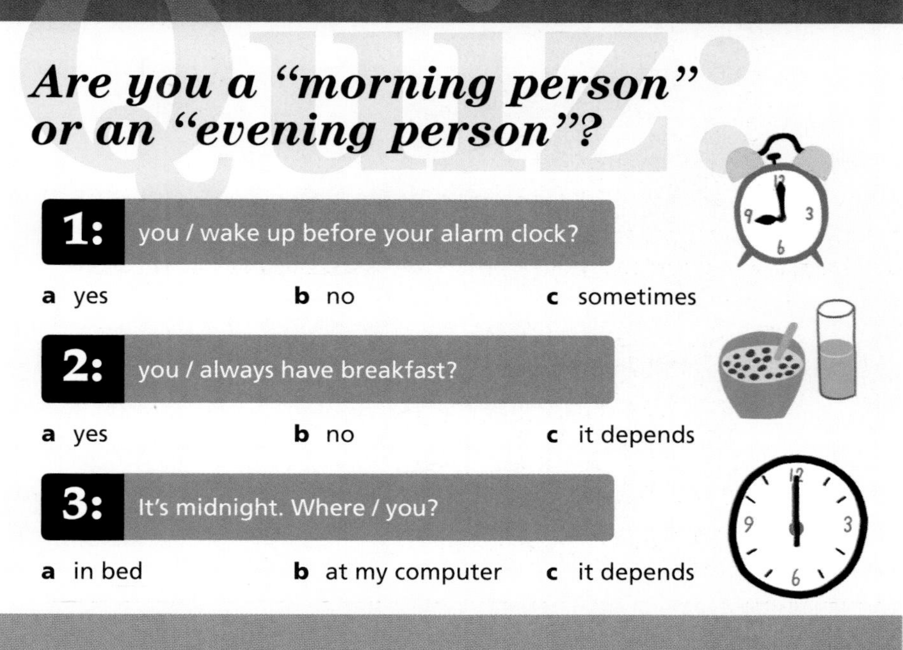

Quiz:
Are you a "morning person" or an "evening person"?
1: you / wake up before your alarm clock?
a yes
b no
c sometimes
2: you / always have breakfast?
a yes
b no
c it depends
3: It's midnight. Where / you?
a in bed
b at my computer
c it depends

UNIT 9b, Exercise 11, page 109

Student A

1 Look at this room. Answer Student B's questions.

2 Look at these two rooms. Student B has one of these rooms. Ask questions to find out which one. Use *Is there a . . . ?* and *Are there any . . . ?*

UNIT 10c, Exercise 9, page 122

Pair A

1 Listen to Pair B. Who are the people?

2 Look at the notes. Tell Pair B about these two people. Don't say the names.

Date of birth	1595
Place of birth	Virginia, North America
Biographical information	a prisoner of the English married to an English farmer, John Rolfe
Name	Pocahontas

Date of birth	January 19, 1807
Place of birth	Virginia, North America
Biographical information	leader, the Army of Northern Virginia, Confederacy, American Civil War also was in war between Mexico and the US
Name	Robert E. Lee

UNIT 12d, Exercise 6, page 148

Student A

1 You work in a museum's ticket office. Look at this information and answer Student B's questions.

Great Explorers Exhibition

Tickets: adults $2.50; children $1.50

Brochures: $2.00

Audio program: English, French, German, Spanish

2 You are a group of two adults and four children. You are going to Bambridge Castle. Ask Student B questions to find out when the last bus leaves and how much the tickets cost.

Buses to Bambridge Castle

Every hour 9:15 – ....

Tickets: one-way $ .... *; round-trip $* ....

Round-trip ticket + admission to castle $ ....

UNIT 1a, Exercise 15, page 11

Student B

1 Spell these jobs to your partner.

a filmmaker

b engineer

c doctor

d teacher

2 Listen to your partner. Write the jobs.

e .... f ....

g .... h ....

UNIT 2b, Exercise 13, page 25

Student B

1 Your friend (Student A) is on vacation. Prepare questions with these words. Then have a telephone conversation with Student A.

1 where?
2 OK?
3 cold?
4 beach / beautiful?
5 hotel / nice?

2 Look at the photo. You are on vacation in New York. Look at the sentences (1–4) and choose an option. Then have a telephone conversation with your friend (Student A) about your vacation.

1 You're *OK / happy*.
2 It's *hot / cold*.
3 The city is *nice / beautiful*.
4 Your hotel is *nice / OK*.

UNIT 3b, Exercise 9, page 37

Student B

1 Look at photo A. Ask your partner questions about the photo with *who, where, what,* and *how old*.

A

2 Look at the information about photo B. Answer your partner's questions about this photo.

John
Anna
in Alaska, US
the officiant (person marrying the couple)
John's 28 and Anna's 27

B

UNIT 8c, Exercise 9, page 98: answers

Are you a "morning person" or an "evening person"?

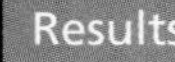

Results

Mostly A: You are a morning person. Evening activities are hard for you. Office jobs are good for you.

Mostly B: You are an evening person. Morning activities are difficult for you. Good jobs for you are jobs in hospitals, the arts, and the media.

Mostly C: You are not a morning person or an evening person. Most people are this way.

UNIT 4b, Exercise 10, page 49

Student B

1 Look at photo A. Use the questions on page 49 to ask your partner about this tower.

A

2 Look at the information about photo B. Answer your partner's questions about this tower.

B

- The Minaret of the Samarra Mosque
- It's in Samarra in Iraq.
- It's not open to tourists at the moment.
- The spiral shape is famous. Samarra is a UNESCO World Heritage Site.

UNIT 5c, Exercise 7, page 62

Student B

1 Listen to your partner. Make notes (1–5) about this microwave oven.

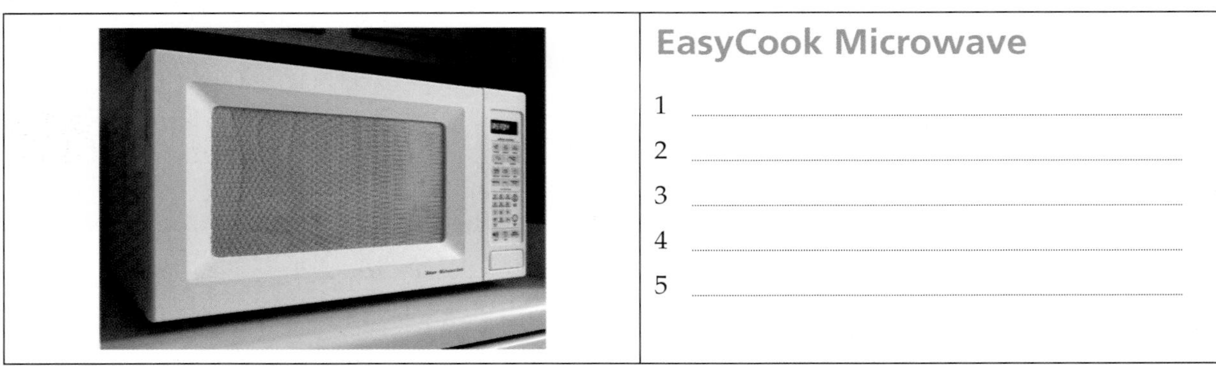

EasyCook Microwave

1 ....

2 ....

3 ....

4 ....

5 ....

2 Tell your partner about this microwave oven. Use *can* and *has*.

shopping_online.com

ProfessionalChef Microwave

Product features:

memory (100 options) ✓
10 power options ✓
cook and heat food ✓
make cakes ✓
buy online ✓

3 Look at the two microwave ovens. Do you think they are cheap or expensive?

UNIT 6c, Exercise 9, page 74

Student B

1 Look at the information about the New York Marathon and the Masters. Answer your partner's questions.

	1	2 the New York Marathon	3	4 the Masters
1 Where?	....	New York	....	Georgia, USA
2 When?	....	November	....	April
3 What kind of event?	....	a race	....	a competition
4 Prize?	....	money	....	money, a green jacket
5 Sport?	....	running	....	golf

2 Look at the photos and the information about sports events 2 and 4. Ask your partner five questions about events 1 and 3. Complete the information. You get 5 points if you identify the event after one question, 4 points if you ask two questions, etc.

UNIT 8c, Exercise 9, page 98

Student B

Write the questions (4–6) and choose your answers.

Then ask your partner the questions. Write your partner's answers and check the results on page 157.

Quiz:

Are you a "morning person" or an "evening person"?

4: What time / you / get up on the weekend?

a early **b** late **c** the same time as usual

5: What / the main meal of the day for you?

a lunch **b** dinner **c** it depends

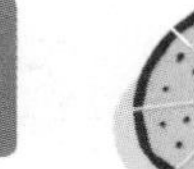

6: you / fall asleep in front of the TV at night?

a yes **b** no **c** sometimes

UNIT 9b, Exercise 11, page 109

Student B

1 Look at these two rooms. Student A has one of these rooms. Ask questions to find out which one. Use *Is there a . . . ?* and *Are there any . . . ?*

2 Look at this room. Answer Student A's questions.

UNIT 10c, Exercise 9, page 122

Pair B

1 Look at the notes. Tell Pair A about these two people. Don't say the names.

Date of birth	July 24, 1783
Place of birth	Caracas, South America
Biographical information	married to a Spanish woman: Maria Teresa leader of four countries: Colombia, Venezuela, Ecuador, and Bolivia first president of Venezuela
Name	Simón Bolívar

Date of birth	February 22, 1732
Place of birth	Virginia, North America
Biographical information	leader, the American army, War of Independence first president, US
Name	George Washington

2 Listen to Pair A. Who are the people?

UNIT 12d, Exercise 6, page 148

Student B

1 You are a group of two adults and three children. You are American and one of the children is German. Visit the Great Explorers Exhibition at a museum. Ask Student A questions to find out about tickets, brochures, and the audio program.

Great Explorers Exhibition

Tickets: adults $__________ ; children $__________

Brochures: $__________

Audio program: English, __________ ,

__________ , Spanish

2 You work in the ticket office of a bus company. Look at this information and answer Student A's questions.

Buses to Bambridge Castle

Every hour 9:15 – 6:15

Tickets: one-way $4.25; round-trip $7.00

Round-trip ticket + admission to castle $8.50

UNIT 1

a/an (articles)

a + single noun with consonants: *b, c, d, f,* etc.
***a** driver, **a** filmmaker*
an + single noun with vowels: *a, e, i, o, u*
***an** artist, **an** engineer*

Practice

1 Complete the sentences with ***a*** or ***an***.

1 I'm ________ scientist.
2 I'm ________ writer.
3 I'm ________ explorer.
4 I'm ________ artist.
5 I'm ________ photographer.

I + *am*, *you* + *are*

I	**am ('m)**	John.
You	**are ('re)**	a student.

Practice

2 Complete the sentences with ***I'm*** or ***You're***.

1 ALEX: ________ Alex.
MIREYA: Hi, Alex.
2 ROBERT: ________ Mattias Klum.
MATTIAS: Yes, I am.
3 CAROLYN: Hi!
ALEX: ________ Carolyn.
4 MIREYA: Hello.
ROBERT: Hi! ________ Robert Ballard.
5 ALEX: I'm a photographer.
ROBERT: ________ Alex Treadway.

he/she/it + *is*

He	**is ('s)**	Brazilian
She	**is ('s)**	from Japan.
It	**is ('s)**	in Italy.

Practice

3 Write sentences with ***He's, She's,*** and ***It's***.

1 Dechen (f) / from Ladakh
2 Manu (m)/ Nepalese
3 Dechen / Indian
4 Jagat / in Nepal
5 Manu / from Jagat

I + *am*, *you* + *are*, *he/she/it* + *is* (*be*)

I	**am ('m)**	John.
You	**are ('re)**	a student.
He	**is ('s)**	Brazilian.
She	**is ('s)**	from Japan.
It	**is ('s)**	in Italy.

Practice

4 Complete the sentences with ***am, are,*** and ***is***.

1 Hi! I ________ Elena.
2 Paul ________ an engineer.
3 He ________ from Hong Kong.
4 It ________ in China.
5 You ________ English.

my, your

I'm Jared. **My** name's Jared.
You're Maria. **Your** name's Maria.

Practice

5 Complete the sentences with ***my*** and ***your***.

1 ________ name's Lisa. I'm from Peru.
2 Hello! You're my teacher. ________ name's Mr. Jones. I'm Tomas.
3 Hello! ________ name's Paolo.
4 Hi. I'm Juan. What's ________ name?
5 ________ cell number is 695-836-7362.
6 John, what's ________ home number?

UNIT 2

we/they + *are*

We **They**	**are ('re)** **are ('re)**	in Canada. from Brazil. Italian.

Practice

1 Complete the sentences.

1 This is Jack. This is Bill. ________ are Canadian.
2 France and Spain ________ in Europe.
3 Bruno and Paola are from Italy. ________ Italian.
4 I'm with my teacher. ________'re in a classroom.
5 Jane and Barry are American. ________'re from the United States.

be

I	**am ('m)**	
You	**are ('re)**	
He **She** **It**	**is ('s)**	in Canada. from Brazil. Italian.
We **You** **They**	**are ('re)**	

Practice

2 Choose the correct option.

1 My name is Carlos and I *am / is / are* a student.
2 Toshiba *am / is / are* Japanese.
3 You *am / is / are* a student.
4 My teacher *am / is / are* from Chicago.
5 I'm with my friend. We *am / is / are* in China.

be negative forms

I You	**am not ('m not)** **are not (aren't)**	a teacher. from Europe. in China.
He She It	**is not (isn't)**	
We You They	**are not (aren't)**	from Europe. in China.

Practice

3 Rewrite the sentences with the verb in the negative form.

1 Jack's a student.
2 We are Spanish.
3 I'm happy.
4 Susana and Gina are from Peru.
5 You're a writer.

be questions and short answers

Am I **Are** you **Is** she/he/it **Are** we/you/they	in a hotel? nice? from Peru?	Yes, I **am**. No, **I'm not**. Yes, she/he/it **is**. No, she/he/it **isn't**. Yes, we/you/they **are**. No, we/you/they **aren't**.

Practice

4 Write questions with the correct form of ***be***. Then answer each question with ***yes*** and ***no***.

1 Simona / from Bolivia?
2 John / a teacher?
3 you / on vacation?
4 your hotel / nice?
5 Susana and Gina / in Paris?

plural nouns

Add *-s*.
a friend → *friends*

Change *-y* to *-ies*.
a city → *cities*

Add *-es* to nouns that end in *-s*, *-ch*, and *-ss*.
a bus → *buses*

Practice

5 Write the plural of these nouns.

1 a lake	4 an airport	7 a mountain
2 a country	5 a beach	8 a tent
3 a car	6 a photo	9 a student

UNIT 3

possessive *'s*

Alexandra is Philippe's daughter.
Simone and Jacques are Alexandra's grandparents.

Note: The possessive *'s* is not a contraction of *is*.
Who's Fabien? = Who is Fabien?
He's my brother. = He is my brother.
He's Jean-Michel's son. = He is Jean-Michel's son.

Practice

1 Look at the family tree. Write sentences.

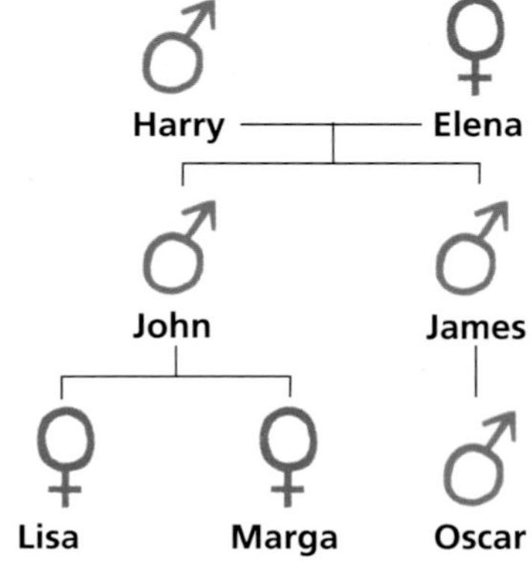

1 James / Oscar / father
2 John and James / Elena / sons
3 Lisa and Marga / Harry / granddaughters
4 Lisa / Marga / sister
5 Elena / Oscar / grandmother

his, her, our, their

This is	**my** **your** **his** **her** **our** **their**	friend.

Practice

2 Choose the correct option.

1 This is a photo of my brother at *her / his* wedding.
2 My wife is Russian. *Her / My* name is Olga.
3 We are happy. It's *his / our* daughter's wedding.
4 Hi, Zara. Is it *her / your* birthday today?
5 My parents are on vacation. It's *his / their* wedding anniversary.

irregular plural nouns

a child → ***children***
a man → ***men***
a woman → ***women***
a person → ***people***

Remember: Add *-s* or *-es* and change *-y* to *-ies* to make regular plural nouns.

Practice

3 Complete the singular and plural nouns.

1 How old are the wom________ in the photo?
2 Who are the pe________ at the wedding?
3 This chil________ is three years old.
4 Who is the pe________ in this photo?
5 James and Eliza are my chil________ .

UNIT 4

prepositions of place

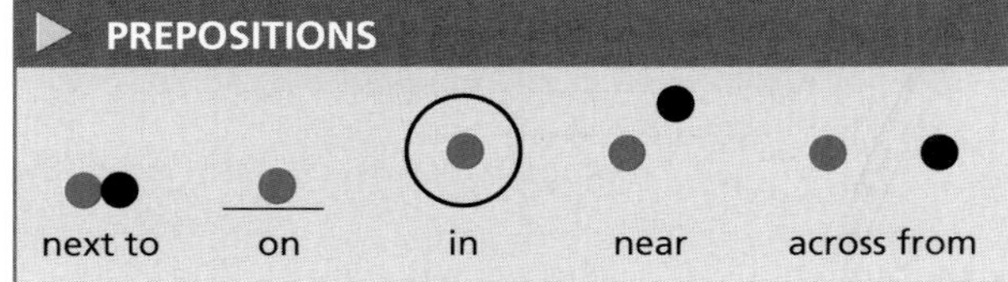

The museum is ***next to*** *the market.*
The market is ***in*** *a building.*
The movie theater is ***near*** *the bank.*
The café is ***across from*** *the bus station.*

Practice

1 Look at the picture. Complete the sentences.

1 The bank is ________ the hotel.
2 The bank is ________ the Tourist Information Center.
3 Two people are ________ the park.
4 The parking lot is ________ the hotel.
5 The Science Museum is ________ the parking lot.
6 Three people are ________ the movie theater.

this, that

This book is in Portuguese.
That's Big Ben!

Use *this* for things that are near you but *that* for things that aren't near you.

Practice

2 Look at the picture in Exercise 1. Read the words of the people in the park. Choose the correct option.

1 "*This / That* park is nice."
2 "*This / That* is my bank."
3 "Is *this / that* your book?"

question words

What*'s that?*
Where*'s the bank?*
When*'s the park open?*
Why*'s the Statue of Liberty famous?*
Who*'s this?*
How old *is he?*

Practice

3 Match the questions (1–5) with the answers (a–e).

1 Where's O'Hare airport?
2 What's your address?
3 How old is your brother?
4 Who's that in the park?
5 When are banks open in your country?

a From Monday to Friday.
b It's in Chicago.
c It's 36 Oxford Street.
d My sister and her children.
e He's 27.

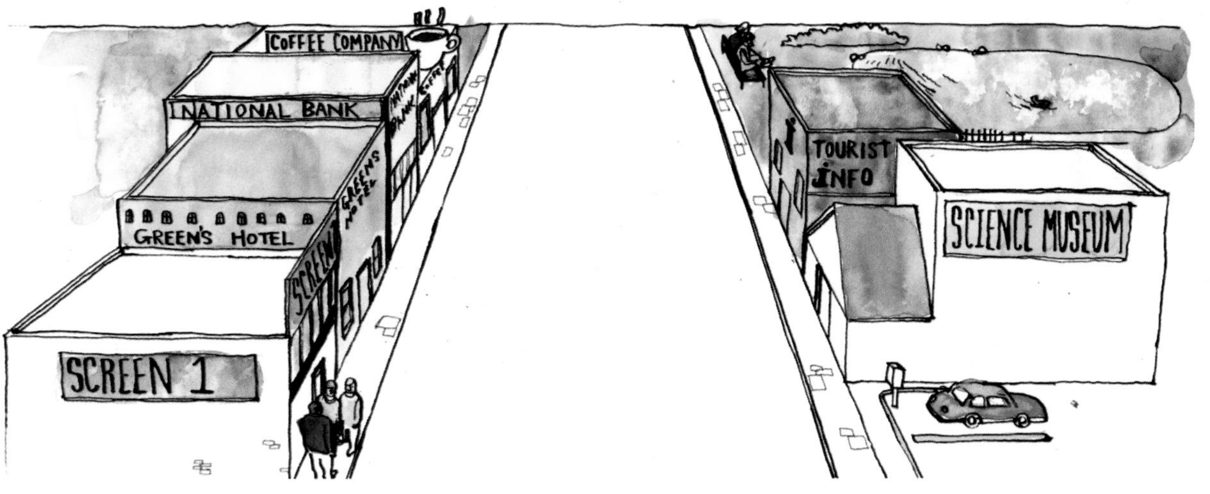

UNIT 5

can/can't

Affirmative		Negative	
I/You He/She/It We/You/They	**can** cook.	I/You He/She/It We/You/They	**can't** cook.

can't = cannot

Practice

1 Choose the correct option.

1 Babies *can / can't* run.
2 Children *can / can't* see.
3 Cars *can / can't* fly.
4 Animals *can / can't* speak.

can questions and short answers

Questions			Short answers		
Can	I/you he/she/it we/you/they	cook?	Yes, No,	I/you he/she/it we/you/they	**can.** **can't.**

Practice

2 Write questions and answers.

1 he / sing ✓
2 you / drive a car ✓
3 they / play table tennis ✗
4 she / cook ✗
5 we / speak English ✓

have/has

I/You We/You/They	**have**	a cell phone. batteries.
He/She/It	**has**	

Practice

3 Complete the sentences with *have* and *has*.

1 I .... two cameras.
2 My laptop .... a webcam.
3 My friends .... three children.
4 My sister .... a great job.

adjective + noun

*My **headphones** are **new**.*
*I have **new headphones**.*
Note: Adjectives have only one form: *I have ~~news~~ headphones.*
The word order is adjective + noun, NOT noun + adjective: *I have ~~headphones new~~.*

Practice

4 Put the words in order to make sentences.

1 is / camera / this / Japanese / a
2 fantastic / phone / my / a / memory / has
3 MP3 player / you / great / a / have
4 is / Jack's / man / an / grandfather / old

very, really

$600	This camera is It's	expensive. great/fantastic.	
$2,000	This camera is	**really** **very**	expensive.
	It's	**really** ~~very~~	great/fantastic.

Practice

5 Rewrite the sentences with ***very*** or ***really*** where possible.

1 This laptop is light. (really)
2 Their house is big. (very)
3 My friend's new phone is fantastic. (really)
4 That microwave is great. (very)
5 We have an old car. (really)

UNIT 6

like

Affirmative
I/You/We/You/They **like** fruit.
Negative
I/You/We/You/They **don't like** vegetables. (don't = do not)

Practice

1 Write sentences with the correct form of ***like***.

1 I / basketball ☹
2 We / tennis ☺
3 I / coffee ☺
4 They / cake ☹

like questions and short answers

Questions				Short answers
Do	I you we you they	**like**	pizza?	Yes, I/you/we/you/they **do**. No, I/you/we/you/they **don't**.

Note:
"Do you like pizza?" "Yes, I do." NOT *"Yes, I ~~like~~."*

Practice

2 Write questions with the words. Then answer the questions.

1 cheese / they ✓
2 fruit / you ✗
3 fish / they ✓
4 rice / they ✗

he/she + like

Affirmative		Negative	
He She	**likes** books.	He She	**doesn't like** music.
		(doesn't = does not)	

Questions			Short answers
Does	he she	**like** fish?	Yes, he/she **does**. No, he/she **doesn't**.

Practice

3 Three of these sentences are missing ***does*** or ***doesn't***. Rewrite them with the missing word.

1 Zeb likes Arizona.
2 Joanna like action movies.
3 your teacher like music?
4 Ryan like swimming.

object pronouns

Diana likes	**me.** **you.** **him.** **her.** **it.** **us.** **you.** **them.**

Practice

4 Look at the underlined nouns. Complete the sentences with an object pronoun.

1 I like <u>birds</u>, but my friend doesn't like ....
2 <u>We</u> can't see you. Can you see .... ?
3 <u>She</u>'s a popular writer, but I don't like ....
4 Do you like <u>pop music</u>? Yes, I love ....
5 <u>Matt Damon</u> is fantastic in the *Bourne* movies. I love ....

UNIT 7

simple present *I/you/we/you/they*

Affirmative			Negative		
I You We You They	**speak**	Sami.	I You We You They	**don't speak**	Sami.
			(don't = do not)		

Practice

1 Rewrite the sentences using the form in parentheses.

1 I live near a beach. (negative)
2 You don't have a car. (affirmative)
3 My friends speak English. (negative)
4 We study during the holidays. (negative)

simple present questions *I/you/we/you/they*

Questions				Short answers
Do	I you we you they	**live**	in Sweden?	Yes, I/you/we/you/they **do**. No, I/you/we/you/they **don't**.

Practice

2 Write questions with the words. Then write the answers.

1 in Egypt (you / live) ✓
2 to college (they / go) ✗
3 Spanish (I / study) ✓
4 friends in this class (we / have) ✓
5 at this school (you / teach) ✗

simple present with question words

What **Where** **Who** **Why** **When**	**do**	I/you/we/you/they/people	**do?** **go?** **meet?**

Practice

3 Read the questions and answers. Complete the questions with a question word.

1 "............ do you do?"
"I work in a school."
2 "............ do you go on vacation?"
"In the summer."
3 "............ do you do on summer vacation?"
"I play golf."
4 "............ do you play golf with?"
"I play golf with my brothers."
5 "............ do your brothers live?"
"They live near me."
6 "............ do you play golf?"
"I like it."

UNIT 8

simple present *he/she/it*

Affirmative		Negative	
He/She/It	**gets up** at 7:30	He/She/It	**doesn't work.**
		(doesn't = does not)	

Add *-s*.
get up → *gets up*

Add *-es* to verbs that end in *-ch* and *-sh*.
teach → *teaches, finish* → *finishes*

The verbs *go, do,* and *have* are irregular.
go → *goes, do* → *does, have* → *has*

Practice

1 Write the correct form of the verb in parentheses.

1 Kristen ______ (not / go) to work during the day.
2 She ______ (work) in the evening.
3 She ______ (not / work) in a school.
4 She ______ (teach) adults at a college.
5 She ______ (start) work at 5:30 and she ______ (not / finish) until ten o'clock.

prepositions of time

at + time	**at** 6:30
on + day	**on** Tuesday/Tuesdays
in (the) + part of day, month, season	**in** the morning, **in** July, **in** the summer

Note: *at night*

Practice

2 Complete the text with the correct preposition.

Alan works in the city. He gets home [1] ______ seven o'clock [2] ______ the evening. He has dinner [3] ______ 8:30 and [4] ______ winter he watches TV. He goes out for dinner [5] ______ Fridays. He can go to bed late because he doesn't work [6] ______ Saturdays.

frequency adverbs

100%
*I **always** have breakfast.*
*We **usually** get up early.*
*My friend **often** works late.*
*I **sometimes** travel for my job.*
*My friend **never** writes emails.*
0%

Note: The word order is adverb + verb, except with *be*: *I am never late*, NOT *I ~~never am~~ late.*

Practice

3 Put the words in order to make sentences.

1 in the morning / coffee / have / usually / I
2 travels / colleague / my / for her job / often
3 homework / never / our / gives / teacher / us
4 always / I / at night / read
5 studies / my / at home / friend / sometimes

simple present questions *he/she*

Questions			Short answers
Does	he she	**teach?**	Yes, he/she **does.** No, he/she **doesn't.**

Questions with question words
What does he/she **do**?
Where does he/she **go** in the summer?

Practice

4 Read the sentence. Then write a question with the words in parentheses.

1 Carl doesn't have breakfast at 7:30. (8:30 ?)
2 Anna doesn't finish work at 6:30. (what time ?)
3 Julia doesn't go to bed late. (early ?)
4 Michael doesn't work in an office. (where ?)
5 My brother doesn't read novels. (what ?)

How ... ?

***How** does he take photos?*
***How many** people do you work with?*
***How often** does your friend call you?*
***How old** is that tiger?*
***How much** is this book?*

Practice

5 Read the sentence. Then write a question with the words in parentheses and an expression with *How ...* .

1 I have 200 friends on Facebook. (you ?)
2 I'm 23. (you ?)
3 This camera is $99. (that camera ?)
4 I call my sister every day. (your sister ?)
5 I take videos with my phone. (you ?)

UNIT 9

there is/are

Singular	Plural
There's a book in my bag. (**There is**)	**There are** some books in my bag.

Practice

1 What's in my suitcase? Write sentences.

1 a map ✓
2 clothes ✓
3 a camera ✓
4 a pair of sandals ✓

there is/are negative and question forms

Negative singular	Negative plural
There isn't a bus. (**There is not**)	**There aren't** any hotels. (**There are not**)
Questions and short answers singular	**Questions and short answers plural**
Is there a sofa? Yes, **there is.** No, **there isn't.**	**Are there** any trains today? Yes, **there are.** No, **there aren't.**

Practice

2 What's in my suitcase? Write questions. Then answer them.

1 a hat ✗
2 a passport ✓
3 pairs of shoes ✓
4 tickets ✗

imperative forms

***Book** the hotel online.*
***Don't travel** by bus.*
(don't = do not)

Practice

3 Read the instructions from a travel guide for some tourists. Choose the best option.

1 *Don't forget / Forget* your passports.
2 *Don't arrive / Arrive* at the airport on time.
3 *Don't be / Be* late.
4 *Don't wait / Wait* a moment, please.

UNIT 10

was/were

Affirmative
I/He/She/It **was** Korean.
You/We/You/They **were** Korean.

Practice

1 Complete the paragraph with ***was*** or ***were***.

Sally Ride [1] .... the first American woman in space. She [2] .... born in 1951. Her first space flight [3] .... in 1983. She [4] .... the writer of five books for children. They [5] .... about space and science.

was/were negative and question forms

Negative
I/He/She/It **wasn't** famous.
You/We/You/They **weren't** famous.
(wasn't = was not, weren't = were not)

Questions			Short answers
Was	I he she it	happy at school?	Yes, I/he/she/it **was**. No, I/he/she/it **wasn't**.
Were	you we you they		Yes, you/we/you/they **were**. No, you/we/you/they **weren't**.

Practice

2 Complete the sentences with ***was, wasn't, were,*** and ***weren't***.

1 " .... Neil Armstrong the first man in space?"
"No, he ...."
2 My parents are from Hong Kong. They .... born in Europe.
3 " .... you born in 1986?"
"Yes, I ...."
4 " .... the first televisions in color?"
"No, they ...."
5 I .... very good at music in school and I can't play a musical instrument.

UNIT 11

irregular simple past verbs

Affirmative	
I/You/He/She/It/We/You/They	**went** to the Alps. **had** a good vacation.

do → did; find → found; go → went; have → had; leave → left; make → made; see → saw; take → took

Practice

1 Complete the sentences with the simple past form of the verb.

1 We .... (take) a lot of photos.
2 The tourists .... (go) for a walk.
3 I .... (have) lunch at home yesterday.
4 We .... (see) a great movie last week.
5 I .... (make) dinner last night.
6 My father .... (leave) for work.

regular simple past verbs

Affirmative
I/You/He/She/It/We/You/They **walked** in the mountains.

Add *-ed* or *-d*.
*start → start**ed**, live → live**d***

Change *-y* to *-ied*.
*study → stud**ied***

Practice

2 Complete the sentences with the simple past form of the verbs in parentheses.

Last weekend we [1] .... (go) for a walk in the mountains. We [2] .... (start) early in the morning. We [3] .... (walk) for two hours. Then we [4] .... (have) a snack. We [5] .... (find) a bag on the walk. We [6] .... (take) the bag to the police station. They [7] .... (find) a lot of money in the bag.

simple past negative and question forms

Negative
I/You/He/She/It/We/You/They **didn't take** a vacation last year.
Questions
Did I/you/he/she/it/we/you/they **drive**?
Short answers
Yes, I/you/he/she/it/we/you/they **did**. No, I/you/he/she/it/we/you/they **didn't**. (didn't = did not)

Note: In the negative and in question forms, we use the simple past of *do* (*did*) + verb (*go*, *drive*, etc.), NOT *They didn't ~~took~~ a vacation last year.*
Did they ~~took~~ a vacation last year?

Practice

3 Complete the interview with an explorer.

Q: [1] .... (you / travel) a lot last year?
A: Yes, I [2] .... I went to 17 countries.
Q: Wow! [3] .... (you / go) to South America?
A: Yes, we did. We went to Ecuador, Peru, and Chile.
Q: [4] .... (you / write) a blog about your trip?
A: No, I [5] .... , but I made a website.

simple past with question words

Questions with question words			
What **Who** **Where** **When** **Why**	**did**	I/you/he/she/it/we/you/they	**see?** **go?**

Practice

4 Write questions for these answers. Use a question word and the correct form of the underlined verb.

1 We <u>met</u> lots of interesting people.
2 They <u>went</u> to Cancun in Mexico.
3 She <u>saw</u> some beautiful buildings.
4 We <u>arrived</u> at the hotel at night.
5 I <u>went</u> there because I like the food.

UNIT 12

present continuous

Affirmative / Negative		
I He/She/It You/We/You/They	**am / 'm not** **is / isn't** **are / aren't**	**cooking.** **eating.** **reading.**

We use the present continuous for activities in progress at the time of speaking.

Practice

1 Complete the sentences with the present continuous of the verb in parentheses.

1 The teacher .... (talk).
2 Javier and Cheng .... (not write).
3 I .... (listen).
4 Juan and Paolo .... (read).
5 Tomas .... (not watch) a video.

Questions			Short answers		
Am	I		Yes,	I he/she/it you/we/you/they	**am.** **is.** **are.**
Is	he/she/it	**cooking?**			
Are	you/we/you/they		No,	I he/she/it you/we/you/they	**'m not.** **isn't.** **aren't.**

Practice

2 Write questions with these words. Use the information in Exercise 1 to answer the questions.
1 Tomas / watch a video
2 I / listen
3 Javier and Cheng / write
4 the teacher / talk
5 Juan and Paolo / read

present continuous with future time expressions

I'm meeting my friends	**tomorrow.** **on Saturday (morning).** **this/next weekend.** **on June 8.**

We use the present continuous + future time expressions for future plans.

Practice

3 Read each sentence. Does it refer to now (N) or the future (F)?

1 I'm playing tennis on Sunday.
2 We aren't watching this TV show.
3 My friends are coming this weekend.
4 Is your family having a party tonight?
5 What are you doing in June?
6 My sister is staying with us.

Unit 1

1

Hi! I'm Mike.

2

M: Hi. I'm Mattias. I'm a filmmaker.
C: Hi. I'm Carolyn. I'm a writer.
R: Hello. I'm Robert. I'm an explorer.
M: Hi. I'm Mireya. I'm a scientist.
A: Hello. I'm Alex. I'm a photographer.

3

explorer filmmaker
photographer scientist
writer

4

A: Hello.
C: Hi.
A: I'm Alex Treadway.
C: Oh, you're a photographer!
A: Yes.

5

Y: Hi.
M: Hello. I'm Mattias Klum.
Y: Oh, you're a filmmaker!
M: Yes, for National Geographic.

6

a b c d e f g h i j k l m n o p q r s t
u v w x y z

7

1 **P:** I'm Paola.
Q: Can you spell that?
P: Yes. P–A–O–L–A.

2 **B:** I'm Bryan.
Q: Can you spell that?
B: Yes. B–R–Y–A–N.

3 **S:** I'm Sean.
Q: Can you spell that?
S: Yes. S–E–A–N.

4 **A:** I'm Ana.
Q: Can you spell that?
A: Yes. A–N–A.

8

Brazil Brazilian
Canada Canadian
China Chinese
Egypt Egyptian
France French
Germany German
Great Britain British
Italy Italian
Japan Japanese
Mexico Mexican
Oman Omani
Spain Spanish
the United States American

9

zero one
two three
four five
six seven
eight nine
ten

10

A: What's your phone number?
B: My cell phone number is 619 408 7132.
A: 6–1–9 4–0–8 7–1–3–2. OK! And what's your work number?
B: It's 661 467 9285.
A: 6–6–1 …
B: … 4–6–7 9–2–8–5.
A: Great. Thanks.

11

R: Good morning. What's your name, please?
L: Hi. My name's Schultz.
R: Can you spell that?
L: Yes. S–C–H–U–L–T–Z: Schultz.
R: What's your first name?
L: Liam: L–I–A–M.
R: Thank you. What's your job?
L: I'm a photographer. I'm from *Today* magazine.
R: OK. Sign here, please.
L: OK. Thanks. Bye.
R: Goodbye.

12

R: What's your name, please?
R: What's your first name?
R: What's your job?

13

Y: Hi, Katya. How are you?
K: Fine, thanks. And you?
Y: I'm OK. This is Silvia. She's from Madrid.
K: Nice to meet you, Silvia.
S: Nice to meet you too.

Unit 2

14

the ocean
an island
a beach
a mountain
a city
a lake

15

We're in Egypt.
We're from India.
We're happy.
They're on vacation.
They're Australian.
They're French.

16

1 We aren't in Tunisia.
2 It isn't a beach.
3 Brad isn't on the camel trek.
4 I'm not in this photo.

17

a It's twelve degrees in London today.
b Phew! It's cold! It's thirty-five degrees today.
c It isn't hot. It's eighteen degrees.
d It's twenty-seven degrees here.
e Wow! It's eighty degrees in Sydney today.
f It's nice out. It's sixty-five degrees.

18

G: Hi! Where are you now? Are you in France?
L: Yes, I am. I'm in the Alps. It's beautiful!
G: Are you OK?
L: No, I'm not. It's two degrees!
G: Wow! Is it cold in your hotel?
L: No, it isn't. The hotel is nice.
G: It's eighty-six degrees in Sydney today.
L: Oh! That's hot!
G: Are Kara and Ona in France?
L: No, they aren't. They're on a beach in Morocco!

19

1 **Q:** Are you OK?
A: Yes, I am.

2 **Q:** Is Kara in France?
A: No, she isn't.

3 **Q:** Are you and Paul in Sydney?
A: Yes, we are.

4 **Q:** Is Greg in London?
A: No, he isn't.

5 **Q:** Are Kara and Ona in Morocco?
A: Yes, they are.

6 **Q:** Is your hotel nice?
A: Yes, it is.

20

lakes airports
cars countries
beaches buses

21

cities doctors
friends hotels
mountains offices
phones students
tents

22

A: Good evening.
S: Good evening. My name's Sato. This is my ID.
A: Thank you. Where are you from, Mr. Sato?
S: I'm from Tokyo.
A: Ah! Is this your address?
S: Yes, it is.
A: What's the zip code?
S: It's 170–3293.
A: OK. Are you on vacation here?
S: No, I'm not. I'm on business.
A: What's your telephone number in the US?
S: It's 718 157 0963.
A: Thanks. Is this your email address?
S: Yes, it is: e p sato at hotmail dot com.
A: OK. Sign here, please. Here are your keys.
S: Thanks. What's the license plate number?
A: It's with your keys—BD6 ATR.
S: Thanks.

23

vacation address
car email
key number
telephone

Unit 3

 **24**

Danvir and Mohan are brothers. Ravi and Danvir are father and son. Ravi and Mohan are father and son.

 **25**

Alexandra Cousteau is part of a famous family. She's Jacques Cousteau's granddaughter. Jean-Michel Cousteau is Jacques Cousteau's son. He's a filmmaker. Jean-Michel's children are Fabien and Celine. Fabien's a marine explorer. Celine's an explorer. Jean-Michel's brother Philippe is dead. Philippe's children are Alexandra and Philippe Jr. Alexandra's an environmentalist. Her brother is an environmentalist too. And Alexandra's grandmother Simone was the first woman scuba diver.

26

1 Simone is Philippe's mother.
2 Celine is Jean-Michel's daughter.
3 Alexandra is Jacques's granddaughter.
4 Simone is Fabien's grandmother.

27

1 They're at a wedding.
2 He's at a meeting.

28

A: Congratulations!
B: Thank you. We're very happy.
A: Ah, she's lovely. What's her name?
B: It's Juba.
A: Hello, Juba.

29

1 **A:** Emma and I are engaged.
B: Wow! Congratulations!
A: Thanks very much.
B: I'm very happy for you. When's the wedding?
A: We're not sure … maybe in August.

2 **C:** Hello!
D: Hello, come in.
C: Happy anniversary!
D: Oh, thanks!
C: How long is it?
D: Twenty-five.
C: Wow! Twenty-five years.

3 **E:** Happy birthday, Freya!
F: Thank you.
E: How old are you? Nineteen or twenty?
F: Actually, I'm twenty-one.
E: Oh, great!

30

Congratulations!

Happy anniversary!

Happy birthday!

Unit 4

 **31**

Shanghai is a city in China. Shanghai is big, but it isn't the capital city—Beijing is the capital of China. Shanghai is a rich city. A lot of the buildings in Shanghai are new. The Pearl TV tower is in Shanghai. It's famous in China. Tourists from around the world visit Shanghai. They visit the river and the Pearl TV tower.

32

1 **A:** Excuse me?
B: Yes?
A: Where's the train station?
B: It's on Exeter Street.
A: Is it near here?
B: Yes, it is.
A: OK. Thanks.

2 **C:** Excuse me?
D: Yes?
C: Is the information center near here?
D: Yes, it is. It's near the park.
C: OK. Thanks.

3 **E:** Excuse me?
F: Yes?
E: Is the parking lot on this street?
F: No, it isn't. This is Exeter Street. The parking lot's on Milk Street. It's next to the park.
E: Thank you very much.

4 **G:** Excuse me?
H: Yes?
G: Where's the bank?
H: I'm not sure. Oh! It's across from the market.
G: Is it near here?
H: Yes, it is.
G: OK. Thanks.

33

T: Hi.
A: Good morning.
T: Is this a map of the city?
A: No, it isn't. That's a map of the city.
T: OK. And where's Tokyo Tower?
A: It's near the Prince Park … here it is.
T: Oh yes. Is it open on Sunday?
A: Yes, it is.

34

1 **A:** Excuse me. Is that a map of Tokyo?
B: Yes, it is.

2 **A:** Is this a train schedule?
B: No, it's a bus schedule.

3 **A:** Is that guidebook in English?
B: Where?
A: The book next to you.
B: No, it isn't. It's in Spanish.

35

T: Are museums open on Monday?
A: Yes, they are. They're open every day of the week.
T: OK. Are stores open every day?
A: Yes, they are. They're open every day of the week too.
T: Are banks open on Sunday?
A: No, they aren't. They're open Monday to Friday in the morning and afternoon. And they're open on Saturday morning.

36

1 Q: What time is it?
A: It's five o'clock.

2 Q: What time is it?
A: It's one thirty.

3 Q: What time is it?
A: It's seven fifteen.

4 Q: What time is it?
A: It's nine forty-five.

5 Q: What time is it?
A: It's two twenty.

6 Q: What time is it?
A: It's six o'clock.

37

1 A: Hi. Can I help you?
C: Two coffees, please.
A: Large or small?
C: Small.
A: Anything else?
C: No, thanks.

2 A: Hi. Can I help you?
C: Can I have a bottle of water, please?
A: Anything else?
C: Yes. A salad.
A: OK. Four dollars, please.

3 A: Can I help you?
C: A tea and a fruit juice, please.
A: Anything else?
C: Yes. Two pastries, please.
A: OK. Here you are. Seven dollars, please.
C: Here you are.

38

1 Can I help you?
2 Can I have a water, please?

Unit 5

39

Look at this fantastic photo. It's not a toy or a robot—this is a man. His name's Yves Rossy—or Jetman—and he can fly. Rossy is from Switzerland. Here, Rossy is above the Swiss Alps. He's in the air for a short time—only five minutes. But it's fantastic!

40

1 Robots can speak.
2 Robots can carry things.
3 People can't fly.
4 I can speak English.
5 My grandfather can't run.

41

L: Hi. Welcome to "Technology Today." I'm Lewis Jones and this morning I'm in a university technology department. I'm here with Christine Black and Tomo, a Japanese robot. Hi, Christine.
C: Hi, Lewis.
L: Christine, tell me about this robot.
C: Well, Tomo is from Japan. She's from a new generation of robots. They can do things that people can do.
L: "She"? Or "it"?
C: Aha! We say "she." She's a robot.
L: OK. So, she's from Japan. Can she speak Japanese?
C: Oh yes, she can speak Japanese and English.
L: OK. Can she sing?
C: Yes, she can.
L: And can she play the piano?
C: Yes, she can.
L: Wow! I can't sing or play the piano. Can she swim?
C: Well, Tomo can't swim, but some robots can swim.
L: OK. Well, my last question is about the name. What does "Tomo" mean?
C: It means "intelligent" in Japanese.
L: OK, Christine, thanks very much.
C: Thanks!

42

a two dollars and thirty cents
b thirteen pounds fifty
c fifteen euros
d three euros seventy-five cents
e seventeen dollars eighty cents
f eighteen dollars

43

1 It's thirty dollars.
2 It's forty dollars.
3 It's fifteen dollars.
4 It's sixteen dollars.
5 It's seventy dollars.
6 It's eighteen dollars.

44

1 A: Can I help you?
C: How much is this alarm clock?
A: This is a clock radio. It's fifty dollars.
C: Hmm, that's a little expensive. Thanks.
A: That's OK. No problem.

2 A: Can I help you?
C: Yes, I'd like this video camera, please.
A: Certainly.
C: Is it HD?
A: Yes, it is. The image quality is fantastic.
C: Great.
A: OK, that's ninety-five dollars and fifty cents, please.
C: Here you go.

3 C: Excuse me.
A: Yes, can I help you?
C: How much are these flash drives?
A: They're five ninety-nine each.
C: Can I pay with euros?
A: Yes, of course.

Unit 6

45

These fans are passionate about soccer. Their team is the Kaizer Chiefs. Soccer and rugby are big sports in South Africa today. Soccer is an international sport—about 270 million people play soccer in more than 200 countries. The soccer World Cup is every four years. The World Cup prize is millions of dollars—$30 million for the World Cup in South Africa! Many international soccer players are millionaires. Soccer is a sport of passion and money!

46

I: Hi, Steve. Congratulations on your prize.
S: Thank you very much.
I: So, you are passionate about vegetables. But do you like fruit?
S: Yes, I do. I like fruit. I have a lot of fruit in my garden.
I: We know you don't like pumpkin pie. Do you like fruit pie?
S: No, I don't. But people in my family like fruit pie a lot.
I: So, giant vegetables are very important to you. But what about other food? What do you like?

47

I: Do you like fruit?
I: Do you like fruit pie?
I: Do you like meat?
I: Do you like pasta?
S: Oh well, I like salad.
I: Do you like meat?
S: No, I don't—but I like fish.
I: And pasta? Do you like pasta?
S: Yes, I do. I like spaghetti and I like macaroni too.
I: OK, thanks very much, Steve.
S: Thank you!

48

1 He likes fish.
2 He likes Botswana.
3 He doesn't like cold places.
4 He likes water.
5 He likes coffee.

49

1 A: Let's watch TV tonight.
B: That's a good idea. What's on?
A: A movie with Emily Blunt is on at eight o'clock.
B: Oh, I love her. She's fantastic.

2 C: Let's play ping-pong tomorrow.
D: No, thanks. I don't like ping-pong.
C: OK. How about soccer?
D: Sorry. Sports are boring.

3 E: Let's have spaghetti this weekend.
F: No, don't like pasta. It's horrible.
E: OK. How about pizza? Do you like pizza?
F: Yes, it's great.

50

She's fantastic.

Sports are boring.

It's horrible.

It's great.

Unit 7

51

The Holi festival—or festival of colors—is in March. It's a very happy festival. It's a celebration of spring and new life. People say "goodbye" to winter and "hello" to spring. In India, the winter months are December, January, and February. The Holi festival is one or two days. It's a big celebration in parts of India and in other parts of the world.

52

They don't understand traditional Sami life.

They don't live in France.

We don't study Sami.

I don't have a car.

53

I: Hello, Miriam. Nice to meet you.
M: Hello.
I: Do you work at Kakenya's school?
M: Yes, I do. I teach there. We have five teachers.
I: Do you like it?
M: Yes, I do.
I: Do boys study at the school?
M: No, they don't. The school is for girls.
I: Only girls?
M: Yes, only girls.
I: That's unusual!
M: Yes, it is.
I: Do the girls live with their families?
M: No, they don't. They live at the school.
I: OK. And do they go home in summer?
M: Yes, they do. They go home to their villages.
I: Do the girls learn English at the school?
M: Yes, they do. And in the summer we teach extra classes in English too.
I: OK. Thank you, Miriam.
M: Thank you.

54

I: Hi, Carl.
C: Hi.
I: Do you study at a college?
C: No, I don't. I'm at a university.
I: Do you have classes every day?
C: No, I don't. I have classes on Monday, Wednesday, Thursday, and Friday.
I: Do you like your classes?
C: Yes, I do.
I: Do you live near your university?
C: Yes, I do.
I: Do you live with your family?
C: No, I don't. I live in a dorm.
I: Do you go home for the summer?
C: Yes, I do. I go home for the summer and in December.

55

1 Do you study at a college?
2 Do you have classes every day?
3 Do you like your classes?
4 Do you live near your university?
5 Do you live with your family?
6 Do you go home for the summer?

56

1 I live in Canada. My favorite time of year is winter. It's cold and snowy.
2 I'm studying in South Africa. I like spring. It's sunny and it isn't cold.
3 I'm studying in Australia. Summer is the wet season. It's hot and rainy. I don't like it!
4 I live in Great Britain. In autumn here, it's cloudy. It's windy too, but I like it. We don't have a dry season!

57

1 Ooh, I'm cold.
2 I'm tired.
3 I'm thirsty.
4 Uff, I'm hot.
5 Ugh, I'm wet.
6 Oh, I'm bored.
7 Mmm, I'm hungry.

58

M: What's the matter?
F: It's cold and I'm thirsty.
M: Why don't you have a cup of coffee? Here you are.
F: Thanks.
M: Paul, are you OK?
P: No, I'm not. I don't feel well.
M: Why don't you eat a sandwich? Here.
P: No, thanks. I'm not hungry. I'm cold and I'm wet.
M: What's the matter, Anna?
A: I'm bored.
M: Why don't you go to the beach? Go swimming.
A: In the rain?!? Mom!
M: I don't understand you all. We're on vacation!

59

Why don't you have a cup of coffee?

I don't feel well.

I don't understand you all.

Unit 8

60

I: Do you like your job?
M: Yes, I love my job. I'm a farmer. I don't work in an office. I work outside. I work in Nevada, in the United States. Every day is different in my job.
I: What do you do?
M: We work with animals. Today farmers use modern technology. We have cell phones and computers. We don't use tractors—we use helicopters!

61

1 He works in Chile.
2 He starts work at nine o'clock.
3 He finishes work at 1:30.
4 He goes to bed at two o'clock.
5 He gets up at 8:45.

62

M: Who's Cynthia Liutkus-Pierce? Does she work at this university?
W: Yes, she does.
M: I don't know her. Does she teach languages?
W: No, she doesn't.
M: What does she do?
W: She's a geologist.
M: Oh, OK. Does she give lectures?
W: Yes, she does. And she works in Africa.
M: Oh, does she go to Africa every year?
W: Yes, she does. She goes in the summer.
M: I know some geologists in Africa. Where does Cynthia go?
W: I don't know. I think she goes to Tanzania.
M: Oh, my friends are in Angola.

63

1 **R:** Good morning, PJ International. Can I help you?
C: Yes, can I speak to Ed Carr, please?
R: I'm sorry. He's in a meeting.
C: OK, thank you. I'll call back later. Goodbye.
R: Goodbye.

2 **R:** Hello, Green Wildlife Park. Can I help you?
C: Good morning. Can I speak to Mr. Watts, please?
R: Yes, one moment, please.
C: Thank you.

3 **R:** Good morning, City College. Can I help you?
C: Yes, can I speak to Mrs. Jackson, please?
R: I'm sorry. She's out of the office at the moment.
C: OK, thank you. I'll call back later. Goodbye.
R: Goodbye.

64

1 **R:** Good morning, PJ International. Can I help you?
C: Yes, can I speak to Ed Carr, please?
R: I'm sorry. He's in a meeting.
C: OK, thank you. I'll call back later. Goodbye.
R: Goodbye.
3 **R:** Good morning, City College. Can I help you?
C: Yes, can I speak to Mrs. Jackson, please?
R: I'm sorry. She's out of the office at the moment.
C: OK, thank you. I'll call back later. Goodbye.
R: Goodbye.

65

please he's yes Fridays works thanks

Unit 9

66

1 I travel from Boston to New York for my job. I go every week. I usually go by train because I can work on the train.
2 I'm studying in Australia and I travel in the summer. I love Asia! I travel by bus. It's really interesting. You meet a lot of people.
3 I live in San Francisco. I don't like flying, so I never travel by plane. I don't really travel.
4 I'm from Barcelona, but my parents live in Mallorca. I visit them every summer. I usually go by boat.

67

There's a camera.

There's a laptop.

There are three scarves.

There are two shirts.

There's a pair of shoes.

There's a skirt.

There are some T-shirts.

68

S: OK, that's the flight. Let's look for a hotel now. Is it for two nights or three?
L: Three nights: Friday, Saturday, and Sunday. Are there any hotels near the airport?
S: Yes, there are. But they're expensive. Just a minute … no, there aren't any cheap hotels near the airport. They're all expensive. This one is four hundred dollars a night!
L: Wow! Well, what about a youth hostel? Is there a youth hostel near the airport?
S: OK, let's see. I don't think so … no, there isn't. I don't like youth hostels. They aren't very comfortable.
L: OK. Let's look downtown. Are there any cheap hotels there?
S: Yes, of course there are.
L: Well, that's good. And is there a bus to downtown?
S: A bus from the airport? Yes, there is. There's a bus every twenty minutes from the airport to downtown. There isn't a train, but that's OK.
L: And there are taxis, too.
S: I think the bus is fine. OK, let's look at these hotels.

69

1 TV
2 bathtub
3 bed
4 chair
5 table
6 lamp
7 desk
8 sofa
9 closet
10 armchair
11 shower
12 fridge

70

L: Wow, this room is really big! Oh, it's two rooms! The bed is in here, look!
S: It's fantastic!
L: I know. And it isn't really expensive …
S: Are you sure?
L: Yes. Oh, I like these lamps!
S: Yes, they're really unusual!
L: This sofa is very comfortable. And what's this? Oh, it's a fridge.
S: Are there any drinks in it? I'm really thirsty.
L: Yes, there are some bottles of water. Here.
S: Thanks.
S: Where's the TV?
L: I don't know. There isn't one.
S: What? There isn't a TV!

71

R: Good afternoon, sir. Can I help you?
G: Hello. Yes, I'd like a wake-up call at 7:30, please.
R: In the morning? Certainly, sir. What's your room number?
G: 327.
R: OK, 327 … wake-up call for 7:30.
G: And I'd like to have dinner in my room this evening.
R: Of course. There's a menu in your room. It's on the desk.
G: Oh, yes!
R: Call 101 for room service.
G: Fine. I'd like to use the Internet too.
R: No problem, sir. There's wi-fi in all the rooms.
G: Great. Oh, and is there a bank near the hotel?
R: Yes, there's one on this street. It's next to the movie theater.
G: OK, thanks a lot.

72

I'd like a wake-up call at 7:30, please.

I'd like breakfast in my room.

I'd like to use the Internet, too.

Unit 10

73

1950 color television
1963 video recorders
1973 cell phones
1975 digital cameras
1993 MP3 players
1995 digital television
2006 Blu-ray discs

74

1 She was born in 1939. She was in a team of Japanese mountaineers. They were all women.
2 He was born in 1480. He was Portuguese, but he was an explorer for the Spanish king Carlos I.
3 She was born in the United States on September 29, 1955. She was the leader of an expedition to the South Pole in 1993. The expedition was all women.
4 He was from Norway and he was born on July 16, 1872. His father was a sea captain.

75

He was born in 1480.

He was an explorer.

He was Portuguese.

They were explorers.

They were from Russia.

76

first, second, third, fourth, fifth, sixth, seventh, eighth, ninth, tenth, eleventh, twelfth, thirteenth, fourteenth, fifteenth, sixteenth, seventeenth, eighteenth, nineteenth, twentieth

77

twenty-first, twenty-second, twenty-third, twenty-fourth, twenty-fifth, twenty-sixth, twenty-seventh, twenty-eighth, twenty-ninth, thirtieth, thirty-first

78

I: Aneta, who was your hero when you were young?
A: When I was about ten years old, my hero was Michael Johnson. He was a great athlete.
I: Was he the Olympic champion?
A: Yes, he was. And he was the world champion eight times.
I: Were you good at sports at school?
A: Well … yes, I was. I was on the basketball team at school.
I: Joe, who was your hero when you were young?
J: When I was young, my hero was David Attenborough. He was on television. His shows about animals and nature were fantastic.
I: Was it his first job?
J: No, it wasn't. His first job was with books, but he wasn't happy in that job.
I: Which is your favorite David Attenborough show?
J: I think it's *Life on Earth*. But all his shows were really interesting.
I: That was in 1979 … were you born then?
J: No, I wasn't! But I have the DVD.
I: Clare, who was your hero when you were young?
C: My heroes weren't famous. They were my teachers at my school. The teachers were really nice and friendly. Mrs. Harvey was my art teacher. She was very funny. And she was married to my English teacher, Mr. Harvey.
I: Were they good teachers?
C: Yes, they were. They were fantastic.

79

1 Was he the Olympic champion? Yes, he was.
2 Was it his first job? No, it wasn't.
3 Were they good teachers? Yes, they were.

80

1 **T:** Hello!
S: Hi, I'm sorry I'm late. The bus was late.
T: That's OK. Take a seat.

2 **C:** Oh, hi Ravi.
R: Hi Clare.
C: Umm, the meeting was at 2:30. Where were you?
R: Oh, I'm sorry. I was very busy.
C: It's OK. It wasn't an important meeting.

3 **A:** Mmm, this coffee is good!
B: Yes, it is.
A: So, what about yesterday? We were at your house at ten o'clock. Where were you?
B: I'm very sorry. We weren't at home. We were at my sister's house!
A: It's OK. Don't worry.

81

1 I'm sorry I'm late.
2 The bus was late.
3 I was very busy.
4 We weren't at home.

Unit 11

82

Scientists discover hundreds of new plants and animals every year. A large number of these discoveries are in Indonesia. In fact, scientists in Papua New Guinea usually find about two new plants or animals every week. It's a fantastic place. There aren't many people in the area and it isn't easy to get there. Scientists sometimes arrive and leave by helicopter!

83

The scientists at the University of Innsbruck started their investigation. They took photos and they studied the body. They discovered the body was a man. They called him "Ötzi" because the body was in the Ötztal mountains in the Alps. The scientists finished their report. It was very interesting.

Ötzi was a small man. He was about 45 years old when he died. He was from the north of Italy and he lived about 5,000 years ago. The scientists think he walked to the mountains. The scientists think he died in spring. They also think an arrow killed him.

84

1 call called
2 die died
3 discover discovered
4 finish finished
5 kill killed
6 live lived
7 start started
8 study studied

85

I: Hi, Jamie.
J: Hello.
I: Did you watch Alastair's videos?
J: Well, I didn't see the first or second video, but I saw a video about swimming in the River Thames.
I: Did you like it?
J: Yes, I did. I liked it a lot. The next weekend, I didn't stay at home. I drove to a lake near my house and went swimming.
I: Was that an adventure?
J: Yes, because usually I go to the swimming pool. It was very different in the lake.
I: Did you make a video too?
J: Yes, my friend went with me. He filmed me on his phone and we sent the video to Alastair online.

86

1 Did you watch Alastair's videos?
2 Did you like it?
3 Did you make a video too?

87

1 **A:** Did you and Sonia have a good time in Sydney last week?
B: Yes, we did, thanks. But we didn't go swimming.
A: Oh? Why not?
B: There was a shark in the water!

2 **C:** Did you and Jack have a good vacation last year?
D: No, we didn't.
C: Oh? Why not?
D: Well, we stayed at home. We didn't have any money!

3 **E:** Did you and Alice have a nice dinner last night?
F: Yes, we did. It was delicious. And we didn't pay!
E: Oh? Why not?
F: My boss paid!

88

We didn't go swimming.

We didn't have any money.

We didn't pay!

Unit 12

89

The young women in this photo work in a factory from Monday to Saturday. But today is Sunday—it's the weekend. On Sunday, they usually meet and go out for the day. Most stores, museums, and movie theaters are open, so there are a lot of things to do. In different countries, the weekend is on different days. In some countries—for example, Oman—the weekend is Thursday and Friday. In Algeria, Egypt and Qatar, the weekend is Friday and Saturday. These Chinese factory workers have one day off, but office workers have Saturday off too. The Saturday and Sunday weekend is quite new in China—it started in 1995.

90

I: Ayu, tell us about these photos.
A: Well, this is my mother. She's in the kitchen. She's cooking.
I: What's she making?
A: She's making lunch. We have a big family lunch every Saturday.
I: And who's this?
A: That's my husband, Amir, in the bathroom. He's bathing our daughter.
I: How old is your daughter?
A: She's eighteen months old. And this is my father with his friend. They're talking and drinking coffee.
I: What are they sitting on?
A: They're sitting on the mats we use in Indonesia. And then this photo is Amir's brother with his son.
I: What are they doing? Are they reading?
A: No, they aren't. They're playing a game on Amir's computer. This is my sister. She's in the bedroom. She's ironing. I usually help her.
I: And what about this last one?
A: This is my brother. He's wearing shorts. He and his friend are washing their bikes. They do that every Saturday.
I: Which is your favorite photo?
A: Oh, I think it's the one of my husband and my daughter because they're both smiling and happy.

91

A: Hi Lauren, it's Alex.
L: Oh, hi! Where are you?
A: I'm on the bus. I'm going home from work. So, what are you doing this weekend?
L: Well, I'm going shopping tomorrow.
A: Of course. You always go shopping on Saturdays.
L: No, I don't! Anyway, Sports Gear is having a sale tomorrow.
A: Really?
L: Yes, they're selling all the winter sports stuff at half price.
A: Wow! And what about on Sunday?
L: I don't know. What are you doing?
A: Well, do you remember Helen Skelton? She went down the Amazon River last year.
L: Oh yes.
A: She's giving a talk about her trip on Sunday evening. I'm going with my brother. Would you like to come?
L: Where is it?
A: At the Natural Science Museum. Tickets are free.
L: OK! Why not?

92

I'm going home from work.

What are you doing this weekend?

I'm going shopping tomorrow.

What are you doing?

I'm going with my brother.

93

a **C:** Four tickets to the museum, please.
S: Four adults?
C: Oh sorry, no. Two adults and two children.
S: OK. That's ten dollars, please. Would you like a brochure for the Home Life exhibition?
C: Yes, please.
S: Would you like it in English? We have brochures in French, German, and Japanese, too.
C: Oh, French, please.
S: Here you are.
C: Thanks.

b **C:** Three round-trip tickets to Lindisfarne, please.
S: Are you coming back today?
C: Yes, we are. Is there a bus after six o'clock?
S: Yes, there is. There's a bus every hour. The last one is at nine o'clock.
C: OK.
S: Are you going to the castle and gardens? Would you like to buy the tickets now?
C: Oh, yes. Great.
S: It's a special weekend ticket. That's thirty-four dollars, please.
C: Here you are.
S: Thank you.

c **S:** Good morning.
C: Hi. It's busy today! Are there any free tennis courts?
S: Yes, there are. The people on court 4 are finishing now.
C: OK, great. A ticket for two people, please.
S: Would you like it for one hour or two hours?
C: Umm, just a minute … Ellen, do you want to play for one hour or two?
E: One is fine.
C: OK. So just one hour, please.
S: That's sixteen dollars.
C: Thanks.

94

Would you like a brochure for the Home Life exhibition?

Would you like it in English?

Would you like to buy the tickets now?

Inside Photo: 3 tl (DAVID DOUBILET/National Geographic Creative), 3 tc (Richard nowitz/National Geographic Creative, 3tc (XPACIFICA/National Geographic Creative), 3 tl (Melissa Farlow/National Geographic Creative), 3 cr (Michael S. Lewis/National Geographic Creative), 3 bl (Willard Culver/National Geographic Creative), 3 bc (TIM LAMAN/National Geographic Creative), 3 br (CARY WOLINSKY/National Geographic Creative), 8 tl (Mike Thesis/National Geographic Creative), 8 bl DreamPictures/Photographer's Choice/Getty Images), 8 bc (Michael Nichols/National Geographic Creative), 8 br (Michael Nichols/National Geographic Creative) 9 t (DAVID DOUBILET/National Geographic Creative), 11 tl (© StockPhotosArt - Technology/Alamy), 11 br (© i creative/Alamy), 11 cr (© Gino's Premium Images/Alamy), 11 tr (© medical images/Alamy), 11 cl (Alamy), 11 bl (© Nikreates/Alamy), 12 tl (©ALEX TREADWAY/National Geographic Creative), 12 bl (©ALEX TREADWAY/National Geographic Creative), 13 bl (©Blend Images/Alamy), 13 cl (Larry Lilac/Alamy), 13 cr (Sean Nel/Alamy), 13 cl (©Ilya Andriyanov/Shutterstock.com), 13 tr (©TANSEL ATASAGUN/Shutterstock.com), 13 tl (amana images inc./Alamy), 13 tc (©David Gee 1/Alamy), 13 tr (©foodfolio/Alamy), 15 tl (Andres Rodriguez/Alamy), 15 cl (Custom Medical Stock Photo/Alamy), 15 cl (LSC Office/LatinStock Collection/Alamy), 15 bl (RubberBall/Alamy), 16 tr (Eric Audras/PhotoAlto/Alamy), 16 tl (©Corepics VOF/Shutterstock.com), 19 tl (©Dieter/Shutterstock.com), 20 bc (©Monkey Business Images/Shutterstock.com), 20 cl (©Forster Forest/Shutterstock.com), 20 cr (©ollyy/Shutterstock.com), 20 tc (©Dmitry Kalinovsky/Shutterstock.com), 22 t (Tim Hall/Stockbyte/Getty Images), 20 tl (©Dmitry Kalinovsky/Shutterstock.com), 21 t (richard nowitz/National Geographic Creative), 23 b (Simeone Huber/Getty Images), 24 bkgd (Andrew Kornylak/Aurora Photos/Alamy), 25 c (Alamy Limited), 27 tl (Mauro Ladu/Alamy), 26 t (marianne pichot/Fotolia), 27 tr (Peter Adams/Digital Vision/Getty Images), 27 cr (annie griffiths/National Geographic Creative), 27 bkgd (dmitri alexander/National Geographic Creative), 28 cl (Christoph Papsch/vario images GmbH & Co. KG/Alamy), 29 tl (Jeremy Woodhouse/Holly Wilmeth/Blend Images/Alamy), 29 bl (Aki/Alamy), 28 tl (©iStockphoto.com/carterdayne), 28 bl ©iStockphoto.com/Alan_Lagadu), 30 (DreamPictures/Photographer's Choice/Getty Images), 32 cl (©Luiz Rocha/Shutterstock.com), 33 t (©AP Images/Biswaranjan Rout), 35 b(©Wong Adam/Redlink/Encyclopedia/Corbis), 34 c (KeenPress/National Geographic Creative), 37 b (christian kober/Alamy), 39 tr (Alessio D'Amico/AAD Worldwide Travel Images/Alamy), 39 b (Karen Kasmauski/Terra/Corbis), 40 tr (Kuttig - Travel - 2/Alamy), 42 Full (lynn johnson/National Geographic Creative), 43 tr (lynn johnson/National Geographic Creative), 43 cr (joel sartore/National Geographic Creative), 44 tl (Kellie Netherwood), 45 t (XPACIFICA/National Geographic Creative), 45 t (XPACIFICA/National Geographic Creative), 46 tr (©anshar/Shutterstock.com), 46 tr (Sami Sarkis (4)/Alamy), 46 tl (Alamy), 46 tc (Dave Porter/Alamy), 46 tc (The Photolibrary Wales/Alamy), 46 cr (dbimages/Alamy), 46 cl (Randy Olson/National Geographic Image Collection/Alamy), 46 c (geogphotos/Alamy), 46 c (Hufton + Crow/VIEW Pictures Ltd/Alamy), 46 cr (Ferenc Szelepcsenyi/Alamy), 46 br (Bailey-Cooper Photography/Alamy), 46 br (Bailey-Cooper Photography/Alamy), 47 tr (Ian Dagnall/Alamy), 47 br (Anna Stowe Botanica/Alamy), 49 tl (gianluca colla/National Geographic Creative), 50 bl (bruce dale/ngs image collection/National Geographic Creative), 51 b (Carole Anne Ferris/Alamy), 52 tl (Rhys Stacker/Alamy), 52 cl (Marsden, David/Bon Appetit/Alamy), 52 cr (Lucie Lang/Alamy), 52 cr (©Swellphotography/Shutterstock.com), 52 bl (David Lee/Alamy), 52 bc (Lenscap/Alamy), 52 br (whiteboxmedia limited/Alamy), 53 c (Dennis Cox/Alamy), 54 Full (Mike Theiss/National Geographic Creative), 52 cl (©iStockphoto.com/Lee Rogers), 65 b (Alamy), 57 t (Laurent Gillieron/AFP/Getty Images), 58 tl (randy olson/National Geographic Creative), 59 tl (Holsten, Ulrike/Bon Appetit/Alamy), 59 tc (Photodisc/Digital Vision/Getty Images), 59 tr (i love images/couples/Alamy), 59 cl (©gorillaimages/Shutterstock.com), 59 c (Corbis Bridge/Alamy), 59 c (FirstShot/Alamy), 59 cr (IS098Q1YB/Image Source/Alamy), 59 bl (Yoshikazu Tsuno/AFP/Getty Images), 60 cl (Ron Bedard/Alamy), 60 tc (Vincenzo Lombardo/Getty Images), 60–61 Spread (Martin Benik/Alamy), 62 tl (A. T. Willett/Alamy), 70 b (Boston Globe/Getty Images), 71 tl (incamerastock/Alamy), 71 tr (Brian Jackson/Alamy), 71 cl (foodfolio/Alamy), 71 cr (Westmacott/Alamy), 71 cl (OnWhite/Alamy), 71 cr (Edd Westmacott./Alamy), 71 cl (Helen Sessions/Alamy), 71 cr (foodfolio/Alamy), 71 br (blickwinkel/Alamy), 74 tl (ZUMA Press, Inc./Alamy), 74 tc (PhotoKratky/Alamy), 74 tr (Speedpix/Alamy), 74 cl (Horizon International Images Limited/Alamy), 74 c (Jordan Weeks/Alamy), 75 c (Goran Tomasevic/Reuters/Corbis), 75 t (©Alison Wright/Corbis), 76 t (Fuse/Getty Images), 78 (Mr Standfast/Alamy), 79 tl (robfood/Alamy), 79 tc (Marco Secchi/Alamy), 79 tr (Rawdon Wyatt/Alamy), 80 tl (Brian J. Skerry/National Geographic Creative), 81 t (DIBYANGSHU SARKAR/AFP/Getty Images), 82 tr (Franz Aberham/Photographer's Choice/Getty Images), 82 br (Franz Aberham/Photographer's Choice/Getty Images), 83 cl (Outdoor-Archiv/Alamy), 84 b (Philip Scott Andrews/National Geographic Creative), 85 br Kablonk/Purestock/Alamy), 87 tl (Radius Images/Alamy), 87 cl (D. Hurst/Alamy), 87 cl (Ian Cook/All Canada Photos/Getty Images), 87 bl (Antony SOUTER/Alamy), 88 t (Peter Macdiarmid/Getty Images), 89 tr (i love images/Fitness/Alamy), 89 br (Catchlight Visual Services/Alamy), 90 (Eric CHRETIEN/Gamma-Rapho/Getty Images), 92 tl (White Star/Monica Gumm/imagebroker/Alamy), 93 t (Melissa Farlow/National Geographic Creative), 94 bkgd (XPACIFICA/National Geographic Creative), 95 cl (Jim Richardson/National Geographic Creative), 96 tl (EMORY KRISTOF/National Geographic Creative), 97 tl (Hill Street Studios/Erik Isakson/Blend Images/Alamy), 97 bl (Olaf Doering/Alamy), 97 bc (Jim Wileman/Alamy), 97 br (IS2010-12/ImageSource Plus/Alamy), 98 tl (mike lane/Alamy), 98 cl (Rainer Martini/LOOK Die Bildagentur der Fotografen GmbH/Alamy), 98 cl (John Giustina/The Image Bank/Getty Images), 98 bl (D. Hurst/Alamy), 99 t (STEVE WINTER/National Geographic Creative), 99 br (STEVE WINTER/National Geographic Creative), 100 tc (david hancock/Alamy), 100 tr (Nick Dolding/Photodisc/Getty Images), 100 cl (Shoosmith Snack Foood Collection/Alamy), 100 cr (Michael Hartmann/imagebroker/Alamy), 100 bl (PCN Photography/Alamy), 100 br (David Hoare/Alamy), 101 tr (Sherwin Crasto/Reuters/Corbis), 102 (Michael Nichols/National Geographic Creative), 104 tl (Cary Wolinsky/National Geographic Creative), 105 t (Michael S. Lewis/National Geographic Creative), 106 tr (©Photoexpert/Shutterstock.com), 106 tr (©Coprid/Shutterstock.com), 106 tl (©Karkas/Shutterstock.com), 106 tl (©Coprid/Shutterstock.com), 106 tc (©Karkas/Shutterstock.com), 106 tc (©Gemenacom/Shutterstock.com), 106 cr (©Karkas/Shutterstock.com), 106 cr (©Simone Andress/Shutterstock.com), 106 cl (©Karkas/Shutterstock.com), 106 cl (©Ruslan Kudrin/Shutterstock.com), 106 bc (©BortN66/Shutterstock.com), 106 bc (©Gordana Sermek/Shutterstock.com), 106 bc (©Karkas/Shutterstock.com), 106 br (©sagir/Shutterstock.com), 106 br (©sagir/Shutterstock.com), 106 bl (©zhaoyan/Shutterstock.com), 106–107 (Kevin Steele/Aurora Photos/Alamy), 108 tl (Jan Greune/LOOK/Getty Images), 108 tr (Stefan Espenhahn/imagebroker/Alamy), 109 tr (RichardBakerHeathrow/Alamy), 109 tc (Rob Cousins/Alamy), 109 tr (Y.Levy/Alamy), 109 cl (©Stanislav Komogorov/Shutterstock.com), 109 c (ACE STOCK LIMITED/Alamy), 109 cr (©Rohit Seth/Shutterstock.com), 109 cl (Degree/eStock Photo/Alamy), 109 c (Peter Alvey/Alamy), 109 bl (Moritz Hoffmann/LOOK Die Bildagentur der Fotografen GmbH/Alamy), 109 bc (Guns4Hire/Alamy), 109 br (©Jiri Pavlik/Shutterstock.com), 109 tr (numb/Alamy), 109 br (Curtseyes/Alamy), 109 c (©romakoma/Shutterstock.com), 111 t (AARON HUEY/National Geographic Creative), 111 bl (AARON HUEY/National Geographic Creative), 111 bc (©alexkar08/Shutterstock.com), 111 bc (Olivier Renck/Aurora/Getty Images), 111 br (ITAR-TASS Photo Agency/Alamy), 112 t (Larry Lilac/Alamy), 113 cl (adam eastland/Alamy), 113 bl (DAVID NOBLE/nobleIMAGES/Alamy), 113 bc (chris warren/CW Images/Alamy), 114 (KENNETH GARRETT/National Geographic Creative), 116 tl (ian nolan/Alamy), 10 t (MONIKA KLUM/National Geographic creative), 122 cr (Alamy), 126 bkgd (Alamy Limited), 129 t (TIM LAMAN/National Geographic Creative), 131 tl (Press Association Images), 131 tr (KENNETH GARRETT/National Geographic Creative), 131 cr (KENNETH GARRETT/National Geographic Creative), 135 t (STEPHEN ALVAREZ/National Geographic Creative), 135 bl (STEPHEN ALVAREZ/National Geographic Creative), 135 br (STEPHEN ALVAREZ/National Geographic Creative), 137 tr (Chase Jarvis/UpperCut Images/Alamy), 138 (©Pierre-Yves Babelon/Shutterstock.com), 140 tl (MICHAEL MELFORD/National Geographic Creative), 140 tr (©James Peragine/Shutterstock.com), 141 t (CARY WOLINSKY/National Geographic Creative), 142 tl

(GREG DALE/National Geographic Creative), 142 tr (GREG DALE/National Geographic Creative), 142 cl (GREG DALE/National Geographic Creative), 142 cr (GREG DALE/National Geographic Creative), 142 bl (GREG DALE/National Geographic Creative), 142 bl (GREG DALE/National Geographic Creative), 143 br (GREG DALE/National Geographic Creative), 144 b (Werner Dieterich/Photographer's Choice/Getty Images), 147 bkgd (TYRONE TRNER/National Geographic Creative), 147 tr (TYRONE TURNER/National Geographic Creative), 148 t (Alistair Brydon/Alamy), 150 (Camilla Watson/John Warburton-Lee Photography/Alamy).

Illustration: Alastair Humphreys p 132, Alex Treadway p 10, Alfredo Fernandez Valmayor p 96, Beehive Illustration pp 14, 19, 21, 24, 31, 48, 50, 55, 56, 62, 64, 70, 72, 79, 80, 82, 83, 86, 91, 95, 99, 103, 115, 118, 127, 134, 139, 151, 164, Brant Allen p 072, Carol Liutkus p 96, David Russell pp 15, 20, 47, 55, 83, 92, 111, 123, 130, 151, Eye Candy Illustration pp 38, 41, 43, 44, 48, 49, 56, 73, 76, 79, 81, 88, 91, 94, 151, 163, Kellie Netherwood p 44, Matthew Hams pp 14, 16, 19, 33, 34, 44, 50, 51, 62, 72, 73, 88, 105, 145, 155, 159, 162, 163, OSCAR HERNÃNDEZ p 77, Samsung Electronics pp 154, 158, Simeone Huber p 23, Zeb Hogan p 73.